ISBN 978-1-330-75747-5
PIBN 10101504

1 MONTH OF
FREE
READING

at

www.ForgottenBooks.com

By purchasing this book you are eligible for one month membership to ForgottenBooks.com, giving you unlimited access to our entire collection of over 1,000,000 titles via our web site and mobile apps.

To claim your free month visit:

www.forgottenbooks.com/free101504

English
Français
Deutsche
Italiano
Español
Português

www.forgottenbooks.com

Mythology Photography **Fiction**
Fishing Christianity **Art** Cooking
Essays Buddhism Freemasonry
Medicine **Biology** Music **Ancient**
Egypt Evolution Carpentry Physics
Dance Geology **Mathematics** Fitness
Shakespeare **Folklore** Yoga Marketing
Confidence Immortality Biographies
Poetry **Psychology** Witchcraft
Electronics Chemistry History **Law**
Accounting **Philosophy** Anthropology
Alchemy Drama Quantum Mechanics
Atheism Sexual Health **Ancient History**
Entrepreneurship Languages Sport
Paleontology Needlework Islam
Metaphysics Investment Archaeology
Parenting Statistics Criminology
Motivational

A LITERARY
HISTORY OF EARLY CHRISTIANITY.

STANDARD WORKS.

Fifth Edition, 8s. 6d.

A HISTORY OF ROMAN LITERATURE. From the Earliest Period to the Times of the Antonines. By the Rev. C. T. CRUTTWELL, M.A., Late Fellow of Merton College, Oxford.

"Mr. Cruttwell has done a REAL SERVICE to all students of the Latin language and literature. . . . Full of good scholarship and good criticism."—*Athenæum.*

"A most serviceable—indeed, INDISPENSABLE—guide for the student. . . . The 'general reader' will be both charmed and instructed."—*Saturday Review.*

COMPANION VOLUME.

Second Edition, 8s. 6d.

A HISTORY OF GREEK LITERATURE. From the Earliest Period to the Death of Demosthenes. By FRANK BYRON JEVONS, M.A., Tutor in the University of Durham.

"Beyond all question the BEST HISTORY of Greek literature that has hitherto been published."—*Spectator.*

Fourth Edition, 10s. 6d.

THE VOCABULARY OF PHILOSOPHY: Psychological, Ethical, and Metaphysical. With Quotations and References for the Use of Students. By WILLIAM FLEMING, D.D., Late Professor of Moral Philosophy in the University of Glasgow. Revised and Edited by HENRY CALDERWOOD, LL.D., Professor of Moral Philosophy in the University of Edinburgh.

In large 8vo, handsome cloth, 21s.

PREHISTORIC ANTIQUITIES OF THE ARYAN PEOPLES. By Dr. O. SCHRADER. Translated from the Second German Edition by F. B. JEVONS, M.A.

*** Dr. Schrader's pictures of the Primeval Indo-European Period in all its most important phases—The Animal Kingdom, Cattle, The Plant-World, Agriculture, Computation of Time, Food and Drink, Clothing, Dwellings, Traffic and Trade, The Culture of the Indo-Europeans, and The Prehistoric Monuments of Europe (especially the Swiss Lake-Dwellings), Family and State, Religion, The Original Home—will be found not only of exceeding interest in themselves, but of great value to the Student of History, as throwing light upon later developments.

"Dr. SCHRADER's GREAT WORK."—*The Times.*

"A MOST REMARKABLE BOOK."—*St(einthal)—Zeitschrift für Völkerpsychologie und Sprachwissenschaft.*

"One of the BEST WORKS published of late years. . . . Every one who, for any reason whatsoever, is interested in the beginnings of European Civilisation and Indo-European Antiquity, will be obliged to place Dr. SCHRADER's book on his library shelves. The work addresses itself to the general reader as well as to the learned."—*Gustav Meyer—Philologische Wochenschrift.*

LONDON:

CHARLES GRIFFIN & CO., LIMITED, EXETER STREET, STRAND.

A LITERARY HISTORY

OF

EARLY CHRISTIANITY:

INCLUDING THE

FATHERS AND THE CHIEF HERETICAL WRITERS

OF THE ANTE-NICENE PERIOD.

For the Use of Students and General Readers.

BY

CHARLES THOMAS CRUTTWELL, M.A.

RECTOR OF KIBWORTH, LEICESTER, AND RURAL DEAN; FORMERLY FELLOW OF MERTON
COLLEGE, OXFORD.

AUTHOR OF "A HISTORY OF ROMAN LITERATURE," ETC.

In Two Volumes.

VOL. I.

LONDON:

CHARLES GRIFFIN AND COMPANY, LIMITED,

EXETER STREET, STRAND.

1893.

TO THE MOST REVEREND

EDWARD,

LORD ARCHBISHOP OF CANTERBURY.

VISITOR OF MERTON COLLEGE,

WHOSE PROFOUND LEARNING IS NOWHERE MORE AT HOME

THAN AMONG

The Ancient Fathers,

THIS

HISTORY OF THE LITERATURE OF THE EARLY CHURCH

IS BY HIS PERMISSION

RESPECTFULLY DEDICATED.

PREFACE.

THE encouraging reception given to my "History of Roman Literature," published in 1877, suggested the extension of the same plan to the more complicated field of the Literature of the early Church.

So far as I am aware, there is no English work which exactly covers the same ground; and I hope that the present volume may be found to supply a real want, both for students of theology and for general readers who desire to see for themselves what the first exponents of Christian doctrine after the Apostles believed and taught.

Upwards of seven years have been spent in collecting the materials for this work. The original authorities have in all cases been carefully studied, and, in addition, information has been gathered from such of the best known and most recent Church histories, dictionaries, and monographs as were within my reach. Where more than the general outlines of the thought have been borrowed, I have sought in every instance to acknowledge my indebtedness.

The purpose I have had in view is mainly literary—that is, I have endeavoured to point out the leading intellectual conceptions which animate the various writers, to indicate the degree of success attained by each, and to estimate the permanent value of each one's contribution to the growing edifice of human thought and knowledge.

The student will find included in the list of Christian writers, besides the Church Fathers, a considerable number

of heretical teachers whose works have perished, but whose
ideas are more or less correctly preserved in the controversial treatises of their opponents.   Though rightly repudiated
as heretical, these speculations entered so closely into the
Church's daily life, and both by attraction and repulsion
influenced so strongly the statements of Catholic doctrine,
that it was felt impossible to pass them by with a mere
cursory notice.   It is hoped that the analysis of them, remote
and fantastic as they seem to us, will not prove wearisome to
the reader.

The Ante-Nicene period is, on the whole, more varied in
character than that which immediately follows it.   The two
main streams of Christian thought, represented respectively
by the Greek and Latin Churches, have already begun to
diverge from their common watershed.   In Origen and Tertullian they have hewn out valleys which he who climbs the
intervening heights can still simultaneously survey, but they
have not yet become two rivers watering different regions, as
is the case when we come to compare, let us say, Athanasius
with Augustine.

At the present day, the most fruitful Christian thought is
moving on the lines of the Greek Fathers.   The controversies
which have attended the publication of *Lux Mundi* have
suggested to men's minds the inadequacy of the Augustinian
theology to satisfy the desire for spiritual enlightenment.
A deeper, wider, more truly human theology is required.   In
the pages of Clement of Alexandria, of Origen, and especially
of Athanasius, such a theology is already provided.   The
Incarnation, as the self-revealing of Divine wisdom and love
in terms of a nature fitted by its kinship to the Deity to be
the vehicle of such revelation—this is the central truth of
Christianity as apprehended by the great thinkers of Alexandria.   Christ the Redeemer of all humanity,—humanity

recalled to its true self in and by Christ,—the will once more set free by the living power of an indwelling Spirit, Who opens out infinite possibilities of development by revealing to man the true law of his being—such are some of the inspiring thoughts of Greek theology, which respond to our purest aspirations, and reconsecrate man's intellect to the service of God.

An able writer [1] has taken exception to the clothing of the Church's doctrine in the forms of Greek metaphysics. But we may fairly ask: In what other form could it have been clothed? The intuitions of Revelation, to be presented to the universal consciousness, must needs be recast in the form of thought which nearest approaches universality. And the world has yet to devise an instrument better fitted to achieve this lofty task than the language of Greek philosophy, fashioned to the processes of exact thought by the continuous labour of the highest minds for nine centuries, and, for Christians at least, stamped with the inspired approval of the disciple whom Jesus loved. The answer to Dr. Hatch's objection can hardly be better expressed than in the words of an American writer: [2] "The influence of Hellenic speculation in determining the true nature of the Person of Christ is not a thing smuggled surreptitiously into the domain of Christian thought—an alien element, to be carefully eliminated, if we would understand the original revelation in its simplicity and purity. It enters into the Divine process of preparation for the Advent of Christ as a constituent factor; it is essential to a right interpretation of the Christian Idea in its widest and highest application."

The interpretation of revelation is a process continuous with revelation itself. It is vain to wish for the establish-

---

[1] The late Dr. Hatch, in his *Hibbert Lectures.*
[2] Professor Allen, in his *Continuity of Christian Thought.*

ment in theology of the simple, instinctive religious language of the Old and New Testaments. This language always will be, as it always has been, the spontaneous expression of devout souls as they address their prayers or praises to the All-Merciful Father. But until the modern world can achieve, as perhaps it may, on the basis of inductive science, a metaphysical terminology superior to that of ancient Greece, we may well be content to accept the historic definitions of the Church, only removing what can be proved to be adventitious or unwarranted by the sense of Scripture. This was indeed the professed object of the leaders of the Reformation, but they were not able sufficiently to disengage themselves from their environment to perceive that the views they received as primitive were in truth largely coloured by an Augustinian medium, which refracted and often obscured the light.

The process which they inaugurated was in its very nature incomplete, and it would neither be possible nor desirable to arrest its course. In taking her stand upon Holy Scripture as distinct from any special reading of its sense, the Anglican Church admits the possibility of a progressive interpretation corresponding to the infinite fecundity of Scripture itself. And the true successors of the great divines of the sixteenth and seventeenth centuries are surely those who are turning upon Holy Scripture the entire light of the purified human intelligence, and trying to make it speak for itself in those clear tones to which, once heard, the mind of man cannot but respond.

No reverent soul will presume to limit the meaning of Scripture to that primary sense historically present to the mind of the writer, which it is the mission of our present Biblical criticism incontrovertibly to establish and uniquely to emphasise. If it could be so limited, Scripture would cease to be for us what it undoubtedly is, the Word of GOD. But it is surely a fallacy to conclude that those who bid us study the Bible as we study any other book, mean also to assert that the Bible *is* nothing more than any other book. They are really reverting under changed conditions of thought to the example of the Greek Fathers, who brought to the study of Scripture those canons of interpretation which the highest science of their day applied to all the noblest products of the human mind, to Homer, to the poetic Cycle, to the entire lore of the antique world. No doubt their method was imperfect, transitory, destined to be superseded; but the principle on which they acted, that of employing the highest available culture in the task of interpreting Scripture, was true and valid, and therefore sure to reappear when the course of intellectual development made its reappearance possible.

The methods at present in favour, no doubt, appear to those engaged in applying them as wholly satisfying and final. And the language used by many Biblical critics undoubtedly justifies a cautious attitude with regard to a subject so momentous on the part of those who are responsible for the custody of the body of doctrine handed down to them. At the same time, since it is by reason and reason alone that the words of Scripture as of all other literature must be judged, the instructed Christian will not mistrust the disciplined use of that divine gift which then is most truly free when it serves most impersonally in the cause of truth.

It is my belief that both in the English Church and outside it there is a large and increasing number of earnest persons who fully recognise the connection between the writings of the Fathers and their own religious position, but who desire to approach the study of them from a somewhat less technical point of view than that usual in theological works. To such, whether professed students or not, I venture to submit this survey of early Christian literature as embodying a chapter second to none in significance in the history of man's spirit, and contributing results of undying value to the treasure-house of man's intelligence.

KIBWORTH RECTORY,
Easter 1893.

TABLE OF CONTENTS.

INTRODUCTION.

BOOK I.—THE APOSTOLIC FATHERS.

CHAPTER I.

GENERAL REMARKS.

CHAPTER II.

CLEMENT OF ROME (FL. A.D. 95 ?).

xiii

CHAPTER III.

THE PSEUDO-CLEMENT.

CHAPTER IV.

THE EPISTLE OF BARNABAS (A.D. 75 ?).

CHAPTER V.

THE DIDACHE, OR TEACHING OF THE TWELVE APOSTLES (A.D. 90 ?).

CHAPTER VI.

IGNATIUS (A.D. 40–115 ?).

CHAPTER VII.

POLYCARP (A.D. 69 ?-155).

CHAPTER VIII.

PAPIAS AND THE ASIATIC ELDERS (A.D. 70–150?)

CHAPTER IX.

THE "SHEPHERD OF HERMAS."

BOOK II.—THE HERETICAL SECTS.

CHAPTER I.

JEWISH PERVERSIONS OF CHRISTIANITY—EBIONISM.

CHAPTER II.

THE CLEMENTINE LITERATURE.

b

CHAPTER III.

THE EARLY APOCRYPHAL LITERATURE.

CHAPTER IV.

ON GNOSTICISM IN GENERAL.

CHAPTER V.

FIRST DIVISION: GNOSTIC SECTS NOT IN ANTA-GONISM TO JUDAISM—SIMON—CERINTHUS—DOCETISM.

CHAPTER VI.

BASILIDES AND THE PSEUDO-BASILIDEANS.

CHAPTER VII.

VALENTINUS AND THE VALENTINIANS.

PAGES

The most influential of the early heretics—Philosophy of religion—
Facts of his life—His theology—The doctrine of Æons—The
Pleroma—Sophia and Achamoth—The Demiurge—His theory of
Redemption—His anthropology—His doctrine of the Messiah—
The Soter—The Spiritual and Hylic natures—Marcus—Heracleon
—Ptolemæus—His theory of the Law . . . . .

CHAPTER VIII.

SECOND DIVISION: THE ANTI-JUDAIC GNOSTIC SYS-
TEMS: OPHITES—CARPOCRATES—BARDAISAN—
JULIUS CASSIANUS.

The Ophites hardly to be considered as Christians—Carpocrates—
Immorality of his views—Epiphanes—Sethites, Cainites, and
Nicolaitans—Bardaisan or Bardesanes—His Book of the Laws of
Countries—Less heretical than other Gnostics—His sect almost
confined to Syria—Julius Cassianus holds Encratite views—Pistis-
Sophia—Questions of Mary . . . .

CHAPTER IX.

MARCION AND HIS SCHOOL.

The noblest of the Gnostics—His genius not speculative but practical—
Incidents of his career—Borrows his philosophy from the Syrian
Cerdo—Relations with Polycarp—The Creator of the world an
Evil Being—His Docetic Christology—The love of God opposed to
His justice—The Old Testament contrary to the New—Marcion's
Gospel—His antitheses—Apelles—Controverted by Rhodon—Her-
mogenes—His Stoic affinities—Theory of the eternity of matter

CHAPTER X.

THE EARLY UNITARIAN TEACHERS.

Monarchianism—Two forms of it, one approximating to Deism, the
other to Pantheism — The sect of the Alogi — Theodotus of
Byzantium—Artemon: his rationalistic theology—Relation of
the Roman Church to Monarchianism — Beryllus of Bostra—
Refuted by Origen—Paul of Samosata—His life and character—
His Christology—Conflict between him and the Catholic bishops
—His relations with Zenobia—Intervention of Aurelian—Praxeas
— The Patripassian theory — Tertullian's treatise "Against
Praxeas"—Noëtus—Sabellius—His explanation of the Trinity—
His Christology—General summary of heretical teaching .

BOOK III.—THE APOLOGISTS (A.D. 130–250).

CHAPTER I.

THE APOLOGETIC LITERATURE—GENERAL REMARKS.

CHAPTER II.

THE DIFFERENT CLASSES OF APOLOGISTS.

First Classification of apologetic writings into those addressed to the Civil Power and those addressed to the public—*Second Classification* into those addressed to Jews and those addressed to heathens—*Third Classification* into those which are based on the Immanence of Deity and those which are not, corresponding to Eastern and Western Christianity—To first class belong Justin, Athenagoras, Clement, and Origen—To an intermediate section belong Tatian, Irenæus, the writer to Diognetus, and to some extent Tertullian—The former section admits Greek philosophy to be a divinely appointed medium of truth, the other section denies this—The second class of apologists includes Arnobius and Lactantius and (at a later date) S. Augustine—The treatment of Christian evidences varies in accordance with this fundamental

CHAPTER III.

*THE EARLIEST APOLOGISTS—ARISTIDES—QUADRA-
TUS—AGRIPPA CASTOR—ARISTO OF PELLA.*

CHAPTER IV.

*ATHENAGORAS—EPISTLE TO DIOGNETUS—DIONYSIUS
OF CORINTH—MAXIMUS—THEOPHILUS.*

CHAPTER V.

JUSTIN MARTYR (A.D. 110-164).

CHAPTER VI.

TATIAN (A.D. 110-180?).

CHAPTER VII.

THE BEGINNINGS OF CHURCH HISTORY.
HEGESIPPUS (A.D. 115?-A.D. 185?).

CHAPTER VIII.

THE LATER SCHOOL OF S. JOHN—MELITO TO
POLYCRATES.

CHAPTER IX.

IRENÆUS (A.D. 125-203?).

APPENDIX TO CHAPTER IX.

LETTER OF THE GALLICAN CHURCHES.

CHAPTER X.

THE GRÆCO-ROMAN SCHOOL — MURATORIAN FRAGMENT — HIPPOLYTUS, CAIUS, VICTOR, AND OTHERS.

(A.D. 170-235?).

CHAPTER IV.

ORIGEN—HIS THEOLOGICAL SYSTEM, INFLUENCE AND LITERARY GENIUS.

PART II.

CHAPTER V.

THE SUCCESSORS OF ORIGEN.

BOOK V. — LATIN CHRISTIANITY.

CHAPTER I.

LATIN THEORY OF THE CHURCH.

CHAPTER II.

THE AFRICAN CHURCH—Q. SEPTIMIUS FLORENS TERTULLIANUS (A.D. 160–230 ?).

Part I.

CHAPTER III.

TERTULLIAN'S WRITINGS.

PART II.

CHAPTER IV.

CYPRIAN (A.D. 200 ?–257).

CHAPTER V.

ROMAN CHURCH—MINUCIUS FELIX—NOVATIAN.

CONTENTS.

CHAPTER VI.

ARNOBIUS (FL. A.D. 200?)—*LACTANTIUS* (A.D. 240–325?)—
COMMODIAN (A.D. 260?)—*VICTORINUS PETAVIENSIS.*

PAGES

A LITERARY
HISTORY OF EARLY CHRISTIANITY.

INTRODUCTION.

THE literature of the first three centuries of the Church differs in this respect from all other literatures, that it is wholly theological and religious.[1] The remark may be applied with almost equal accuracy to the centuries that immediately follow. And if to these we add the entire mediæval period, with all its complex life, we shall still find the same statement substantially true. No doubt, in this latter period, some forms of secular thought emerge and find a more or less articulate utterance. But speaking broadly and popularly, we may assert that the long succession of ages from the time of the New Testament to the Revival of Letters, if not absolutely restricted to theological modes of expression, is dominated throughout by a theological spirit. This is surely a very striking phenomenon. Theological ideas are not so easily grasped as to form the natural clothing of man's thought, nor so comprehensive as to cover its entire field. Nor, if we survey the history of those other literatures which have most powerfully influenced mankind, shall we find any adequate parallel. The literatures of India, of Persia, of Islam, though springing from a religious source, and long confined within a religious sphere, include many other elements. Even the Scriptures of the Old Testament and

---

[1] So absolutely is this the case, that the authorship of the "Cesti," a book attributed on good authority to Julius Africanus, has been strongly questioned on the sole ground that it deals with secular topics. See Bk. iv. ch. 5.

Apocrypha display numerous features that are not wholly spiritual. They embrace history, law, politics, poetry, legend. How comes it; then, that for so immense a period Christian literature was so predominantly theological?

The cause is twofold. On the one hand, the transcendent power of the central Christian truth, which set itself to transform the entire attitude of the human mind to knowledge; on the other, the inevitable reaction from the long and exclusive dominion of the secular intelligence. The world into which Christianity entered was emphatically a secular world. Its philosophy, its poetry, its law, were all the products of man's natural wisdom, and addressed themselves to his hopes and fears as concerned with this present world. For his spiritual instincts, for his aspirations after holiness, they made no provision. It is true that among the higher minds many lofty ideas on religion had been reached. Noble souls, true seekers after God, strove to raise men's minds to the heights of contemplation, and, by explaining the order of the universe, to inculcate indifference to external things and arouse an enthusiasm for the supreme good. But these heroic spirits stood almost if not quite alone. It is doubtful whether they greatly influenced the lives even of the small number who could understand their thoughts. It is certain that they left wholly untouched the vast multitude beneath. The subject nations of the Empire, mechanically united but spiritually heterogeneous, were ready enough to yield obedience to Cæsar's power; but when, amid the chaos of fallen religions, they asked for a god to worship, no god was offered them but that very Cæsar whom their own hands had fashioned —an undoubted, unmistakable idol.

It was impossible that such a system could end otherwise than in failure. Men asked for bread and were given a stone. The age was, indeed, profoundly conscious of its misery.[1] The great spiritual void could be filled neither by material prosperity nor by a multitude of inconsistent super-

---

[1] The second and third centuries after Christ, though differing in some respects, are sufficiently alike in their moral condition to be grouped together in a general survey.

stitions. The literature that has come down to us represents the thoughts of the cultivated, the fortunate, the noble. Yet it displays with few exceptions a spirit of indignant, hopeless despair. The utmost that philosophy could do for man was to teach him how to yield to fate; and if self-respect forbade him to yield, he must seek an escape by a voluntary death. Suicide was erected into a virtue, it was even glorified as man's highest privilege, more than compensating him for his outward inferiority to the gods. A profound melancholy or a forced hilarity pervade the poetry of this period; bitter anger or unavailing regret form the burden of its historians. The soul of life seemed dead. The world had become a huge machine, whose vast proportions mocked the puny efforts of individuals.

If the favoured few were thus depressed, what must we imagine to have been the condition of the undistinguished, inarticulate multitude? Undoubtedly the Empire had given them one great benefit in increased personal security. But this had been bought at too high a price. They had sacrificed all freedom, even the illusion of it.[1] They looked to Rome for the entire mechanism of their outward life, while their national gods were lost to them through their indiscriminate adoption into the Roman pantheon. Thus bereft of political life, bereft of religious belief, they sank into the idle frequenters of circus and arena, or sought in degrading superstitions the alternate terror and amusement which reflected but too truly the motive forces of their life.

The task which the Apostles and their followers set before them from the outset was to regenerate the human mind. It was not to alter some of its convictions, or even to give men certainty instead of doubt, knowledge instead of ignorance, but it was to destroy the dominion of falsehood and to set up that of truth; in S. Paul's emphatic language, to make *a new creation*. The efforts of all former teachers had

---

[1] Luc. Phars. ix. 204, 205—

> " Olim vera fides Sulla Marioque receptis
> Libertatis obit : Pompeio rebus adempto,
> Nunc et ficta perit."

been limited to a small circle of disciples. Even the divinely given mission of Moses was confined to a single race. But from the first the proclamation of Christianity was not made to a few but to all; and therefore it was necessary that its watchword should be not merely true in itself, but disengaged from everything that could localise, limit, or obscure it. To bring this about, it was necessary, as it were, to dig out and expose to view the root-principle of the Pagan world, and then to plant another principle equally comprehensive in its place. The root from which the entire civilisation of heathendom grew is rightly declared by Tertullian to be idolatry. "*They worshipped the creature rather than the Creator,*" the transient instead of the permanent, the phantom instead of the reality.[1] This is S. Paul's summary of heathenism, and it cannot be surpassed in its insight. It is what we worship that at bottom decides our attitude to the external world. This truth, which had been recognised in earlier and better periods, had in the time of the Empire become wholly obscured. It was this truth which the Church placed in the van of her teaching, "*We know what we worship.*"[2]

In order to bring home to man the power of this truth for his salvation, it was necessary to penetrate every department of thought and conduct with its inspiring influence, and this involved nothing less than the reconstruction of the whole framework of humanity, or, as Plato expresses it, "the turning round of man's whole soul towards the light."[3] For such a task as this a religious literature of three, four, or five centuries can hardly seem too long; and though we may regret that the process was not completed in the generous spirit in which it was begun,[4] yet its greatness cannot be denied, nor the patient study of its methods be deemed a waste of time.

---

[1] Rom. i. 25. Εἴδωλον = a phantom, a shadow, *not* a graven image.
[2] S. John iv. 22.　　　　[3] 3 Plat. Rep. vii. p. 518, D.
[4] The attitude of the early fathers as of the Apostles themselves towards the human spirit is far more generous and sympathetic than that of the Latin Church from Tertullian onwards.

The writings of the Ante-Nicene Fathers do not exhibit that variety of view, that sympathetic play of intellect, which lends such a deathless charm to the secular literature of Greece and Rome. But these very deficiencies bring into relief the overwhelming power of that central inspiration which could restrain the pride of learning, and force into a single channel the most versatile gifts. This constant self-repression has prevented the intellectual relation of the Fathers to their contemporaries from being justly estimated. Already in the second century Christian thinkers rank among the abler men of their day, and in the third and fourth they are indisputably superior to their Pagan rivals. It is not that men like Clement, Origen, Cyprian, and Tertullian were not fully capable, had they so chosen, of adorning many fields of literature; but that, filled with the master-impulse of illuminating things human by things divine, they concentrated all their powers on the work of tracing man's whole field of knowledge direct to its fountain-source.

In one sense, indeed, and that the most obvious one, it must be allowed that they failed. For *we* are able to discern what they were not, that there exists a sphere of human truth as real, as legitimate as that of divine truth; nay more, that these two spheres so interpenetrate one another, that many domains which once formed branches of divinity are now clearly seen to belong to human learning, and yet they have by no means lost their living connection with the Divine Spirit.[1]

Yet in another and perhaps a higher sense they may be said to have succeeded; for, though their method is often faulty and their results erroneous, they did good service to man's progress by keeping open the conception of a *revelation*, *i.e.*, a source of truth outside the human mind. No one would connect Christianity directly with the rise of inductive science; and yet it is precisely in the patient observation of

---

[1] *E.g.*, ethics, social and historical science. The application of this thought to the realm of physical science is yet to come. But already the theologian is beginning to realise his right in the "Reign of Law," as most precious revelation of the Mind of God.

the Divine operations, and in the unreserved acceptance of them when made known, which are so characteristic of modern science, that we may trace the influence of Christianity, and establish the main difference between modern and ancient science; for while ancient science forced nature into conformity with its own *à priori* conceptions, modern science is content to interpret the universe without professing to measure it.

Therefore, in estimating the permanent value of this Church literature, we shall do well to keep before us the object it strove to attain, and to judge of its importance to progress not only by its direct contributions to knowledge, but also by the effect it had in lifting mankind to that loftier spiritual platform, by means of which the triumphs of the modern intellect have been achieved.

The point of view from which the ecclesiastical writers will be considered in the present volume will not be primarily theological, nor, indeed, wholly religious. Regard will be had also to their general bearings on the history of the human mind; and although the writings passed under review will be almost entirely theological, yet the extent to which this element enters into modern thought is of itself sufficient to prove that the long battle of theological and ecclesiastical controversy was not waged in vain.

In striving to obtain a comprehensive view of a series of writings so extensive and various, the critic will be fain to dwell with greater interest upon the purely spiritual, the philosophical, or the controversial side, according to the bent of his own sympathies. He will concentrate his attention on the metaphysical subtleties of the Eastern Church, or on the rhetorical and dogmatic treatises of the Western, according as his turn of mind is speculative or practical. But, while appreciating these great and important differences, he will bring into clear relief the still greater and more vital underlying unity which binds together forms of genius so divergent, and creates a type of literature which is more than Eastern or Western, more than Hellenic or Barbaric, more than ancient or modern, that which is conveyed by the title, no less accurate than familiar, "The Literature of the Universal Church."

The history of this literature presents three well-marked stages — first, the period of birth, of creative energy and force; secondly, the period of growth, of controversy and struggle; and thirdly, the period of maturity, which is also that of authority and rule.

The first period includes the *Origines* of Christianity down to the close of the Apostolic era. It witnesses the launching of the new-born truth into the ocean of the world, and it covers all the phenomena of Christianity that are truly original.[1] With this period, flooded as it is with divine light, we are not here directly concerned; but, inasmuch as it forms the mainspring and source of all subsequent developments, it will be as well to state what were its grand original ideas, which have entered into and enriched the spiritual inheritance of mankind. They are four in number:[2]—

1. The idea of the Divine Son of God taking man's nature in order to redeem it.

2. The idea of the Brotherhood of redeemed mankind as sons of God in Christ.

3. The idea of the Church, *i.e.*, a society independent of all local or natural ties, founded on a purely spiritual basis.

4. The idea of love to God and man as the one sufficient motive for realising human perfection.

Of these four cardinal points of Christianity, all due to Christ Himself, three at least were absolutely new to mankind. The other, viz., the Church, had already been anticipated by Sakya Mouni five centuries earlier in a distant part of the world, though in connection with a very different moral ideal.

We may here remark that it is precisely these root-ideas of Christianity which, amid all the changes of human life, persist in showing their inherent vitality and consequent

---

[1] Besides the Scriptures of the New Testament, we refer to the practical labours of the Apostles, and particularly those of S. John in the latter part of the first century, which appear in the establishment of Episcopacy, and probably of liturgical worship.

[2] The reader will not suppose that this catalogue is presented as in any sense exhaustive. It rather represents the points in which Christianity stands out as original when compared with the Old Testament.

superiority to all later superstructures built on them. Translated out of the sphere of Divine Revelation into that of moral or social science, and only too often wrested into a shape that seems to belie their origin, they are nevertheless mightily at work in human society to-day, and evidently hold its future in their hand. To what shall we ascribe the growing reverence, almost adoration, paid to human nature as such, in glaring contrast to its dishonour in the ancient world, if not to an unconscious acknowledgment that the Incarnation of Jesus Christ was no isolated Divine Fact, enacted far off in the heaven of heavens, but a process inherently connected with the Divine Idea of manhood, which by it, and by it only, has been made capable of realisation?

To what shall we ascribe the tremendous power of modern social and democratic movements if not to an irresistible, albeit perverted, acceptance of a universal brotherhood founded upon an equality—social, moral, and political? to what the growing impatience of dogmatic restrictions, if not to an overmastering desire that the Church Universal shall express itself in its ideal form as the entire human race? to what the pervading anxiety for the preservation of peace, if not to the conviction that man's destiny can best be wrought out by love, and not by hate? Doubtless these motives are not always present to men's minds in their Christian form. On the contrary, to multitudes who profess them every embodiment of the Christian faith is highly distasteful. Yet if we look below all accidental differences to the essential springs of the human spirit, we shall be justified in connecting these mighty developments with their source in Palestine eighteen centuries ago.

The second period, the period of growth and struggle, includes the second and third centuries, A.D. It begins with a few isolated writings, which in form and tendency are closely connected with the preceding age. They are those ranked as sub-apostolic; and in spite of their pronounced inferiority to the New Testament Scriptures, such was the prestige they enjoyed from their antiquity and devotional fervour, that large portions of the Church regarded them as inspired, and allowed their use in Divine service. But to us their importance is above all things historical. We find in them no new spiritual ideas, no broad outlook on the future of Christianity. They form a kind of back-water of apostolic inspiration, a transitional phase between the truly creative epoch and that process of laborious adaptation to its environment which next engages the attention of the Church of Christ.

It is this second period with which alone the present work is concerned, the period usually known as Ante-Nicene. Its activities were spread over a wide area, and radiated from well-marked centres, each with its own spiritual character. It was conditioned by the existence alongside of it of two hostile forces, the one external, the other internal, the necessity of repelling which brought out and consolidated its inner unity. But this unity was always the free consensus of independent convictions arrived at by discussion, and brought into relief by the exigencies of controversy; it was rarely or never the mechanically imposed unity of centralised power enforced by anathemas. Hence the complexity and indeterminateness of the dogmatic system of this period, which, though in its main points firmly fixed in the conscience of the Churches, had not yet found precise formulation in authoritative symbols. In this period, moreover, there is no exclusive predominance of any one Church, so that local forms of thought and expression find all the greater play.

This very cause, however, adds considerably to the difficulty of grasping the leading features of the period as a whole, since we are confronted with writers from Palestine, Syria, Asia Minor, Greece, Alexandria, Carthage, Gaul, and Rome, each displaying his national peculiarities, not yet planed down by the oppressive weight of Roman or Byzantine preponderance. We have individuality not only in style but in thought. We have differences of standpoint in principles little short of fundamental, and yet over all we have the broad, unformulated, yet morally coercive unity of apostolic teaching and tradition. This unity is so real that it generates as if by instinct a decided rejection of the heretical element not only on the part of such orthodox writers as Irenæus and Cyprian, but on the part of those who, like Origen and Tertullian, were deservedly censured for the unsoundness of their views.

At the same time, this very heretical element which the Church rejected demands our careful consideration. Unless we understand it, we shall not be able to appraise at their true worth those recent criticisms of dogmatic Christianity which regard it as a compromise between Israel's revelation and Pagan thought. This description, so unjust when applied to the doctrine of the Church, is strictly accurate when applied to the Gnostic systems. The brilliant authors of those systems were far from accepting the opprobrious name of "heretic," fixed on them by the orthodox. They maintained, and no doubt with sincerity, that theirs was the higher, the purer, the more spiritual Christianity; and they contended that, in harmonising the truths revealed by Christ with the fundamental conceptions of philosophy, they were placing religion upon its only sure basis, the processes of a purified reason.

It is evident that there must have been some irreconcilable antagonism of first principles between these able theorists and thinkers intellectually so closely akin to them as Clement and Origen, in order to produce in the latter their firm attitude of uncompromising resistance. And this antagonism unquestionably arose from the relations of the two parties to the doctrines of Pagan philosophy. The one absorbed the vital essence of Christianity into a vast cosmogonical scheme, into which it was made to fit; the other drew out and amplified the Christian idea by the methods of Greek metaphysic without absorbing or destroying it. And this capital distinction cannot be clearly discerned unless the schemes of Gnostic Christianity are placed side by side with that of the Church, and the comparative influence of Paganism in each is thus brought out. Our present object will not be to defend the orthodox system, or to pass strictures upon the heretical, but, by sketching briefly yet accurately the views of both, to exhibit the factors in that complex process by which the essential ideas of Christianity were brought to a more complete statement.

There can be no doubt that from an early period Christian writers were indebted to Greek metaphysical science. How far back in Christian history this indebtedness extends has long been, and still is, matter of controversy. In the New Testament there are two writings which exhibit an affinity real or apparent with the Græco-Judaic philosophy of the school of Philo, the Gospel of S. John and the Epistle to the Hebrews. There have been writers of mark who believe that in both these instances the distinctive doctrine of the Divine Logos is borrowed from Alexandria. In the case of S. John this hypothesis has been ably refuted; and Semitic scholars have shown that expressions and modes of thought existed within the Jewish range which were capable of the development they assume in his writings without being borrowed from Philo. In the case of the Epistle to the Hebrews, there is no doubt much more to be said in favour of an Alexandrian influence; but even there the metaphysical aspect is subordinate to the theological, and the Epistle can be adequately criticised without reference to Philo.

But so soon as we leave the New Testament and turn to the Apologetic literature, we are face to face with a very different state of things. What before was at best dubious, is now unquestionable. If we examine the same Logos-doctrine as expounded by Justin, Tatian, or Origen, we find no vestige of a Semitic colouring. The conception is recast in the crucible of Greek metaphysics, and evolved in accordance with the searching dialectic of the schools. And this is done as a matter of course, as the most natural thing in the world. Moreover, the same process is repeated with all the leading ideas of the Christian faith.

Take, for example, the dogma of Creation. To the Jew this was not conceived of so much in the way of an explanation of the Universe as in the light of an authoritative *dictum* of the Eternal Creator. To the Greek Christian it offers itself both as a truth to be established and as a problem to be explained. He connects it by various lines of reasoning,

sometimes heretical, sometimes orthodox, with the essential
nature of the Supreme God, and shows that it flows necessarily from that nature when properly understood. It becomes,
therefore, not only a supernatural revelation, but an intellectual truth.

The same remark is true of the doctrine of the Trinity,
the Incarnation, original sin, redemption, and all the other
mysteries of the Christian faith. An attempt is always made
to connect them intelligibly with the formal revelation to the
Church on the one hand, and with the processes of the human
intelligence on the other. The methods and terminology of
metaphysics are applied with the greatest freedom, and carried
into the very citadel of Revelation; and so thoroughly is the
amalgamation between the two spheres effected, that, as
Dean Milman has declared with scarcely an exaggeration,
in the fourth century of our era Christianity had become a
Greek religion. Nor is there anything in this that need surprise us. No thinkers can transcend the forms of thought
in which their minds have learned to move. The Jew could
not; still less could the Greek. But in the latter case it
was the less necessary, since, of all forms of thought in which
the human mind has worked, that which comes nearest to
universality is that wrought out in the laboratory of the
Hellenic mind. Thus, in speaking of Dogmatic Christianity
as a Greek religion, little more need be implied than that
the great spiritual truths that came forth clothed in the
popular dialect of the Jews were re-stated in terms of the
universal human intelligence.

As the outcome of this energising of Greek culture upon
Christian *data*, we have the presentation of Christianity not
only as a life to be lived but as a system of connected truth
—a complete explanation of the universe. This is our great
debt to the writers of this period. They do not all stand on
one elevation; they are content at first with presenting their
belief in the form of spiritual epistles on the model of those
of the New Testament, or with issuing forensic pleadings for
the toleration of their cult. But they soon gird themselves
to the larger task of determining the place of Christianity

among the competing systems of the day, and proving it to be not only the superior of them all, but the only one that is able to explain what in the rest is false, and to include all that in them is true. The genius of the writers increases with the exigencies of their task; the slender insight into Greek philosophy possessed by Aristides widens into the broad sympathetic touch of Justin, or the able but hostile polemics of Tatian and the writer to Diognetus. And this again gives place, as time rolls on, to the gigantic learning and comprehensive grasp of Clement, and the tender but discriminating sympathy of the beautiful soul of Origen, to be succeeded in its turn by the brilliant scorn—offspring not of ignorance but of profound knowledge—which gleams in the pages of Tertullian, and the large-hearted but superficial eclecticism which makes at once the strength and weakness of Lactantius.

To this second period we owe also the ennobling practical conviction that truth is attested by suffering for the truth's sake. The long line of martyrs who died for their faith, not only, as Tertullian declared, sowed by their blood the seed of the Church, but they also brought home to the minds of all unprejudiced heathens the actual living presence of that Lord who enabled His servants to overcome the whole power of the world, and to display before the turbid and chaotic fury of a hopelessly despairing age the spectacle of a serene certitude, sure of its object, and content to die in realising it. The lesson thus given to mankind has not been lost. Though we cannot declare a doctrine to be true solely because men suffer for it, yet it has generally been found that those beliefs for which good men have willingly suffered death have, as a matter of fact, been true, and so the sacred union between divine truth and human witness to it through the path of suffering or contempt has become, as it were, ingrained as an axiom in the consciousness of mankind.

The third period, which it is beyond the province of the present volume to discuss, comprehends the great dogmatic treatises of the Church, and to its saints and theologians we owe the vast conception of a Christian civilisation—that is, a reconstruction of the whole fabric of human life, within and without, upon the basis of the Incarnation of Jesus Christ, the mightiest idea that has ever been presented to this earth, and which, in the future as in the past, will surely carry us onward to its distant but inevitable consummation. On this, however, we cannot here enlarge.

It may perhaps be said:—Granting the effect of the patristic writings on the moral progress of mankind, is not their scope too restricted to make the study of them profitable to any but theological students? We may concede at once that the Fathers will never be popular authors. In spite of the excellent translations that are available, in spite of the brilliant essays and commentaries on them by some of our greatest divines, and in spite of the real concern of most Englishmen with the subject of religion, people invariably prefer lines of reading more akin to their habitual modes of thought. The Fathers have the mould of ages on them. Their theological dialect suggests remoteness from ordinary life; the doubts and controversies they raise, set forth in the terms of an extinct metaphysic, belie their real permanence and seem to hark back to a buried past. The prolix tone of the discussions, the arid polemics which seem to lose themselves in a mist of wordy disputation, repel the reader who is accustomed to the energetic compression of classical, or the rich freedom of modern literature. All these causes combined lead to very general injustice being done to the profound wisdom and intense moral grandeur which shine forth in the literature of the early Church, and more than atone for its general deficiency in beauty of style.

But although, in an age of hurry and over-pressure, it is difficult to find time for the study of original works, or even to so read between the lines of a translation as to seize on the element of living thought and make it our own, yet it by no means follows that the works themselves have lost their value, or that an account of them is not of general interest.

The exact contrary is nearer the truth. At no time since the Reformation have the works of the Fathers assumed a more important position in the defence of the Christian religion than they do now. At no time has the value of their testimony been more decisively felt. The point of attack has veered round of late years, and hostile criticism directs its shafts against the historical authenticity and credibility of the evangelic records. The writings of the first three centuries have been subjected, by both parties, to a fresh and most thorough examination, with the purpose of establishing or refuting the claims of the Gospels to be accounted authentic history. The question of the canon of the New Testament has been reopened, and the discussion has turned on its attestation by witnesses summoned from the early ages of the Church. The whole series of writers, orthodox and heretical, have been cross-examined, with results which have thrown a remarkable and unexpected light on the subject in dispute. The Christian believer must needs be deeply concerned in this great controversy as to the date of the New Testament writings. And although he may not feel competent to study the evidence at first hand, he will assuredly feel a personal interest in appreciating those sources of information, on whose verdict so vital an issue depends. As has been said, the aim of the present work is not theological or evidential controversy, but literary criticism. Those who desire to satisfy their minds as to the genuineness of the apostolic writings must read the works of those eminent scholars who have enriched so magnificently the theological treasury of the English Church. The object of this book is simply to review the succession of writings which, commencing at the close of the first century, struck out an ever wider range, until it culminated in the great philosophical and theological productions of the Alexandrian and African churches.

It will be necessary, therefore, to disengage the writers as far as possible from their connection with existing controversies, and to point out how they became the torchbearers of progress, mental and moral, through a night which threatened extinction to both. It will be useful to keep in view the aspect of the Church Fathers as men placed like ourselves, amid highly stimulating and anxious surroundings, men of earnestness, men of intelligence, who were bent on understanding the needs of their time, who believed that in the doctrines which had brought them peace they had found the only key to its perplexities and its yearnings.

Yet, in truth, if we abstract ourselves from the special forms of thought then prevalent, and look steadily at the essential nature of the problems raised for solution, we shall find the most striking resemblance between the Imperial period and our own. Both in its external movements and in its inner spirit the era of the rise of Christianity comes nearer to the nineteenth century than to any intervening period.

Let us look first at the side of material civilisation. The whole world was under one system of law, and a uniform administration effaced national idiosyncrasies. One language, the Greek, was widely spread if not universal, and that no dead dialect, but a living and growing idiom, albeit fallen from its first estate.

Then, as now, the life of man was concentrated in cities, and the country districts were rapidly losing touch with the higher thought. Communication between different parts of the world was, comparatively speaking, easy, safe, and direct. Travel was less expeditious than it is now, but scarcely less general. It was pursued not only for purposes of commerce, but for pleasure, for health, for the acquisition of knowledge. The habit of studying at foreign universities was, perhaps, commoner then than it is now. Books, no doubt, were scarce, but their place was to some extent supplied by the local lecturer or the itinerant sophist. Moreover, the universal habit of open-air life brought people into such constant contact that information of any kind soon became public property, and opinion speedily ripened in the crowded street. The popular will had no difficulty in finding a voice; and one effect of it was the general tendency to vulgarise what was great or noble. The standard of excellence was diffused but reduced. The proud and exclusive families of the Republic still survived in name, but in reality they were almost extinct. The *parvenu* and the cosmopolite were everywhere predominant. The coarse ideals of wealth and luxury supplanted, as they are supplanting now, but in a still grosser manner, the self-discipline of a sterner age. The female sex had asserted its social independence, not without success. Roman law was in several respects favourable to women's rights. On all sides levelling influences were at work. The proletariate of the world was rapidly asserting itself as the supreme arbiter of desert. All sorts of competitors catered for its tastes—mountebanks, sophists, magicians, philosophers, astrologers, theosophists; and all of them, to secure a favourable hearing, were obliged to adopt the same tone, and that anything but a high one. To court applause it was necessary to play to the gallery. The earnest soul of Aurelius found no fit audience for its meditations. He therefore addressed them to himself.[1]

On its spiritual side, the parallel between the two epochs is yet more striking, as also is the contrast. In both the mental condition is one of unrest; in both this unrest is due to the same cause, decay of religious belief, combined with an uncontrollable desire to penetrate the mystery of our being. The Pagan creed never had more than an æsthetic hold over men's hearts, consequently it was no hard task to undermine it. The Christian faith is not surrendered without a deeper conflict, a darker sense of desolation. But if we scrutinise the different substitutes now offered for it, we shall detect more than one of the very systems to which men of old turned in their search for lost truth.

At bottom there are but three solutions of the problem of the universe. First, there is Theism, with its distinguishing doctrines of free creation, and moral personality of God and man. It does not profess to account for the origin of matter, and is content to trace the existence of evil to the determinations of an independent will. Next, there is Pantheism, which in its lowest sense becomes materialism, identifying the Deity with the universe as the unconscious working of unvarying law, and in its higher sense becomes Spinozism, or the taking up of all apparent contradictions into an absolute

---

[1] They are entitled τῶν εἰς ἑαυτόν βιβλία.

B

unity which excludes alike Divine Personality and human responsibility. Thirdly, there is Dualism, whether undisguised, as in the Manichean theory of two equal Deities of diverse nature, or veiled beneath an abstract unity, which seeks (but without success) to account for matter by a process of emanation or projection. Of this the moral result is inevitably asceticism, for its moral theory at any rate cannot escape from the underlying assumption that matter is essentially evil.

Those are terrible moments for the human spirit, when it is left to its own resources to choose between these three positions. When Christianity first appeared upon the scene, the disintegration of belief was already far advanced. Many of those who embraced the new faith had passed through the other solutions, and some strove earnestly to combine it with one or other of them, unaware of their fundamental incompatibility.

In the modern world we see the Christian position once more placed in competition with new forms of the same opposing principles. We see a widespread desire, nay rather, an intense anxiety, to retain the moral side of Christianity while relinquishing its Theistic basis. But the Theosophist, the Agnostic, and the higher Pantheist will find their point of view anticipated, and many of their objections already answered, in the arguments of the Alexandrian Fathers. They will find that only by an illusory syncretism or fusing together of discordant elements, can room be found for a Christian system of conduct that does not spring directly from the fountain-head of the Incarnation. They will thus be forced to conclude that either Christianity is, what it professes to be, a unique phenomenon; or else it must be ranked as merely one among many religions which, whatever their comparative merit, are surveyed from a neutral standpoint by the truly critical eye.

The last and most deadly enemy of the rising Christianity was Neo-Platonism, just because of its all-comprehensive, all-resolving spirit, which gave it an apparent universality while yet it was in truth utterly unsubstantial. Precisely in the same manner, we now see its place taken by the Science of Religions, which, so long as it maintains a strictly scientific attitude, is of the highest value; but which will inevitably melt into nothing if it assumes to transcend the scientific sphere and to come forward as a religion of religions, an all-including body of truth.

In conclusion, we may affirm that the reader who approaches the study of the Fathers with the object of investigating their testimony to the historical character of Christ's life on earth, and the authenticity of the records which embody it, will find a rich recompense for the difficulty and obscurity of his subject; he will perceive in the objections made against it by able heathen opponents an anticipation of many of those with which we have of late years become so familiar. As he reads on, the obsolete trappings of antiquity will seem to drop off, and the essential freshness of the evidence and its general applicability to our own time will abundantly appear. And if his bent of mind lead him rather to theological than to historical disquisitions, he will observe, perhaps with surprise, the profound learning, the acute conceptions, and the power of spiritual insight that characterise writings which he has been led to regard as mere monuments of technical skill, with little bearing on the vital questions of his own daily life.

It needs some historical imagination to reproduce to our own minds the exceeding disadvantage at which, from a human point of view, the Christian cause was placed, and the marvellous energy, surely divine in its source, with which one obstacle after another was confronted and overcome. At first, by the patient endurance of unmerited suffering (the triumphant realisation of Plato's glorious vision of truth in the Gorgias), and afterwards by the hand-to-hand conflict of argument with argument, of ideal with ideal, of thought with thought; until the light won its way slowly but surely through the darkness that encompassed it, and the Cross was proved to be in the realm of man's intellect what it had already shown itself in the realm of his moral nature, the Eternal Symbol of his supreme and only good.

BOOK I.

THE APOSTOLIC FATHERS.

CHAPTER I.

THE APOSTOLIC FATHERS—GENERAL REMARKS.

As has been stated in the introduction, there is a long gap between the close of the apostolic writings and the commencement of ecclesiastical literature proper. The intervening period is one of silent growth, broken only by a few scattered voices. We could have wished for fuller information, both as to the founding of Church institutions and the formulating of Christian doctrine. As it is, we are left a good deal to conjecture. Nor is the amount of knowledge obtainable from the few documents that remain by any means equal to what might have been expected. It was with Christianity as with so many other great things : the period of its early growth was involved in obscurity, and when it awoke to self-consciousness, it had forgotten the events of its infancy, or retained them only in scattered recollections. The vivid light that encircles its first preaching gives way to a dim twilight, in which the growth that is fast proceeding finds but feeble expression in words.

The **Apostolic Fathers,** as they are usually called, though *sub-apostolic* would be a more correct name, supply in a partial and fragmentary way the blank in our sources of information. They are persons occupying as a rule prominent positions in the Christian world, and their works are for the most part occasional writings called forth by special circumstances. This is true, at least, of the Apostolic Fathers proper. There are some other Christian writings which from their antiquity and peculiar character are classed as sub-apostolic, but come more properly under the head of regular treatises and show quite a different tone of mind and teaching. To the former class belong the Epistle of Clement, with which we may rank the short homily also ascribed to him ; the Epistles of Ignatius, and the Epistle of Polycarp. These stand in a class by themselves. To the second belong the Epistle of Barnabas so called, the Shepherd of Hermas, the Exposition of the Divine Oracles by Papias, and, last but not least, the anonymous manual of Christian life known as the *Didaché.*

The dates and authenticity of nearly all these writings have been hotly disputed. Few of them have much definite attestation, which makes it all the more desirable that the attainable evidence, such as it is, should be sifted with an unbiassed mind. Unfortunately, in the case of two out of the three primary documents, so many points of ecclesiastical interest are involved in the discussion as to their authenticity that the argument has been as much theological as literary, and *à priori* considerations have been mixed up with matters of historical evidence.

The monumental work of Lightfoot has brought into prominence both the importance of these Fathers and the general results of the critical study of them. The constant use made in these pages of the Bishop's conclusions will be apparent to any one familiar with them, and need not be referred to again.

General Characteristics.—Before commencing a detailed account of these Fathers and their writings, we propose to mention some general characteristics which differentiate them from writers of the succeeding age.

1. They are all (except Hermas) closely connected by personal association with the Apostles or their immediate followers. And no stronger indication can be desired of the surpassing spiritual gifts of the Apostles than the impression they made on those who had intercourse with them. Thus

Clement, whose serene and dignified temper was far from prone to enthusiasm, not only speaks of them with the loftiest praise, but strives to reproduce their thoughts and acknowledges their binding authority. Ignatius, while encouraging himself by their example, nevertheless draws a complete line of distinction between the Apostles and himself. Polycarp seems to have no other desire than faithfully to reproduce and reiterate the treasured sentences of apostolic teaching. Papias insists in the strongest terms on the superior value of apostolic tradition to the voluminous but uncertificated conclusions of those outside their circle. The author of the Didaché, while providing for the possible continuance of the apostolic office in his own time, nevertheless rates its dignity as highly as any one, and speaks of Apostles being received as the Lord.

2. But this recognition of the unapproachable superiority of the Apostles was accompanied by a formal imitation of their writings, which not only differentiates these writers from those that follow, but brings into startling relief the decline in spiritual power that marked the close of the first age. The sole exception is Ignatius, whose fiery zeal and brilliant individuality cause his letters to stand out with a freshness hardly inferior to those of the New Testament. Yet, with all his emphasis of expression, he does not speak as one who is laying down principles for the first time. He is a ruler, but not a creator. The very way in which he magnifies the episcopal office almost forbids one to believe that it was an absolute novelty, though no doubt sufficiently new to need authoritative inculcation. The other writers present few thoughts that can be called original, though many that are highly valuable for hortatory and devotional ends. Barnabas, indeed, or whoever wrote his epistle, strikes out a vein of exegesis which he regards as a signal proof of spiritual insight; but to the modern Christian it appears in the light of an utterly mistaken, not to say puerile, method. Neither he nor Clement is able to grasp the fundamental ideas of the great Apostle, though both have evidently studied them, and Clement at any rate strives faithfully to reproduce

them. This will be sufficiently evident if we compare the 10th, 11th, and 12th chapters of Clement's Epistle, which deal with the grace of faith, with that portion of the Epistle to the Romans which establishes the Pauline doctrine of justification. In the case of Barnabas, the incompetency to understand S. Paul is far more glaring, and amounts almost to contradiction. To S. Paul the Mosaic law, though done away in Christ, was a genuinely divine stage in the great work of redemptive grace. To Barnabas it was not so much a concession to human imperfection, not so much a means of arousing the sense of sin, as a punishment inflicted on the Jews for their failure to apprehend the spiritual character of God's primal revelation. This misapprehension of the relation of the two covenants is not confined to Barnabas. It reappears with damaging effect in the arguments of Justin, and even of Clement of Alexandria; and in a different way it makes itself felt in Irenæus and Tertullian, leading the former thinkers to underrate the value of the legal dispensation, and the latter to reimpose it in a purified form upon the members of the Christian Church.

It seems almost as if there was a spiritual reaction after the immense outpouring of the Divine influence in the great creative age. All at once the tension is relaxed, and in place of the glorious principles of free grace and love as the fulfilment of the law, we find a very earnest and devout but decidedly narrowed conception of the Christian's privileges, and a tendency to erect a new code of ethical commandments to replace the old. This is especially noticeable in the Didaché and Epistle of Barnabas, but is by no means wholly absent from the higher level of thought attained by Clement and Polycarp.

3. We must remark, however, that it is in their intellectual insight alone that these truly holy men display this marked inferiority. In the ethical sphere they are admirable, and well deserve the honour which the Church has given them.

So pure is the spirit that animates the practical exhortations of Clement, Ignatius, and Polycarp that their works were treasured by the faithful as divinely-given helps to righteousness, and those of Clement in especial were read publicly in the Churches, and frequently embodied in transcriptions as supplementary portions of inspired Holy Writ. The same honour was in some quarters accorded also to the writings of Barnabas and Hermas, to the former from his mystical exegesis of the Old Testament, to the latter from his direct claim to inspiration. There is something very beautiful in the calm assured conviction of Clement, in the passionate love of Ignatius for his Saviour, in the pure heavenly wisdom that breathes through Polycarp's short epistle ; and something very touching in the naive simplicity of the Didaché, with its literal acceptance of Christ's precepts and its absolute unworldliness. Never again in the literature of the early Church do we meet with writings which, whatever their intellectual limitations, bear so fresh a stamp of that vision of unearthly purity, that perfect rest in the Father's love, and that life which is hid with Christ in God.

Each of them has bequeathed something to Christianity which the Church could ill spare. To Clement we owe the pervading sense of the Divine Order, manifested in the visible universe, and not less truly operative in the spiritual world, though it requires the eye of faith to discern it ; a great and fruitful thought. Its influence is seen in the stern repression of his own personality, which gives his words, delivered as the utterances of the Church of the world's capital, a solemn grandeur, peculiarly appropriate to the difficult duty of interposing in the quarrels of a sister community. To Ignatius we owe the first impassioned expression of the thirst for martyrdom, which, though carried to excess at times, was the most effective object-lesson of the supreme attachment of the soul to its Lord. We owe to him, also, the clear perception of the necessity of an organised Christianity if the Church was to carry out her task by system as well as by zeal. To Polycarp we owe the example of a faithful ruler of Christ's flock—a rock-like man, deficient in originality, unmarked by eloquence ; but all the more fixed and rooted in the determination to be the incorruptible guardian of the trust committed to him—a truly venerable figure, with face turned back towards the place whence the echo of S. John's voice still sounded in his ears, even while he breasts the billows that surge around his feet. To the Didaché we owe the idyllic picture of a primitive, guileless Christianity, restricted indeed, and only realisable in an obscure and sequestered retreat, but nevertheless inspiring from its artless simplicity, and most instructive from the unexpectedness of much that it reveals.

To the other three writers of this period our debt is by no means so large. The Epistle of Barnabas, however, is interesting, from being the first attempt to explain, after the fashion prevalent in Alexandria, the theological relation of the Old and New Covenants, and also by the evidence it affords in its latter portion of the existence of a rudimentary Christian catechism or scheme of duty, of which the Didaché gives the earliest example.

The work of Papias being unfortunately lost, we are not able justly to estimate its value. But the principle with which he starts is one of great importance. It consists in an emphatic preference for the testimony of eye-witnesses and accredited repositories of tradition over that of second-hand inference, however ably drawn. He may not have been, and probably was not, a very highly qualified sifter of evidence ; but how applicable his principle is to the study of the *origines* of Christianity is abundantly evident from the brilliant imaginative pictures, with every quality except that of historical foundation, which have been so plentifully showered upon the reading public during the last fifty years.

The Shepherd of Hermas belongs to a class by itself. The form in which it is cast, that of visions, similitudes, and commandments, supposed to be communicated by an angel, probably influenced the judgment of the early Church unduly in its favour. Still, making allowance for the lack of culture of the writer, and the narrow circle of dogmatic ideas in which his imagination moves, we are compelled to credit him with a deep sincerity of heart, an overwhelming sense of sin and of the necessity of a true repentance, together with a vein of strong common sense, which enabled him to gauge with tolerable correctness the leading spiritual dangers which beset the Church of Rome, and to protest against them with energy, and occasionally with eloquence.

CHAPTER II.

CLEMENT OF ROME (A.D. 97?)

THIS celebrated Father of the Church has come down to us surrounded with such a halo of romantic legend, that it is necessary, before stating what he was, to determine briefly what he was not. The story which, in mediæval times, did duty for his biography,[1] represents him as a Roman citizen of illustrious birth, who, having listened to the preaching of Barnabas, either at Rome or Alexandria, was seized with a desire to visit Palestine and examine the doctrines of Christianity at their source. He sailed to Cæsarea, and was warmly welcomed by Peter, whose convert and attached disciple he became. Their close friendship suffered no interruption till Peter's death in Rome, shortly before which event the great apostle consecrated **Clement** as his successor in the Roman chair. Clement, with the greatest possible success, filled the office for several years, winning the love, not only of the Christian community, but even of Jews and heathens, until the jealousy of the Prefect caused his banishment to the Crimea, where, after labouring with undiminished zeal, he suffered martyrdom by being cast into the sea.

This story is unquestionably a pure fiction. It originated in Syria among Ebionite sectaries, and the application of criticism to its manifold inconsistencies shows that it lacks even the slender ground of foundation which such stories generally contain.

Of the historical Clement, unfortunately, little is known. But the researches of many eminent scholars in Germany, and, more recently, the exhaustive work of Bishop Lightfoot, enable us to realise with considerable probability not indeed

---

[1] See chapter on "The Clementines."

his personal history, but the surroundings in which he lived, the position he held, and the epoch during which he held it.

In the first place, there is a very old and apparently well-founded tradition as to the Episcopal succession of the Roman Church. This tradition is traceable to Hegesippus,[1] a Jewish Christian who visited Rome during the episcopate of Anicetus (c. A.D. 160) and remained there till the accession of Eleutherus (A.D. 175). During the episcopate of Eleutherus (c. A.D. 175–190) Irenæus also wrote an account of the Roman Succession. In both these lists the first place after the Apostles Peter and Paul is given to one Linus, and the third to Clement, the second being assigned by Hegesippus to Cletus, and by Irenæus to Anencletus, who are doubtless the same person.

This order of succession is followed by Eusebius and St. Jerome, by Epiphanius in the Eastern and Rufinus in the Western Church. It is therefore the traditional order, and must be accorded whatever weight an early and continuous tradition deserves. It is, moreover, supported by the order in which the worthies of the Roman Church are prayed for in the Roman missal, an order which is evidently traditional, and which, if altered, would certainly have been altered in Clement's favour. Furthermore, the only other list which is entitled to consideration (that of Liberius, who was Pope in 354), a list which can with great probability be traced to Hippolytus of Portus (c. A.D. 230), is shown by Lightfoot to owe its divergence from the first list to a blunder.[2] Thus the only evidence we possess is really consistent with itself, and, considering its early origin, may safely be accepted as true. The duration of the two episcopates of Linus and Anencletus (or Cletus) is given as twenty-four years

---

[1] The passage of Hegesippus, which states that he wrote on the Roman succession, is quoted by Eusebius, H. E. iv. 22. It is this list of his which Lightfoot shows is almost certainly the basis of the list in Epiphanius, from which the present names are taken. Epiphanius lived about A.D. 375.

[2] In this list the order is Linus, Clemens, Cletus, Anacletus. Lightfoot has shown that the transposition of Clemens was due to a scribe's error, and the duplication of Anencletus to the same cause.

(probably round numbers), dating from the martyrdom of S. Peter, which may be placed in A.D. 64 or 67. Thus the accession of Clement is brought down to the year 88 or 91; and if we accept as the duration of his episcopate the term of nine years assigned to it by all the lists, we shall find it nearly synchronises with the last decade of the first century.

Thus we have strong external evidence that a person named Clemens was Bishop or President of the Church of Rome in the reign of Domitian, third in succession from the Apostles. And the same evidence declares this Clement to have been the writer of the Epistle to the Corinthians which has come down to us under his name. The letter itself is anonymous; but, in view of the strong testimony to its genuineness, it is accepted as Clement's by all competent judges. Now the writer makes distinct mention of two persecutions in Rome; the first, which took place "very near to the present day," and numbered among its glorious roll of athletes "the two *good* Apostles Peter and Paul."[1] This is evidently the Neronian persecution, in which the universal voice of tradition declares these apostles to have suffered. The second persecution, which was either still raging or just ceasing to rage at the time when the letter was written, is no less evidently that under Domitian, which, while quite as cruel as that of Nero, was carried on, not by a single act of wholesale outrage, but by a succession of insidious attacks under legal forms. So long as this tyrant lived, the Christian community could not feel otherwise than insecure. And this sense of danger, which is very manifest in the epistle, makes it probable that it was composed before the close of Domitian's reign (A.D. 95 or 96).

But here arises a question as to the identity of the writer. History informs us that Flavius Clemens, a near relative of Domitian, and his colleague in the consulship, was accused, together with his wife Flavia Domitilla, on a charge of atheism, and condemned. The husband was put to death,

---

[1] Lightfoot acutely remarks that this epithet, so unlike what a mere panegyrist would employ, betrays the writer's personal acquaintance with the twin founders of the Roman Church.

the wife banished to an island. It was long considered probable that the real crime of Flavius was the profession of Christianity, which heathen writers often confound with atheism, and recent antiquarian discoveries in Rome have made this, in his wife's case, certain. We have, therefore, on the one hand a conspicuous historical personage named Clemens, living under Domitian, condemned to death as a Christian, and on the other, an epistle emanating at the same time from the head of the Roman Church, a namesake of the consul, but of whom nothing else is known. What wonder if the ingenuity of German scholars has suggested that the two are one ?—that Clement the bishop is but a spiritual duplicate of the undoubted man of flesh and blood, Clement the consul?

Tempting as this theory is, it will not bear a close inspection. In the first place, had Clemens the consul been also bishop, it is incredible that no tradition of so remarkable a fact should have survived. Moreover, the two positions at that period were, to a conscientious man, quite incompatible. And, lastly, the whole sphere of thought of the epistle is utterly diverse from that in which a cultured and aristocratic Roman must have moved. The name Clemens had never been uncommon,[1] and now that it was borne by members of the Imperial family, its adoption followed as a matter of course among the innumerable dependents and retainers who formed " Cæsar's household."

We may, therefore, assume that Flavius Clemens, a freedman or dependent of the palace, probably a Hellenistic Jew who had received the Gospel from one or other of the apostolic founders of the Roman Church, and had approved himself therein by long and faithful service, was in due time called to occupy the chief place in the important and rapidly growing Christian community. Whether he was bishop in the modern sense of the term has been doubted, but without sufficient reason. It is true the letter never mentions his name, nor does it speak of any bishop as distinct from the

---

[1] The *Clement* of Phil. iv. 3 was evidently a Philippian Christian. It is a natural but wholly uncritical view which identifies him with the Roman Clement. The confusion is due to Origen.

presbyters; but at this early period, while one Apostle at least still survived, no hard and fast line was drawn between the President of the Presbyteral College and his inferior colleagues. In the next generation the distinction is already clearly marked, as we see from the letters of Ignatius. The language of these letters satisfies the strongest champion of the Episcopal office. Yet even Ignatius does not address the *Bishop* of the Roman Church, but only the presbyters and deacons. We should have expected the opposite of this. The unity of Imperial administration would naturally suggest a corresponding centralisation of Church government. In Rome, if anywhere, we should expect to see Episcopal autocracy first displayed. Instead of this it appears, if not of later growth, at any rate in a less pronounced form than elsewhere. But, if the *Bishop* of Rome is lost sight of, the *Church* of Rome already assumes the rôle of leader and guide of other churches. The tone of Clement's language is distinctly that of a superior, offering counsel, exhortation, and reproof. The Christian Church of the capital of the world seems to have acknowledged from the first a more than local responsibility. This fact gives our epistle a high historical interest, as the earliest and, as it were, spontaneous exponent of this consciousness of pre-eminence.[1] In the next generation Ignatius recognises the practice of the Roman Church as that of "teaching others," and assigns to her a "presidency of love." About half a century later than Ignatius another letter was sent from Rome to Corinth, during the episcopate of Soter, and this also was inscribed with the name, not of the Bishop, but of the Church. The position, then, of bishop in the early Roman Church must not be conceived of after the analogy of the popes of a later period; it would be quite consistent with a modest estimate of itself, and a comparative obscurity of personal fame[2] on the part of its holders.

---

[1] It proceeds in reality not from the Bishop, but from the community. Dionysius of Corinth, quoted by Eusebius (H. E. iv. 23), so refers to it. Similarly Irenæus calls it "The Epistle of the Romans to the Corinthians."

[2] For example, Linus and Anencletus, who are mere names to us.

That Clement was a Jewish and not a Gentile Christian is rendered probable by the whole cast of thought in the letter, and especially by the close familiarity with the LXX. Version of the Old Testament which appears in every page. The argument from Scripture and from Prophecy is to him the main one, though that from reason and natural law is also used with good effect. To him the Scripture is still synonymous with the Old Testament, though he is familiar with several books of the New, notably the writings of S. Peter and S. Paul.

It is not certain whether he quotes from any of the existing Gospels. Probably the sources of Gospel narrative and teaching were still mainly oral. But it is clear that no use was made by Clement of any of the Apocryphal Gospels. His knowledge of the Epistle to the Hebrews is so intimate that some have fancied him the author, or at least the translator of it. This conjecture is not only without foundation, but inconsistent with the style of the letter, which is wholly destitute of those splendid literary qualities which mark the canonical epistle.

The testimony of Clement is of exceeding value towards a correct determination of the relation of the various lines of apostolic teaching. As is well known, a certain school of criticism has divided the early Church into the Petrine and Pauline parties, the antagonism between which threatened to tear it asunder, and was with difficulty bridged over by such *Eirenicons* as the writings of S. Luke and S. Peter's first Epistle. Now S. Clement's letter seems produced expressly to confute this theory. Not only is he unaware of any rivalry between the two great Apostles or their followers, not only does he couple them together as joint founders of the Roman Church, and joint witnesses in their death for Christ, but he has evidently taken great pains to assimilate and harmonise the two lines of teaching, just where they might have appeared divergent. The opposition (if such there is) between faith and works in S. James has died out in Clement ; the two exist side by side as joint elements in perfection. Out of the four broad streams of New Testament doctrine, the Petrine, the Jacobean, the Pauline, and the Johannine, Clement shows a complete grasp of the first three. And if his language is inadequate as an exposition of the deeper aspect of S. Paul's doctrine, this arises from the limitation of Clement's mind, not from any conscious disagreement. His epistle read in conjunction with those of Ignatius and Polycarp proves that Church doctrine was Catholic from the first, so that we must look outside the main stream of development for those factious antagonisms of which so much has been made.

The doctrinal system of Clement is somewhat vague and unformed. This defect, it has been truly remarked, constitutes its highest value. It gives the apostolic teaching in its manifoldness, its fulness, its integrity. It makes no attempt to reduce to system what the Apostles themselves have not reduced. It is a faithful mirror of the current teaching of the early Church. It agrees with Ignatius, with Polycarp, and with the *Didaché*, in preserving an unmodified *corpus* of doctrine, on which the subtleties of Greek intellect and the forensic acuteness of Roman culture had not yet begun to play.

The doctrine of the Trinity receives the same sort of un-defined expression as in the New Testament; yet it is un-mistakably assumed as the basis of faith. The mediatorial and High-priestly work of Christ is also fully grasped, and, so far as we can judge, His pre-existence also. In one passage,[1] indeed, Clement goes beyond the scriptural point of view, and, if the reading be correct, gives some ground for being credited with Patripassian leanings; but new MS. evidence makes it probable that the expression " His suffer-ings " should be referred to Christ and not to God.

Some exception has been taken to the introduction of the Phœnix legend as a type or proof of the Resurrection on the ground of its fabulous character. But to this it is sufficient to reply that men of greater intellect and learning [2] than Clement believed it, and it in no way interferes with the

---

[1] Chap. ii. init. τὰ παθήματα αὐτοῦ (sc. θεοῦ).

[2] Such as, for example, Tacitus.

spiritual authority of the writer's argument. Clement's mind was receptive, not creative; and this fact really enhances the value of his just and comprehensive statement of the main articles of the Christian faith.

Characteristics of his Mind and Genius.

We must not look to this Father for the elucidation of any particular doctrine, but rather for a general comprehensive survey of the Christian system. His is emphatically an "all-round" mind. He is not fascinated by particular aspects of truth, nor led by the claims of one to deny their due to others. Such a temper was needed by the time. The Church of Rome, so far back as the date of the Epistle to the Philippians, contained the two discordant elements of Jew and Gentile Christians, and the misunderstandings between them had probably been accentuated rather than diminished after the Apostle's death. A ruler at once firm and conciliatory, who could hold the balance with impartial sympathy, was imperatively required. Such a one, we can easily believe, was found in Clement.

Of a calm, stately character, naturally fitted for command, he may have had special opportunities for studying the machinery of organisation and government as a dependant of the consul, possibly admitted to his intimate thoughts. It would almost seem that some unusual advantage of this kind had been enjoyed by him. His Jewish descent in itself would be no recommendation to office; but, if we suppose the interest of the consul to have been exerted in his favour, this high testimony may have counteracted a natural prejudice. There can be no doubt that the choice was a singularly happy one. The Church of Rome never had any aptitude towards theological speculation; but she was inevitably destined to take the leading position in the development of ecclesiastical policy. And to Clement belongs the merit or good fortune of possessing exactly the character that was necessary to be impressed upon the church he represented. Consciously or unconsciously, acting under

a strong sense of duty, he vindicated for the Church of the
Metropolis at the outset those mediating and regulating pre-
rogatives, which led on step by step to the towering edifice of
Papal dominion.   His letter, so calm, so equitable, so strictly
impersonal, and yet so instinct with moral authority, recalls
the qualities of those ancient Roman worthies, who, without
any striking individual genius, built up with strangely harmonious sagacity the power of the conquering Republic.
The halo of legendary heroism that gathered round his name
was the tribute of a penetrating instinct on the part of a
later age.

   There is no evidence that the Epistle was ever translated into Latin.   Consequently, after the beginning of the
third century, when Greek ceased to be the spoken language
of the Roman Christians, it seems to have dropped out of
sight, and its place to have been supplied by spurious
documents, which will be referred to in the next chapter.   In several churches of eastern Christendom, however, it was highly valued, and, as we know from Eusebius,
read in the public services, together with the so-called
Second Epistle.

Authorities for the Text.

   Until the year 1875 the sole authority was the celebrated
Alexandrian MS., which contains the whole of the Old and
New Testaments, and appends the two epistles of Clement
after the Apocalypse.   The last part of the first epistle and
the latter half of the second were wanting.   In 1875 a volume
was published at Constantinople, bearing the title, " The two
Epistles of our Holy Father, Clement, Bishop of Rome, to
the Corinthians ; from a MS. in the library of the Most Holy
Sepulchre in Fanar of Constantinople ; now for the first time
published complete, with prolegomena and notes by Philotheus Bryennios, Metropolitan of Serrae."   This MS., which
is known as the Constantinopolitan, has yielded results of
the highest value to Christian theology ; for, besides the
Epistles of Clement, it contains the Epistle of Barnabas,

the Epistle of Mary of Cassobola to Ignatius, and twelve Ignatian Epistles, besides a previously unknown and most precious relic of the first age, "The Teaching of the Twelve Apostles." Shortly after this discovery, a second authority for the complete text of Clement was announced to the world. This was a Syriac translation of the Scriptures of the New Testament in the following order:—

1. The Four Gospels, followed by a history of the Passion, compiled from the four Evangelists.

2. The Acts and Catholic Epistles, followed by the Epistles of S. Clement to the Corinthians.

3. The Epistles of S. Paul, including the Epistle to the Hebrews, which stands last.

At the beginning of the volume are three tables of lessons, one for each of these three divisions.

The First Epistle of Clement is thus headed, " The Catholic Epistle of Clement the Disciple of Peter the Apostle to the Church of the Corinthians," and similarly the second is entitled, " Of the same the Second Epistle to the Corinthians." The date of this translation is uncertain, but Lightfoot thinks it contains two elements, one very ancient and good, the other debased and probably recent.

These three authorities are independent of one another, and between them enable us to fix the text of the epistle with the greatest accuracy. The archetype from which all were derived, though early, cannot be placed further back than the close of the second century; for when it was written, the so-called Second Epistle, if not actually ascribed to Clement, was already annexed to his; and it is quite certain that this writing is considerably posterior to the time of Clement.

The introduction of the two epistles into the calendar of lessons is a testimony to their canonical estimation in the particular Syrian church, perhaps that of Edessa, from which the MS. emanated. But there is no evidence that any other church placed them on the full level of inspired Scripture, far less that the Greek Church as a whole did so.

We conclude the chapter with two extracts, to give the reader an impression of the writer's style. The first is where

he dwells on the orderliness of the visible universe as an
exhortation to man not to interrupt the Divine harmony of
creation : [1]—

"The heavens swaying peacefully under His direction are subject unto Him.   Day and night fulfil under Him their ordered
course, in no wise hindering one another.   Sun and moon, and
starry choir, in accordance with His command, roll harmoniously
along their fixed orbits without any deviation.   The earth bringing to birth at the proper seasons, according to His will, its full
tale of nourishment for man and beast and all the creatures that
inhabit it, puts it forth, making no dissension, nor altering aught
of that which He has assigned to it.   The trackless regions of the
abyss and the unexplored limits of the nether world are bound
together under the same ordinances.   The basin of the boundless
sea, by His creative power gathered into its compartments, does
not overstep the barriers which encircle it, but acts in accordance
with His commands.   For He has said, 'Thus far shalt thou come
and no further, and thy waves shall be broken within thee.'   The
ocean, impassable by man, and the worlds that lie beyond it, are
administered by the same direction of their Master.   The seasons
of spring and summer, autumn and winter, give way in peaceful
succession to each other.   The fixed quarters of the winds in
their proper season fulfil their service without disturbance.   The
perennial streams, formed for enjoyment and health, without fail
supply the breasts that give life to man.   The smallest creatures
fulfil their unions in peace and concord.   All these things the
great Creator and Master of all has commanded to be in peace
and harmony, doing good to all things, and more exceedingly to
us who have taken refuge in His tender mercies through Jesus
Christ our Lord, to whom be glory and greatness for ever and
ever.   Amen."

In the following passage he seems to be competing with
his great predecessor S. Paul in his Epistle to the Corinthian
Christians : [2]—

"Seeing, then, that many gates are open, that of righteousness
is Christ's gate, by which blessed are all they that enter and

---

[1] Chap. xx.   The reader will be reminded of the beautiful lines of
Keble for Septuagesima Sunday, "There is a book, who runs may read,"
&c.   [2] Chaps. xlviii.–l.

direct their way in holiness and righteousness, accomplishing all things without tumult. Let a man be faithful, let him be mighty in expounding knowledge, wise in the discernment of reasonings; let him be strenuous in action, let him be chaste. All the more necessary is it for him to be humble-minded the greater he seems, and to seek the common good and not his own. He that hath love in Christ, let him keep the commandments of Christ. Who can describe the binding power of the love of God? Who is sufficient to express the splendour of its beauty? The height to which love raises us is indescribable. Love joins us to God. Love hides a multitude of sins. Love bears all things, puts up with all things. There is no self-assertion in love, no pride; love knows naught of schism; love fosters not a factious temper; love does all in harmony. In love were all God's elect made perfect; without love nothing is pleasing to God; in love the Lord has taken us for His own. Through the love which He had towards us our Lord Jesus Christ, by the will of God, gave His blood for us, His flesh for our flesh, and His life for our life. You see, beloved, how great and marvellous a thing love is; indeed, there is no describing its perfection. Who is fit to be found therein, save those whom God deems worthy? Let us then seek and implore His mercy, that we may live in love, free from human factiousness. All the generations up to this day have passed, but they who were made perfect in love according to God's grace have the place assigned to the pious, and shall be made manifest in the visitation of Christ's kingdom."

CHAPTER III.

THE PSEUDO-CLEMENT.

As mentioned in the last chapter, the Alexandrian MS., written in the fifth century, contains two "Epistles of Clement," apparently both supposed to be addressed to the Corinthians.[1] The Constantinopolitan MS. of Bryennios intitules both writings as Clement's and to the Corinthians, but not as epistles. The Syriac version heads the second thus, "Of the same the Second Epistle to the Corinthians."

At the earlier date at which Eusebius wrote, this full recognition had not yet been obtained. His words are,[2] "I should mention also that there is said to be a second epistle of Clement; but we do not know that this is recognised like the former; for we do not find the older writers making any use of it." Rufinus and Jerome follow the lead of Eusebius, but with greater emphasis, as is the manner of followers.

The work had, until the year 1875, existed only in a mutilated state; but already more than one editor had suspected that it was no epistle, but a homily or sermon; and the discovery of the lost portion in that year made this suspicion a certainty. It cannot be said to redound to the credit of ancient Church criticism that an epistolary character was first assigned to the work, and then perpetuated by a continuous tradition, without any apparent misgiving.

Whoever the composer may have been, he wrote at Corinth. This is the one correct element in the old title. It has indeed been argued[3] that Rome was the place of composition; but the allusions to the games[4] seem to require a writer on the

---

[1] It is true that the second epistle has no heading : but Lightfoot thinks this is probably due to mutilation, though it might also arise from transcription from an earlier copy, which did not claim to be by Clement.

[2] H. E. iii. 37. [3] By Harnack. [4] In § 7.

spot to give them point. Moreover, it is hard to see why the document should have been connected from the first with Corinth, if there were no reason whatever for it. The Corinthian Church is known to have cherished the custom of reading occasionally, in public worship, compositions by pious men outside the canonical writings, as Clement's epistle, and, at a later date, that of Soter. This homily, if the work of a resident saint, may have gained the honour of such occasional reading, and so have come to be ranked with the genuine Epistle of Clement.

Who the writer was, we cannot even conjecture. Bryennios still thinks he may have been Clement of Rome; but, not to mention other arguments, Clement is evidently a Jewish Christian, and this writer as evidently a Gentile.[1] Hilgenfeld identifies him with Clement of Alexandria, but considerations of tone and style make this altogether incredible. Harnack fancies he may be the Clement alluded to by Hermas,[2] who was to distribute the *Pastor* to foreign cities. But this shadowy individual is almost certainly Clement of Rome, introduced by a slight anachronism, if we suppose the ordinarily accepted date of Hermas[3] to be correct.

-The date of our homily is uncertain, but unquestionably it belongs to a very early period. The attitude assumed towards the Gnostic denial of the resurrection,[4] and the Platonising account of the earthly and heavenly churches,[5] are both characteristic of the time before Valentinus.[6] Again, the free use of the Gospel according to the Egyptians as Scripture, if the writer belonged to the Catholic Church, would only be compatible with a primitive date. It seems clear that he was acquainted with some at least of S. Paul's writings, and perhaps of S. John's. The topics dealt with are primitive, though later than the apostolic period. Any time between A.D. 100 and 140 would suit the indications we

---

[1] *Cf.* §§ 1 and 2.   [2] Vis. ii. 4.   [3] A.D. 140–155.
[4] §§ 8, 9, 14, 16.   [5] § 14.

[6] This heretic imagined an æon called Ecclesia, who was united to the First-born. Had this doctrine been known to the Corinthian writer, he would probably have been more careful in his language.

possess, with a tendency toward the earlier limit of the scale.

A few words may be given to the character and contents of the writing. The interest of these is historic, not intrinsic, for the sermon is as dry and commonplace as any of those of to-day; but the light that it throws on an obscure period of Church history and on the development of doctrine, is not without value. We see a high, though not strictly orthodox Christology, a clear grasp of the connection between the two covenants, a witness to the vast extension of Gentile Christianity, and an appreciation of the dangers of a one-sided and impatient gnosis.

But by far the most interesting point in the composition is the relation of the writer to the canon. In this he shows his posteriority to the true Clement. To the latter the Scripture means the Old Testament, to the former it includes also the New; and not only this, but apparently an apocryphal gospel (that according to the Egyptians), which is quoted several times without suspicion as if it were genuine. From this comes the supposed saying of Christ, that His kingdom should come "when the two are one, and the inside as the outside, and the male with the female, neither male nor female." The words themselves have a spurious ring, and the Encratite interpretation put on them by the homilist reveals a doubtful element in his orthodoxy.

The New Testament quotations and allusions are more numerous than the Old, a clear proof of Gentile origin. They are chiefly from the Gospels, but some are from S. Paul's Epistles. They are loose and often inaccurate, and their application lacks precision. The argument of the sermon is weak, and wearisome to the reader, and the mental power displayed very slight; but, on the other hand, there is a fine moral earnestness, and every mark of a genuine faith. In fact, the stamp of Clement's name served as a guarantee of the author's fidelity to the doctrine of the Catholic Church. He must have been a presbyter,[1] for he

---

[1] §§ 17, 19, where some details of Christian worship are given. "After the God of truth" in § 19, means "After the reading of Scripture." This may be compared with Justin's well-known account in Apol. i. 67.

evidently refers to himself as the deliverer of the sermon, and may have been the bishop for aught that appears to the contrary. The idea that he was a lay-preacher is far less likely, because, although laymen of well-known piety or learning were occasionally allowed to preach, as we know was the case with Origen, yet this indulgence was so rare that it should not be called in to explain what can be explained without it.

Other Writings ascribed to Clement.

The two *Epistles on Virginity*, extant only in the Syriac, were brought to Europe from Aleppo in the last century, and first published in 1752. They were then maintained to be genuine, and the position has been ably defended more than once since. But the frequency of quotations from the New Testament, and the picture presented of the life of the Church, do not agree with the genuine epistle, and point to a later age. They are, however, very ancient, and Westcott thinks they cannot be placed much later than 150 A.D.

The first writer who refers to them is Epiphanius. This Father was well acquainted with Palestine and Syria, the region where they originated. He speaks of "the encyclical letters which Clement wrote, and which are read in the holy churches; . . . he himself teaches virginity; he praises Elias and David and Samson, and all the prophets." This description applies very accurately to the Epistles to Virgins, and not at all to the Epistles to the Corinthians, which indeed Epiphanius had probably never seen. S. Jerome also shows a knowledge of these two letters, though he only once refers to them by name; and one of them is also quoted by Timotheus of Alexandria (A.D. 457). The western churches seem, however, to know nothing of them. What Epiphanius says as to their being everywhere read may either be an exaggeration founded on their use in a few Syrian congregations, or it may be a confusion with the honour accorded to the true Clement.

The existing Syriac text is obviously a translation from

a Greek original, which we may hope will some day come to light.

Besides this pair of epistles, yet another pair may be noticed, viz., those inscribed to James, the Lord's Brother. The first of these, which will be referred to in the chapter on the Clementines, dates probably from A.D. 150–200. In the original Greek MSS. it is prefixed to the Clementine homilies. About the end of the fourth century it was translated into Latin by Rufinus. It gives an account of S. Clement's appointment as successor to S. Peter, and the Apostle's directions as to the general administration of the Church. This letter was incorporated several centuries later into the false Isidorian Decretals, but not without considerable additions. A second letter to James, extant only in the Latin and subsequent to Rufinus, ranks as second in the series of decretals, but is also much interpolated. In the Latin Church these were generally known as "The Letters of Clement." Hence, as Lightfoot truly says, the letters of Clement would have a different meaning for each of the three branches of the Church. To the Greek it would mean "The Epistle and Homily to the Corinthians;" to the Latin it would mean "The two Epistles to James;" and to the Syrian it would mean "The two Epistles on Virginity.' We have shown that of this imposing list one, and one only, is to be accepted as genuine.

CHAPTER IV.

THE EPISTLE OF BARNABAS.

THE curious epistle or treatise which bears the name of **Barnabas** must be regarded as one of the most important documents of the sub-apostolic age. Its title, unlike Clement's, has been hotly disputed. Gebhardt and Harnack, the most recent editors, go so far as to say that none but a prejudiced critic can believe it to be genuine. The learned author of the article in Smith's Biographical Dictionary as evidently leans to its genuineness. Unfortunately, the scarcity of materials for scientific argument must leave the answer to the question a matter of opinion. Where so much depends on a delicate critical sense and acuteness in following up obscure allusions, and so little on clear external proof, a probable conclusion is the utmost that can be expected. We may regret this the more, because the high authority of Barnabas, and his deeply interesting personality as revealed in the New Testament, would have made us hold as a most precious possession any undoubted product of his mind. Following our usual method in similar cases, we shall give a brief summary of the external and internal evidence, noting only the more striking points, and leaving the *minutiæ* to those who are prepared to give the question a thorough study.

The author of the article referred to says, " It is admitted on all sides that the external evidence is decidedly in favour of the idea that the epistle is authentic." Clement of Alexandria bears witness to it on more than one occasion as the work of Barnabas the Apostle.[1] He is followed by Origen,

---

[1] Harnack cites nine passages of Clement containing quotations of this epistle, some of which he has misunderstood (Prolegom. p. xlvii.)

who, in his first book against Celsus,[1] quotes from the "Catholic Epistle of Barnabas" as if it were Scripture. The famous *Codex Sinaiticus*, written in the fourth century, includes it among the books of Scripture, but, by placing it after the Apocalypse of John though before that of Peter and the Shepherd of Hermas, implies that its authority is deutero-canonical, or inferior to that of the universally accepted books. Thus far the testimony in its favour is limited to the Alexandrian Church, to which the Codex Sinaiticus may ultimately be traced. But a wider recognition awaited it, though on a somewhat lower level. Eusebius mentions the epistle in two places.[2] In one he ranks it among the "spurious," in the other among the "disputed" books.

In the first passage he speaks of it as the currently received Epistle of Barnabas,[3] in the second simply as the Epistle of Barnabas. While, therefore, he expresses himself unfavourably as regards its canonicity, he appears to accept without question its authenticity. The testimony of Jerome is also important. In two places[4] he mentions it as classed among "the Apocryphal Scriptures," which phrase must be understood not as implying a want of authenticity,[5] but as denoting its rejection from the canon of inspired and universally received Scripture.

If it be asked, How could Eusebius and Jerome believe the epistle to be the work of the Apostle Barnabas, and yet relegate it to the position of an apocryphal work? the answer may be given that Barnabas, in separating himself from the Apostle Paul, had necessarily impaired that complete fellowship of apostolic doctrine which his association with S. Paul would otherwise have secured.[6] Nevertheless, the fact that as late as the close of the fifth century a place among the

---

[1] Chap. lxiii.   [2] Book iii. 25, 4. Book vi. 13, 6.

[3] ἡ φερομένη Βαρνάβα ἐπιστολή. This has been interpreted as equivalent to ἡ λεγομένη, "the so-called Epistle," but without good reason.

[4] De Vir. Illustr. 6, and in Comm. ad Ezech. xliii. 19.

[5] ψευδεπίγραφον. It is true that Jerome sometimes uses the word "apocryphus" in this sense, but that is not his usual way.

[6] Acts xv. 40.

canonical books is still claimed for the epistle, proves the high estimation in which it was held, the origin of which is hard to explain on any other supposition than that it had always been associated with the name of the great apostolic teacher.

On the other side, several arguments have been advanced, all based upon internal evidence. The most important are those adduced by Hefele, of which the following are the chief:—(1.) That the intellectual level of the work is inconsistent with the attainments of Barnabas, the argument being founded upon ingenious but trifling allegories, and not upon a broad spiritual grasp of the Old Testament. This is one of those *à priori* arguments that it is always hard to refute. No doubt, to the modern reader, armed with the rational methods of scientific criticism, many of the analogies insisted upon in the epistle are not merely unconvincing but ridiculous; but in an age which delighted in mystic exposition, and found latent spiritualities in the barest numerical statistics, these same applications may have seemed instances of profound wisdom; and in any case, they affect rather the scaffolding of his argument than the edifice itself, for there is no want of real insight into the great truths of Christianity, and especially into the connection between the Old and New Dispensations, by which the former receives its meaning as well as its completion only in the latter.

(2.) Hefele's second argument is that the mistakes made in the seventh and eighth chapters about Jewish ceremonies which must have been well known to a Levite who had resided in Jerusalem, are inconsistent with the authorship of one who had been a Levite. If the reader will take the trouble to compare these chapters with the references given to the Old Testament, he will have no difficulty in appreciating the force of this objection. To the learned student of Jewish antiquities the consideration carries still greater weight. It seems inconceivable that one whose express duty it was to carry out with rigid exactness the requirements of the priestly code, should either forget them or misunderstand their nature. The only reply suggested is, that if the authorship of

Barnabas be rejected on this ground, it is impossible to imagine any other author in whose case they would be easier to explain. Some, however, have thought from an expression of chap. iii., which seems to imply that the author was one of these to whom he writes, and therefore a Gentile, that the mistakes arose from a second-hand acquaintance with Jewish rites, natural to a heathen Christian of Alexandria, and were not likely to be detected by an audience equally ignorant with himself. Yet, in the face of the approval of the epistle by such men as Clement and Origen, this view is difficult to maintain.

(3.) Hefele's third argument is drawn from its erroneous teaching with regard to Judaism and the meaning of God's old covenant. Undoubtedly this presents a grave difficulty on the hypothesis of Barnabas' authorship, for the epistle is in direct opposition to the Pauline doctrine of the Law as laid down in the Epistles to the Romans and Galatians, as well as to the view given in the Hebrews. To say with S. Paul, that the legal ordinances were transitory, or with the writer to the Hebrews, that they were typical, is one thing; to say that they were never meant to be outwardly observed at all, is another. Nevertheless, there are points in S. Paul's exegesis which come very near to that of Barnabas.[1] And perhaps the latter may be more correctly regarded as an extreme and one-sided application of the Pauline view than as essentially antagonistic to it. Still, the writer's entire inability to grasp the idea of development so forcibly expounded by S. Paul, must lower our estimate of his spiritual intelligence; and those who would fain cherish their scriptural impressions of S. Paul's majestic companion will certainly be slow to admit the possibility of so great a falling off.

On the whole, therefore, our opinion is that these arguments are fatal to the authorship of Barnabas or any other Apostle. It is quite possible that some Alexandrian Christian

---

[1] *E.g.*, the allegories of Sarah and Hagar, and of the "spiritual following Rock" (Gal. iv. 24, and 1 Cor. x. 4), and more especially the application of Deut. xxv. 4, in 1 Cor. ix. 9.

of the name of Barnabas may have written it, for the work is evidently of Alexandrine origin, its cast of thought and mode of exegesis being such as could hardly have arisen elsewhere, and its earliest and indeed only reception as inspired Scripture being confined to the Alexandrian Church. The date is fixed, by internal evidence, as after the destruction of Jerusalem by Titus, and before that by Hadrian (A.D. 70–132). Several dates between these limits have been assigned. Weizsäcker places it under Vespasian (A.D. 69–79); Volkmar under Hadrian (A.D. 119–138); Hilgenfeld under Nerva (A.D. 96–98).

The main argument of all these theories is drawn from the interpretation of two passages in the fourth chapter. The first is a free quotation from Dan. vii. 24, "Ten kingdoms shall reign upon the earth, and after them shall rise up a little king, who shall lay low three of the kings in one." The second, which follows immediately after, is from Dan. vii. 20. "And I saw the fourth beast wicked and strong and untoward beyond all the beasts of the earth, and how that ten horns sprang up out of it, and out of them a little horn as an offshoot, and how that it laid low three of the great horns in one." And he adds, "Ye ought therefore to understand."

The only satisfactory explanation of this enigmatical passage appears to us to be that given by Lightfoot.[1] He points out that, while the Cæsars are evidently intended, the language is wrapped up in mystery to avoid the danger of high treason. Yet the application must be sufficiently obvious for an intelligent reader to supply it for himself. The last great scene of the world's spiritual history is supposed to be at hand, in which Antichrist is expected to appear and wage the final conflict with the saints. Counting the Cæsars from Julius according to the common reckoning, we arrive at Vespasian·as the tenth. Now this prince associated his two sons Titus and Domitian very closely with him in the Empire, so much so that it scarcely seemed an abuse of terms to speak of them as three "in one."[2] The little horn, which

---

[1] Apostolic Fathers, S. Clement, vol. ii. p. 506 *sqq.*

[2] It will be noticed that the puzzling expression τρία ὑφ' ἓν is inserted

is represented as springing out of the ten, and yet not counting as one of them, in fact as an excrescence or offshoot, is intended to apply to Nero, whose death was not fully believed, either by Christians or heathens, both of whom, for many years, anticipated his reappearance or resurrection, the one with anxious dread, the other with wistful expectation. For, incredible as it may appear, Nero was by no means unpopular with the masses, and two, if not three, posthumous claimants to his name had sufficient following to threaten seriously the peace of the Roman Empire. The Christians, on the other hand, had lost by Nero's death the awful but triumphant spell of conflict for which they had prepared themselves, and which was in their eyes the necessary preliminary of Messiah's reign. Hence the plausibility of this interpretation of Daniel's words, which a writer impressed with their imminent fulfilment might easily hint at to readers equally eager, and equally versed in prophecy with himself.

The result of accepting Lightfoot's view is to fix the date within Vespasian's reign, i.e., not later than A.D. 78 or 79, and probably a few years earlier. This brings the epistle well within the apostolic period, before several of the New Testament writings, and considerably before any of the other relics of the first age; and such a date is not only consistent with the scanty and obscure historical allusions, but also with the crude and undisciplined style of Gnosis, of which the author is so proud. If the epistle were much later, we can hardly believe he would have exposed himself to possible misconstruction as exhibiting Gnostic affinities. But in that early period, when tendencies afterwards differentiated were still allowed to co-exist, it was possible for an ecclesiastical writer to show a lack of precision in dogmatic points, which at a later stage of development would have impaired his claim to orthodoxy. Tried by this test, the Christology of our epistle certainly fails to rise to the Catholic standard; nevertheless there is little doubt that the author accepted

by Barnabas, but does not occur in the original prophecy, as is also the case with the epithet "offshoot," παραφυάς, applied to the little horn.

the Divinity of Christ; but, as in the earlier speeches of the Acts and some of the epistles in the New Testament, the idea is not clearly expanded. The acceptance of the work as inspired Scripture by Clement and Origen is much easier to explain on the hypothesis of its remote antiquity than on that of its origin under Hadrian, a time comparatively so near their own.

Its object is to a large extent controversial, and the opponents whom the writer has in view are not Jewish Christians, but Jews, which is another mark of antiquity. We pronounce it, therefore, though with hesitation, as beseems so knotty a point, the earliest Christian document out of the New Testament.

The authorities for the text are mainly two, the Codex Sinaiticus, in which it is found entire, and the Codex Constantinopolitanus, discovered by Bryennios in 1875, which also contains the entire epistle, and which will be referred to on a later page.[1] Both these important MSS. have been recently discovered. Before this took place the text of Barnabas depended on a variety of codices, all derived, though not all actually transcribed, from the same original in which a leaf had been lost containing the end of Polycarp's Epistle and the first portion of that of Barnabas, which was accordingly lacking in all the derived manuscripts. The missing portion was supplied by the Latin version, which dates from a very early period,[2] and is complete, with the exception of the last four chapters. This last portion, which treats of the Two Ways, may possibly be the earliest form of that extremely popular religious manual. It has certainly been closely followed by the tract entitled "Ordinances of Clement and Ecclesiastical Canons of the Twelve Apostles," on which something will be said in a future chapter.[3] And it exhibits marked affinities with the treatment of the same subject in the *Didaché*. Though the transition from chap. xvii. to

[1] See pp. 36 and 57, and also the note in the chapter on the Apostolic Constitutions.

[2] Possibly as early as the second century.

[3] It is also freely used by the author of the *Duæ Viæ*, or *Judicium Petri*, if this is distinct from the Ordinances.

the new departure in chap. xviii. is certainly very **abrpt**.
yet there is no reason to doubt the authenticity of t se
chapters. The writer may have added them at a somev at
later period, which will account for their omission from **he**
old Latin version. But, as Harnack and Rendall have **e**-
marked, their style corresponds very closely with tha c t
Barnabas, and though they were retouched rather than c)-
posed by him, being doubtless of primitive origin. ye
has made them so completely his own as to render it **wl** l
unnecessary to separate them.

Its General Argument.

The general argument of the treatise is **to** prove at
Judaism, at any rate in its ceremonial aspect, is no' in
expression of the Mind of God, but a carnal **misinterp**: a-
tion of commands that were from the first intended t
wholly spiritual. The great point made by Jewish cor o-
versialists was this :—How can you maintain that Christ 1e
Son of God and revealer of His will, has done away the
when God Himself, the unchanging and eternal Father, it
forth that law as the only condition of salvation ? Wi n
the narrow sphere of Rabbinical exegesis this argument 1s
difficult if not impossible to answer. It was necessar o
take a bolder flight, and survey the Mosaic system fr a
higher standpoint. Three writers address themselves to is
task—the Apostle Paul in the Epistles to the Romans d
Galatians, Justin Martyr in his dialogue with Trypho. and ir
author. By none of the three is the argument very cle y
conducted. The Apostle, who had himself been traine n
the Rabbinical method, seems often to divert his logic f: 1
its natural channel in order to accommodate its movemets
to the technical requirements of an artificial theology. S l.
though the expression is obscure, the master-thought is
clear enough, that Judaism and Christianity are succes e
moments of one eternal self-revealing purpose, and that
superseding of the former by the latter in no way invalid. s
its claim to a divine origin. This line of argument is too str

an comprehensive for the mind of Barnabas. He takes the lower ground of retaliating upon the Jews the charge of in pacity to understand God's will. And he does not confine th to his own time, but carries it back to the very foundati of Judaism. So far from the Jewish position being th that the Christians annulled the Divine Law, it is the J 's' own assertion that is false in attributing that law to Gd. The truly Divine law is entirely moral and spiritual. Tse features, such as circumcision, sacrifices, sabbaths, &c., w ch to the Jews are co-extensive with their religion, were i osed on their minds by the persuasions of an evil angel. T Divine revelation has always spoken in one and the s ie sense, and that the Christian. In establishing this t sis, Barnabas betrays the unsoundness of his critical r thod. It is wholly subjective. It relies upon a supposed ical sense underlying the literal, not as a secondary or taphorical application of it, but as the only true reality, to ich the outward expression is a mere glass-case. Thus precept not to eat swine's flesh has nothing to do with question of food; it means that we are not to defile ourves with those vices of which swine are examples : and this ain is harped on through several chapters—the conclusions ing sound and spiritual, but the process absurd, and the ration wearisome.

Another feature of his exegesis is its discernment of Christnity and the Cross in the Old Testament, and in the most unpected quarters—e.g., in the number of Abraham's servants, hich in Greek numerals gives the first two letters of the me Jesus, viz., I H, and the letter T, which represents His oss. In this peculiar fancy Barnabas is equalled, or indeed rpassed, by Justin, who presses nearly every allusion to a tree a piece of wood into the service of a mechanical Staurology. e shall have occasion, in a later chapter, to note the conicuous falling off in strength of conception from the Pauline pistles to the later anti-Jewish Apologists. Armed as they ere with the powerful weapon of Greek philosophy, from hich S. Paul was debarred, they never succeed in reaching, s he did, a truly comprehensive platform, from which it the new departure in chap. xviii. is certainly very abrupt, yet there is no reason to doubt the authenticity of these chapters. The writer may have added them at a somewhat later period, which will account for their omission from the old Latin version. But, as Harnack and Rendall have remarked, their style corresponds very closely with that of Barnabas, and though they were retouched rather than composed by him, being doubtless of primitive origin, yet he has made them so completely his own as to render it wholly unnecessary to separate them.

Its General Argument.

The general argument of the treatise is to prove that Judaism, at any rate in its ceremonial aspect, is not an expression of the Mind of God, but a carnal misinterpretation of commands that were from the first intended to be wholly spiritual. The great point made by Jewish controversialists was this:—How can you maintain that Christ, the Son of God and revealer of His will, has done away the law, when God Himself, the unchanging and eternal Father, put forth that law as the only condition of salvation? Within the narrow sphere of Rabbinical exegesis this argument was difficult if not impossible to answer. It was necessary to take a bolder flight, and survey the Mosaic system from a higher standpoint. Three writers address themselves to this task—the Apostle Paul in the Epistles to the Romans and Galatians, Justin Martyr in his dialogue with Trypho, and our author. By none of the three is the argument very clearly conducted. The Apostle, who had himself been trained in the Rabbinical method, seems often to divert his logic from its natural channel in order to accommodate its movements to the technical requirements of an artificial theology. Still, though the expression is obscure, the master-thought is clear enough, that Judaism and Christianity are successive moments of one eternal self-revealing purpose, and that the superseding of the former by the latter in no way invalidates its claim to a divine origin. This line of argument is too strong and comprehensive for the mind of Barnabas. He takes the lower ground of retaliating upon the Jews the charge of incapacity to understand God's will. And he does not confine this to his own time, but carries it back to the very foundation of Judaism. So far from the Jewish position being true that the Christians annulled the Divine Law, it is the Jews' own assertion that is false in attributing that law to God. The truly Divine law is entirely moral and spiritual. Those features, such as circumcision, sacrifices, sabbaths, &c., which to the Jews are co-extensive with their religion, were imposed on their minds by the persuasions of an evil angel. The Divine revelation has always spoken in one and the same sense, and that the Christian. In establishing this thesis, Barnabas betrays the unsoundness of his critical method. It is wholly subjective. It relies upon a supposed ethical sense underlying the literal, not as a secondary or metaphorical application of it, but as the only true reality, to which the outward expression is a mere glass-case. Thus the precept not to eat swine's flesh has nothing to do with the question of food; it means that we are not to defile ourselves with those vices of which swine are examples: and this strain is harped on through several chapters—the conclusions being sound and spiritual, but the process absurd, and the iteration wearisome.

Another feature of his exegesis is its discernment of Christianity and the Cross in the Old Testament, and in the most unexpected quarters—e.g., in the number of Abraham's servants, which in Greek numerals gives the first two letters of the name Jesus, viz., I H, and the letter T, which represents His Cross. In this peculiar fancy Barnabas is equalled, or indeed surpassed, by Justin, who presses nearly every allusion to a tree or a piece of wood into the service of a mechanical Staurology. We shall have occasion, in a later chapter, to note the conspicuous falling off in strength of conception from the Pauline Epistles to the later anti-Jewish Apologists. Armed as they were with the powerful weapon of Greek philosophy, from which S. Paul was debarred, they never succeed in reaching, as he did, a truly comprehensive platform, from which it was possible to be at once just to Judaism and unsparing of its narrow limitations. The fault of Barnabas, as of the Gnostics, lies in his failure to connect rationally the appearance and work of Christ in Palestine as a Jew, with his severe depreciation of the Jewish element in the Old Testament. Justin surpasses him in breadth and candour, but also fails in appreciation of Israel's spiritual grandeur, in which, as in other respects, he falls infinitely below S. Paul. We conclude with a translation of chapters iv. and xv., which are favourable examples of his style, and show the higher aspect of his teaching :—

The Christians Possessors of the Covenant Forfeited by the Jews.

" Moreover, I ask you this also, as one of yourselves, and loving you individually and collectively more than my own life, to take heed to yourselves and not resemble some who heap up their sins, affirming that the covenant is theirs and ours.[1] Ours it certainly is. But they (i.e., the Jews) have invariably lost touch with it from the day that Moses received it. The Scripture saith, ' Moses was in the mount fasting forty days and forty nights, and received the covenant from the Lord, viz., the tables of stone written with the finger of the Lord.' But they lost possession of it by turning to idols. For the Lord saith in this wise, ' Moses, Moses, go down quickly, for thy people whom thou hast brought out of the land of Egypt have transgressed.' And Moses understood, and hurled the two tables from his hands. And so their covenant was broken in order that the covenant of Jesus the Beloved might be sealed in our heart in hope of the faith which is in Him. Now, because I write to you, not as a teacher, but in the manner of one who loves you, not to fall short of what you possess, I have taken earnest care to address you, I who am your offscouring. Therefore let us take heed in these last days. For the whole time of our faith will profit us nothing if we do not in the present lawless period resist the coming offences as becomes sons of God, that the Black One[2] may not have an opportunity

---

[1] Referring to the Judaising sects who declared that the Mosaic law was still binding upon Christians.

[2] Viz., the angel that presides over the way of darkness.

of entrance. Let us flee from vanity, let us perfectly hate the works of the evil way. Do not shrink into yourselves in solitude as already justified, but come together, and together inquire concerning the common welfare. For the Scripture saith, 'Woe to those who are wise unto themselves, and learned in their own sight.' So let us be spiritual, let us be a temple perfect for God."

No. 2.—The True Doctrine of the Sabbath.

"Moreover, it is written in the Decalogue concerning the Sabbath, 'And ye shall hallow the Sabbath of the Lord with pure hands and a pure heart.' And in another place He saith, 'If thy sons shall keep my Sabbath, then will I send My mercy upon them.' He makes mention of the Sabbath at the beginning of creation, 'And God made in six days the works of His hands, and finished them on the seventh day, and rested on it and hallowed it.' Mark, my children, the meaning of those words, 'finished in six days.' The meaning is that God the Lord will finish everything in 6000 years. For one day with Him is as 1000 years. He Himself attests this: 'Behold! this present day shall be as 1000 years.' Consequently, my children, all shall be finished in six days, i.e., in 6000 years. 'And rested the seventh day.' This means that when His Son shall come and destroy the opportunity of the ungodly one, and judge the impious, and change the sun and moon and stars, then shall He rest well on the seventh day. Furthermore he saith, 'Thou shalt hallow it with pure hands and a pure heart.' If, then, a man who is not pure in heart can now keep the day which the Lord hath hallowed, then indeed we are utterly in error. See whether we shall not *then* rest well and keep it holy when we shall have been justified and have received this promise; and iniquity shall no longer exist, and all things shall be made new by the Lord; and we shall then be able to hallow it, for we shall first have been sanctified ourselves. Farther, he saith unto them (*i.e.*, the Jews), 'Your new moons and your sabbaths I cannot away with.' Ye see how He speaks. The present sabbaths are not acceptable to Me, but the one which I have made, when I shall cause all things to cease and make the beginning of the eighth day, which is the beginning of another world. Wherefore we also (*i.e.*, Christians) keep the eighth day for rejoicing, in

which Jesus both rose from the dead and manifestly ascended into heaven." [1]

[1] In this point Barnabas agrees with the so-called Gospel of Peter, but is at variance with the tradition of the Church. He again departs from it in his assertion in ch. v. that the Apostles were men of extraordinary sinfulness before Christ called them. Origen (Cels. i. 63) quotes and seems to acquiesce in this view. Probably it appeared to bring into greater relief the power of God's grace. But the instinct of the Church has beyond question rightly repudiated it.

CHAPTER V.

THE TEACHING OF THE TWELVE APOSTLES.[1]

CLEMENT of Alexandria, in the first book of his Stromateis, has the following passage, " This man is spoken of as a thief by the Scripture. The words are, ' My son, be not a liar ; for lying leads to theft.' " The origin of this quotation was long unknown, and the Scripture referred to was a matter of conjecture. Again, Eusebius, in his account of the canon given in the third book of his history, places last among the ecclesiastical but uncanonical books (νόθα) of Scripture a treatise which he calls " *The Teachings, so called, of the Apostles.*" He speaks of it as used in some churches, but excludes it from the class of generally received (ὁμολογούμενα) and even of controverted writings (ἀντιλεγόμενα). A fragment supposed to be from Irenæus also refers to a similar work, called "*The Second Ordinances of the Apostles.*" Various attempts were made by scholars to fix on some of the existing treatises as fulfilling the conditions of these allusions, but without success. It has been reserved for the present generation to bring to light the long-lost fragment, and to connect together the scattered and puzzling notices of what was evidently held to be a quasi-inspired work.

In the year 1875 Philotheus Bryennios, Metropolitan of Nicomedia, made the discovery that in a manuscript kept in the Jerusalem Monastery of the Most Holy Sepulchre in Constantinople was contained, among other works of interest, a short treatise entitled "Teaching of the Lord to the Gentiles through the Twelve Apostles." Bryennios subjected it to a thorough investigation, and did not make it public until 1883. The learned world received it with the greatest interest, and within a very short time it had passed satis-

[1] Διδαχὴ τῶν ιβ ἀποστόλων.

factorily through the ordeal of criticism, and was generally accepted as the original lost treatise, of semi-scriptural authority, referred to by Clement and Eusebius. Though its intrinsic inferiority to the Scriptures is immediately evident, and it seems strange that so poor a composition should have gained even the lowest place on the canonical record, yet its historical importance may be estimated by the fact that most scholars attribute its composition to the last years of the first century, the time when Clement was writing his Epistle, a little after Barnabas, but before Hermas and before Ignatius. Some scholars, it is true, place it a little later, within the first quarter of the second century. However this may be, it may safely be allowed to rank among the earliest documents of the post-apostolic Church.

The treatise is very short, filling but a few pages, but it sheds much light upon the obscure interval that separates the close of the New Testament from the rise of Apologetic literature, perhaps the least known period in the entire history of the Church. It professes to embody the apostolic rule of Christian life, together with directions as to worship and administration of the sacraments. It is intended both for teachers and congregations, and formed the basis of the various more elaborate manuals that were circulated as apostolic in later times. It consists of four divisions—1. A summary of practical Christianity under the title of " *The Two Ways, the Way of Life and the Way of Death.*" 2. A short ritual and liturgical manual. 3. An account of the ecclesiastical organisation of the period. 4. A brief statement of Christian eschatology.

Each of these divisions contains matters of great interest.

1. The first, which borrows its title from the Old Testament,[1] most probably formed an original part of the Apostles' teaching. At all events, it struck very deep roots in the early Church. So much of it is reproduced in the Epistle of Barnabas [2] that we may feel quite sure that, if one writer did

---

[1] Jer. xxi. 8.

[2] Though it is often assumed that the Epistle of Barnabas draws upon the *Didaché*, yet this is by no means certain, and several scholars are of

not borrow from the other, both drew from a still more primitive source, which may have been entitled "The Two Ways of Life and Death," or possibly, as we find it in Barnabas, "The Ways of Light and Darkness." The Shepherd of Hermas also reproduces the idea under the form of "The Straight and Crooked Ways," and the Apostolical Constitutions at a later date betray a close familiarity with it. The moral teaching of the "Two Ways" is substantially that of the Sermon on the Mount, arranged under heads, and intended for the systematic instruction of catechumens. Very little dogmatic theology is introduced, and no creed is inserted. We must not, however, infer from this that no syllabus of the Faith was in use at the time of its composition, but partly that the writer's object was practical rather

opinion that both are based upon a common, and that a pre-Christian, source. The very scanty amount of Christian references in the "Two Ways" of Barnabas, as compared with those in the *Didaché*, makes it probable that the *Didaché* has been remodelled upon the basis of the Sermon on the Mount. Such manuals were in use among the Jews of our Lord's time, and would naturally suggest to a Jewish Christian the form in which to cast a similar production of his own. Hence we are led to ask whether any traces can be found of a *Didaché* earlier than that brought to light by Bryennios. Apparently there are such traces. The Egyptian Church Ordinances, a document allied to the Apostolical Constitutions, on which more will be said hereafter, agrees with Barnabas in omitting all references to the Sermon on the Mount in its account of the "Two Ways," but differs from him in other points in which it agrees with a fragmentary Latin version called *Doctrina Apostolorum*, discovered by Gebhardt, and undoubtedly of high antiquity. This Latin version carries us back as near to the original form of the *Didaché* as we are likely to get, and affords evidence that our existing *Didaché* has been amplified and supplemented in those sections (the "Two Ways") which are common to both. The main factor in estimating the influence of our present *Didaché* is the consideration that it was a local document, intended mainly for the Judæo-Christian churches of Palestine and Syria, and never attained to any wide circulation in the Church at large. Its honoured position among the quasi-inspired books in no way contradicts this view, for its great antiquity, its authoritative tone, its Palestinian origin, were all in its favour. And the numerous amplifications of it which appeared in Syria and Egypt testify to a high appreciation of its contents by those who undertook to adapt it to wider use. Scholars like Clement, Origen, and Eusebius, who made it their business to read all the ecclesiastical literature that came in their way, are almost the sole authorities who name the work.

than doctrinal, and partly that the particular section of the
Church for which he wrote was already familiar with the
leading articles of the faith.

2. The second part, which deals with Baptism, Prayer and
Fasting, and the Holy Eucharist, is not less noticeable for
its extreme conciseness than for the primitive character of
its injunctions.   Baptism is ordered to be performed in the
Triune Name by threefold immersion in running water, or in
default of this, in any pure cold water, or in warm water, if
necessary on account of health.   Failing a supply of water
sufficient for immersion, threefold affusion is allowed.   Both
baptizer and baptized are required to fast previously to the
sacrament.   Nothing is said as to the necessity of baptism by
an ordained minister, or of the spiritual significance of the rite.

The fast days are the Wednesday and Friday in each week.
The Lord's Prayer, given almost exactly as in S. Matthew,[1]
is to be repeated three times every day.   The Eucharist is to
be preceded by a thanksgiving for the cup and for the bread,
and followed by another prayer of thanks for God's mercies.
At the close of the act of worship, the prophets are allowed
to give thanks in their own words.

In this and other injunctions we observe the freedom of
the first age co-existing with the beginnings of ecclesiastical formularies and disciplinary regulations.   The period is
clearly one of transition, when the house is being set in order
with a view to impending changes, though they are not expected at once.   The whole circle of ideas in which the
document moves is precisely what might be expected by
those who accept the main results of criticism as applied to
the *origines* of the Church; but it is in startling contrast
with many of the traditionally accepted views, and cannot
fail, when its influence has had time to work, materially to
modify them.

3. The third part gives directions with regard to apostles
and prophets, how to receive them, how to distinguish the
true from the false, and how to apportion their maintenance.

---

[1] In the doxology, "the kingdom" is omitted, perhaps by accident, and
there are one or two other slight variations.

The observance of the Lord's Day is next enjoined, by breaking of bread, and giving of thanks, after confession made in the presence of the congregation. Then follow directions to appoint bishops and deacons, "to minister the service of the prophets and teachers."

4. The fourth part calls on the faithful to watch for the coming of the Lord, in order that they may partake in the resurrection of the saints, which the writer believes will precede the universal judgment.

From this brief summary, it will be at once perceived that a very primitive state of the Church is here presented. Apostles still exist, but by them we are to understand certain companions or followers of the Twelve, not the Twelve themselves, the name being used in a general sense, as in several passages of the New Testament. The prophetic office is also in full vigour, itinerant apostles and prophets being apparently the chief authorities of the Church. Side by side with these are the bishops and deacons, who have evidently taken their position as permanent officials to exercise local government, as distinct from the general and temporary supervision exercised by the apostles and prophets. The order of presbyters is nowhere mentioned, a sure mark of antiquity, showing their identity with the Episcopi or Bishops.

Another feature which recalls the primitive Church is the non-separation of the Agape from the Eucharistic service, just as in the Epistle to the Corinthians and elsewhere in the New Testament. The permission of extempore prayer of the prophets agrees also with New Testament usage, though both these customs lingered on into the second century.

Other signs of antiquity are, the very slight allusions to any written Gospel (chap. viii. § 2; chap. xi. § 3) and the omission of any direction for reading the Christian Scriptures in the Lord's Day service. With regard to baptism, that of adult converts only appears to be contemplated, though, doubtless, the children of Christian families were from the first admitted to this sacrament with their parents. But there is no explicit reference to infant baptism.

It remains to say a few words about the style and language of the book, and about its place of writing. Though, as already remarked, it was by some churches accepted as Scripture, there is no claim to inspiration advanced in the work itself, and its modest tone contrasts very favourably with the exaggerated pretensions of later manuals. There breathes throughout an air of sincerity, even of simplicity, combined with reverence, which stamps the document as authentic, that is, as being what it professes to be, a summary of what the author had learnt from personal instruction or oral tradition to be the Apostles' teaching. The diction is extremely similar to that of the New Testament. Out of 552 words, Schaff finds 504 identical in usage with those of the New Testament; 15 occur first in the *Didaché*, and 14 occur in the New Testament with different meanings.

The quotations from the Old Testament are two only.[1] Those from the New Testament are more numerous, but are confined to S. Matthew, with whose Gospel the author was almost certainly acquainted. Several reminiscences from other books occur, chiefly S. Luke's writings, and it is probable that he was acquainted with some, at least, of S. Paul's epistles. But he shows no familiarity with the distinctive Pauline doctrines, his point of view approaching much more nearly to that of the synoptic Gospels and the Epistle of S. James.

The place of composition is thought by some scholars to have been Alexandria, but others, with more probability, connect it with Palestine or Syria. The Judæo-Christian communities were not much influenced by Pauline teaching, and the theology of S. James continued for some time to predominate among them. The book must have been known at Antioch, where it was expanded, and finally superseded by the Pseudo-Clementine writings. Some have conjectured that the author was Symeon of Jerusalem, and that he wrote it at Pella for the use of the surrounding heathen converts. In any case it is probably the work of a Judæo-Christian, either a pupil of the Apostles or of their immediate associates. The

---

[1] Mal. i. 11, 14, and Zech. xiv. 5.

great historical interest of the work justifies us in appending a translation of it, which will give the reader an opportunity of judging for himself its merits and importance :—

THE TEACHING OF THE LORD TO THE GENTILES THROUGH THE TWELVE APOSTLES.

PART I.—CHAPTER 1.

1. There are two ways, one of life and one of death : and there is a great difference between the two ways.

2. The way of life is this. First, thou shalt love God who made thee : second, (thou shalt love) thy neighbour as thyself. And all things whatsoever thou dost not wish to be done to thee, those do not thou to another.

3. Now the teaching of these words is as follows. Bless those that curse you and pray for your enemies, and fast for those that persecute you. For what thank is it, if ye love them that love you? Do not even the Gentiles the same? But do ye love those that hate you, and ye shall not have an enemy.

4. Abstain from fleshly and bodily desires. If any one give thee a blow on the right cheek, turn to him the other also, and thou shalt be perfect. If a man compel thee to go a mile, go with him twain. If a man take thy cloak, give him thy coat also. If a man take from thee what is thine, ask it not back, for, indeed, thou canst not.

5. Give to every one that asketh thee and ask it not again : for the Father wills to give to all of his own gracious gifts. Blessed is he that giveth according to the commandment, for he is without guilt. Woe to him that receiveth. For if a man receiveth that hath need, he shall be guiltless. But he that hath no need shall be punished, because he received, and up to the amount; and being in durance, shall be examined as to his deeds, and shall not come out thence till he have paid the uttermost farthing.

6. Moreover it is laid down on this head. Let thine alms sweat within thine hands, until thou knowest to whom thou art giving it.

CHAPTER 2.

1. The second commandment of the teaching is—

2. Thou shalt do no murder, thou shalt not commit adultery, thou shalt not corrupt boys, thou shalt not commit fornication

thou shalt not steal, thou shalt not deal in magic, thou shalt not make philtres, thou shalt not procure abortion, nor slay a child that is born: thou shalt not covet that which is thy neighbour's.

3. Thou shalt not perjure thyself, thou shalt not bear false witness, thou shalt not speak ill of any one, thou shalt not bear a grudge.

4. Thou shalt not be double-minded or double-tongued. For a double tongue is a snare of death.

5. Thy word shall not be false or empty, but filled with accomplishment.

6. Thou shalt not be grasping nor greedy, nor a hypocrite, nor ill-natured, nor proud. Thou shalt not take evil counsel against thy neighbour.

7. Thou shalt not hate any one: but some thou shalt convince, and to some thou shalt give way, and others thou shalt love above thine own life.

Chapter 3.

1. My child, flee from (one that is) evil, and from all that is like unto him.

2. Be not wrathful: for wrath leads to murder. Be not a zealot nor a wrangler nor passionate. For from all these things murders arise.

3. My child, be not lustful, for lust leadeth to fornication: nor of base converse, nor given to raising thy eyes, for from these things adulteries arise.

4. My child, be not a soothsayer: for this leadeth to idolatry; nor given to charms, astrology, or lustrations, nor even be willing to look at them, for from all these things idolatry proceedeth.

5. My child, be not a liar: for a lie leadeth to theft; nor money-loving, nor vain-glorious: for from all these things thefts arise.

6. My child, be not a murmurer, for it leadeth to blasphemy; nor conceited, nor evil-thinking; for from all these things blasphemies arise.

7. But be meek, for the meek shall inherit the earth.

8. Be long-suffering, and pitiful, and guileless, and quiet, and good, and reverencing continually the words which thou hast heard.

9. Thou shalt not exalt thyself, nor give rashness to thy soul.

Thy soul shall not be joined with the lofty, but thou shalt hold converse with the just and the humble.

10. The troubles that befall thee receive as good things, knowing that nothing happeneth without God.

CHAPTER 4.

1. My child, remember him that speaketh the Word of God to thee by day and by night. Thou shalt honour him as the Lord. For in whatsoever quarter the Lordship is spoken,[1] there is the Lord.

2. Thou shalt seek out day by day the faces of the saints, that thou mayest rest in their words.

3. Thou shalt not make a division, but shalt set at one those that quarrel. Thou shalt judge justly, thou shalt not respect persons in convicting of transgressions.

4. Thou shalt not be of two minds whether a thing shall be or not.

5. Be not one to stretch out the hand for receiving and close it up for giving.

6. If thou hast (money), thou shalt give it by thy hand as a ransom for thy sins.

7. Thou shalt not hesitate in giving nor murmur while thou givest: for thou shalt know who is the good recompenser of the reward.

8. Thou shalt not turn away from him that is in need, but shalt share all things with thy brother, and shalt not say that they are thine own : for if we are sharers in the Immortal One, how much more in things mortal?

9. Thou shalt not remove thine hand from thy son or thy daughter, but shalt teach them from their youth up the fear of the Lord.

10. Thou shalt not command with bitterness thy slave or thy maiden, who hope in the same God, lest they fear not the God that is over you both. For He cometh not to call you by respect of persons, but those for whom He has made ready the Spirit.

11. And do ye, slaves, submit to your masters in reverence and fear as to a type of God.

12. Thou shalt hate all hypocrisy and all that is not pleasing to the Lord.

13. Thou shalt not forsake the commandments of the Lord,

---

[1] *I.e.*, where Christ is confessed to be the Lord.

but shalt keep what thou hast received, neither adding thereto nor taking therefrom.

14. Thou shalt confess thy transgressions in the church, and shalt not come to thy prayer with an evil conscience.

This is the way of life.

CHAPTER 5.

1. And the way of death is this. First of all, it is evil and full of curse. Murders, adulteries, lusts, fornications, thefts, idolatries, magic, incantations, plunderings, false-witness, hypocrisies, double-heartedness, craftiness, pride, villainy, conceit, covetousness, base conversation, jealousy, rashness, loftiness, insolence.

2. Persecutors of good men, hating truth, loving a lie, not knowing the reward of righteousness, not joined to goodness nor to just judgment, asking not to do good but evil: far from whom is meekness and patience ; loving vanity, pursuing compensation, not pitying the poor, not sorrowing over him that is in trouble, not knowing Him that made them, murderers of children, destroyers of the creation of God, turning away from him that is in need, grinding down the distressed, flatterers of the rich, unrighteous judges of the poor, full of all sin : may ye be delivered, my children, from all these.

CHAPTER 6.

1. See that no one cause thee to wander from this way of doctrine, for (such a one) teaches thee apart from God.

2. For if thou canst bear the whole yoke of the Lord, thou shalt be perfect ; but if not, do what thou canst.

3. In the matter of meat bear what thou canst. But abstain strictly from meat offered to idols, for it is the service of dead gods.

PART II.—CHAPTER 7.

Baptism.

1. Concerning baptism, baptize in this wise : Having said all these things beforehand, baptize (dip) into the name of the Father, and of the Son, and of the Holy Ghost in living (running) water.

2. But if thou hast no running water, baptize into other water : and if thou art not able (to use) cold, use warm.

3. But if thou hast neither, pour water three times upon the head in the name of the Father, Son, and Holy Ghost.

4. Before baptism, let the baptizer and the baptized fast with such others as can ; and thou shalt require the baptized to fast one or two days beforehand.

CHAPTER 8.

Prayer and Fasting.

1. Let not your fastings be with the hypocrites ; for they fast on the second and fifth days after the Sabbath : but do ye fast on the fourth and sixth days of the week.

2. Neither pray ye as the hypocrites, but as the Lord com- manded in His Gospel, so pray ye : Our Father which art in heaven, hallowed be Thy name, Thy kingdom come, Thy will be done in earth as it is in heaven.   Give us this day our daily bread, and forgive us our debt, as we also forgive our debtors. And lead us not into temptation, but deliver us from evil.   For thine is the power and the glory for ever.

3. Use this prayer three times a day.

CHAPTER 9.

The Eucharist.

1. Concerning the Eucharist, thus give thanks (or "celebrate the Eucharist ").

2. First, concerning the cup—" We give Thee thanks, O Our Father, for the holy vine of David Thy servant, which Thou hast made known to us by Jesus Thy Servant.   Glory be to Thee for ever."

3. Concerning the broken bread—"We give Thee thanks, O Our Father, for the life and knowledge, which Thou hast made known to us by Jesus Thy Servant.   Glory be to Thee for ever."

4. "As this broken bread was scattered upon the mountains, and being gathered together became one, so let Thy Church be gathered together from the ends of the earth into Thy kingdom : for Thine is the glory and the power, through Jesus Christ, for ever."

5. Let no one eat or drink of your Eucharist, except those

who have been baptized into the name of the Lord. For concerning this the Lord hath said, "Give not that which is holy unto dogs."

CHAPTER 10.

1. After ye are filled, thus give thanks :—

2. "We give Thee thanks, Holy Father, for Thy holy Name, which Thou hast caused to dwell in our hearts, and for the knowledge and faith and immortality which Thou hast made known to us by Jesus Thy Servant. Glory be to Thee for ever."

3. "Almighty Lord, Thou hast created all things for the sake of Thy Name. Thou hast given food and drink to men for enjoyment, that they may give Thee thanks, and Thou hast graciously given spiritual food and drink and eternal life through Thy Servant."

4. "Before all things, we give thanks to Thee, because Thou art mighty. Glory be to Thee for ever."

5. "Lord, remember Thy Church, to deliver it from all evil, and to perfect it in Thy love, and gather it together, the sanctified one, from the four winds into Thy kingdom, which Thou hast prepared for it. For Thine is the power and the glory for ever."

6. "Let grace come, and let this world pass away. Hosanna to the God of David. If any is holy, let him come ; if any is not so, let him repent. Maranatha. Amen."

7. Allow ye the prophets to give thanks as shall seem good to them.

PART III.—CHAPTER 11.

Apostles and Prophets.

1. Whosoever shall come and teach you all these things aforesaid, receive him.

2. But if the teacher turn and teach another doctrine to destroy (this), hear him not; but if he teach with a view to adding righteousness and knowledge of the Lord, receive him as the Lord.

3. Concerning the Apostles and Prophets according to the decree of the Gospel, thus do.

4. Let every Apostle who comes to you be received as the Lord.

5. He shall remain one day, and if there be need, another day also ; but if he remain three days, he is a false prophet.

6. And when the Apostle cometh forth, let him not receive anything except bread until he go to rest; if he ask for money, he is a false prophet.

7. And every prophet that speaketh in the Spirit ye shall not try nor doubt: for every sin shall be forgiven, but this sin shall not be forgiven.

8. Not every one that speaketh in the Spirit is a prophet, but only if he have the character of the Lord.   By their characters a false prophet and a true prophet shall be known.

9. And every prophet that ordaineth a table in the Spirit shall not eat thereof: if otherwise, he is a false prophet.

10. And every prophet that teacheth the truth, if he do not what he teacheth, is a false prophet.

11. And every approved true prophet sacrificing at the earthly mystery of the Church, but not teaching to do what he himself doeth, shall not be judged of you: for he hath his judgment with God.   For so also did the ancient prophets.

12. And whosoever shall say in the Spirit, Give me money or any other things, ye shall not hear him.   But if he tell you to give in the matter of others that have need, let no one judge him.

CHAPTER 12.

1. Let every one that cometh in the name of the Lord be received; and then, when ye have proved him, ye shall know him.   For ye have the power of discernment on the right and on the left.

2. If he that cometh be a wayfarer, assist him so far as ye are able.   But he shall not abide with you more than two days, or three, if there be a necessity.

3. But if he be willing to settle among you, being a craftsman, let him work and eat.

4. But if he have no handicraft, consider in your wisdom how he may not live with you as a Christian in idleness.

5. But if he will not do this, he is a trafficker in Christ. Beware of such.

CHAPTER 13.

1. Every true prophet who is willing to settle among you is worthy of his maintenance.

2. So also a true teacher is worthy, even as the labourer, of his maintenance.

3. Therefore all the firstfruits of the produce of the wine-press and the threshing-floor, and of the oxen and of the sheep, thou shalt take and give to the prophets. For they are your high-priests.

4. But if ye have no prophet, give it to the poor.

5. If thou makest a feast, take the firstfruits and give it according to the commandment.

6. Likewise when thou openest a cask of wine or oil, take the firstfruits and give it to the prophets.

7. Of money also and of raiment, and of every possession take the firstfruits, and as it shall seem good to thee, give it according to the commandment.

Chapter 14.

1. On the Lord's day of the Lord [1] gather together and break bread and offer the Eucharist, having first confessed your transgressions, that your sacrifice may be pure.

2. Let every one that hath a dispute with his friend not come together with you, until they be reconciled, that your sacrifice be not profaned.

3. For this is the (word) spoken by the Lord : " In every place and time to bring to Me a pure sacrifice ; for I am a great King, saith the Lord, and My Name is wonderful among the Gentiles."

Chapter 15.

1. Appoint to yourselves bishops and deacons worthy of the Lord, meek men and without covetousness, true and approved. For they also minister to you the ministry (divine service) of the prophets and teachers.

2. Do not therefore despise them ; for they are those who are honoured among you with the prophets and teachers.

3. Reprove one another not in wrath but in peace, as ye have it in the Gospel : and to every one that misbehaveth against another let no one speak, nor let him be heard by you, until he repent.

4. Your prayers and your alms and all your actions so perform ye as ye have it (commanded) in the Gospel of the Lord.

---

[1] ἡ κυριακὴ τοῦ κυρίου, a curious expression.

PART IV.—CHAPTER 16.

1. Watch for your life. Let not your lamps be quenched, nor your loins be loosed, but be ye ready : for we know not the hour in which our Lord cometh.

2. Gather yourselves together frequently, seeking the things that are fitting for your souls ; for the whole time of your faith shall not profit you unless ye be made perfect in the last time.

3. For in the last days shall the false prophets and corrupters be multiplied, and the sheep shall be turned into wolves, and love shall be turned into hate.

4. For by the increase of iniquity men shall hate and persecute and betray each other ; and then shall the deceiver of the world appear as the Son of God, and shall do signs and wonders, and the earth shall be given over into his hands, and he shall do unlawful things which have never happened since the world began.

5. Then shall come the judgment of men into the fiery trial, and many shall be offended and perish. But those who remain in their faith shall be saved from the power of the curse.[1]

6. And then shall the signs of the truth appear : first, the sign of the unrolling of heaven,[2] then the sign of the voice of the trumpet, and the third (shall be) the resurrection of the dead.

7. Yet not of all the dead ; but as it was said. "The Lord shall come, and all His saints with Him."

8. Then shall the world see the Lord coming above the clouds of heaven.

---

[1] Others render : "by the Curse Himself," *i.e.*, Christ, who was made a curse for us.

[2] Others render : "the flying forth in heaven," *sc.*, of those who are alive at the time. See 1 Thess. iv. 17. But this use of the word ἐκπέτασις is doubtful. Others interpret it of the Sign of the Cross.

CHAPTER VI.

IGNATIUS (A.D. 40–115 ?).

OF all the early heroes of the Church, there is perhaps none who excites so much interest as **Ignatius**; there is certainly none whose writings have been the subject of such keen and long-continued controversy. He follows Clement at an interval of about twenty years, but those were years of rapid progress, and, when we compare or contrast the two men and their writings, it is hard to realise that they are separated by less than a generation.

Ignatius is often spoken of pre-eminently as " the Martyr," by which title is indicated not indeed his only, but his most conspicuous claim to the veneration of Christendom. It is not that his readiness, or rather his eager impatience to meet a cruel death, may not easily be paralleled in the lives of other worthies. But it is in the opportuneness, in the celebrity of his death, in the dramatic publicity of his progress as a condemned criminal through some of the most renowned cities of the Empire, in his clear perception that by dying he would best serve the cause he loved, in his unshakable resolve to die, that he reveals the lineaments of a hero, and attains a position in the ranks of martyrdom second only to that of the Proto-martyr himself. Yet strange to say, in spite of his fame, to which even Pagan writers testify, the circumstances that precede his death are almost all we really know about him. His previous life is an utter blank. His death is described by anticipation, but nowhere recorded. The few allusions to him in trustworthy writers of later date do nothing to supplement the deficiencies of contemporary history. The earliest mention of him occurs in the Epistle of Polycarp, written to the Philippian Church about the time of his martyrdom; but it is very slight. Origen twice mentions him by name, and quotes three short passages from the letters. Irenæus, A.D. 180, refers to one well-known passage. The Apostolical Constitutions, written in the fourth century, speak of him as Bishop of Antioch. Eusebius, to whom we are indebted for the first connected notice of his writings, besides considerable quotations, supplies a catalogue of the letters which in his opinion are correctly ascribed to the saint, which is of the first importance to the literary historian. If we could be quite certain that Lucian's Satire on the Death of Peregrinus (written about A.D. 165) alluded to the history of Ignatius, we should have an immensely strong corroboration of the truth of the letters themselves and the tradition which gathered round them. But though probability is strongly in favour of the identification of Peregrinus with Ignatius, it cannot be said to be certainly proved.

After Eusebius, we find Athanasius, in a treatise written probably in A.D. 359, alluding to him by name, and quoting a passage from one of the letters. The subsequent authors who profess to supply information about him mostly either borrow, with amplifications, from Eusebius or Origen, or else allow themselves, in the absence of known facts, a free latitude of imagination; to this latter class belong the Acts of Martyrdom known as the Antiochene and Roman. These were long supposed to convey authentic details of the death and burial of the saint, but a more discerning age justly rejects their testimony as absolutely worthless.

All that we can state with any approach to certainty is as follows. Ignatius was a native of the East, probably of Syria, possibly of Antioch. From the expression "an untimely birth," which, like S. Paul, he applies to himself, we should infer that he was not born of Christian parents, but was converted in adult life, most probably by some sudden and violent interposition. Of his previous life we have no record, but Lightfoot thinks his language about himself implies that he had not been free from the moral laxity which was universal among the Gentile world. It is at any rate characterised by remarkable self-depreciation, which seems to be most easily explained by this theory, though, of course, it does not prove it.

He was unquestionably Bishop of Antioch in Syria at the time of his condemnation, but how long he had held this office is uncertain. The earliest tradition speaks of him as an apostolic man, *i.e.*, one who had had personal intercourse with one or more of the Apostles. The Apostolical Constitutions represent him as having been appointed bishop by S. Paul, but this statement is not entitled to much credit. Neither the date of his appointment nor that of his martyrdom is known; but the latter may with great probability be placed within a few years of A.D. 110, before or after. As there are good grounds for believing that he was advanced in life when he met his death, we may suppose him to have been born somewhere about A.D. 40: in which case he may as a young man have seen S. Peter and S. Paul (for the latter of whom he has the veneration of a kindred though lesser spirit); but it is more probable that his conversion occurred later in life, and that, if associated with any apostle, it was with S. John, whom tradition represents as residing at Ephesus until after the close of the first century. A late tradition attributes to him the introduction of antiphonal singing in the public worship of his church; but it is more than probable that this custom, which was known to the Jews, prevailed at or before his time, not only in Antioch, but over a far wider sphere.[1]

The one and only certain event of his episcopal life is that during some excitement or commotion at Antioch, which roused the passions of the multitude, and disturbed the tranquillity of the Church, he was accused before the local tribunal and condemned to death for professing Christianity. For some reason or other, probably the increasing demand for victims in the amphitheatre, he was not executed at Antioch, but sent to Rome to be thrown to the wild beasts. This sufficiently proves that he could not have enjoyed the

---

[1] See Pliny's letter to Trajan, which speaks of the Christians in Bithynia singing hymns antiphonally (the most probable rendering of *secum invicem,*) to Christ as God.

privilege of Roman citizenship, since in that case he would, like
S. Paul, have had the right of appeal, and, in the event of the
previous sentence being confirmed, would, like him, have suffered death by the sword. He was sent from Antioch under
the custody of a maniple, or company of ten Roman soldiers.
The exact route that he followed is not quite certain, but
may be inferred with great probability from various allusions
in his letters, as well as from their titles. "It is probable"
(says Lightfoot) "that he took ship at Seleucia, the port of
Antioch, and sailed to some harbour on the Cilician or Pam-
phylian coast. From this point he must have travelled across
the continent of Asia Minor. The first place where we find
traces of him is near the junction of the rivers Lycus and
Mæander, where the road divides, the northern route leading
along the valleys of the Cogamus and Hermus *viâ* Philadelphia and Sardis to Smyrna, the southern leading to Ephesus
by way of Tralles and Magnesia." Ignatius followed the
northern route, stopping at Philadelphia and Sardis, and
arriving at Smyrna, where a longer halt was made. There
he was welcomed by Polycarp the Bishop, and the Smyrnean
Church, and was also met by delegates from the churches
lying along the southern route, who had, it appears, received
intimation of his movements, and sent representatives to do
him honour. Ephesus was represented by its Bishop Onesi-
mus and four other officials ; Magnesia by its Bishop Damas
and three others ; Tralles, being more distant, by its Bishop
Polybius only. While at Smyrna, Ignatius wrote four of his
extant letters, those to the Ephesians, Magnesians, Trallians,
and Romans. On leaving Smyrna, he was conducted to Alexandria Troas, whither he was accompanied by Burrhus, a
deacon from Ephesus, and where he was joined by two Christians from his own neighbourhood, named Philo and Rhaius
Agathopus, who were destined to accompany him to Rome
and to share his martyrdom. From Troas he wrote three
letters, two addressed to the Churches of Philadelphia and
Smyrna respectively, and the third to Polycarp. He requested these churches to send emissaries to Syria to congra-
tulate the Church of Antioch on the cessation of persecution,

of which fact he had been informed by his two companions. "From Troas he crossed to Neapolis, and thence travelled to Philippi. While there, he desired the Philippians to send a letter to the brethren at Antioch. Accordingly, soon after Ignatius' departure, they wrote to Polycarp, asking him to convey the Syrian letter for them, and further requesting him to send them copies of the letters Ignatius had addressed to him, together with any other letters he might have with him. With this request he complied. It is not improbably to this circumstance that we owe the preservation of the seven letters of Ignatius."

From this point of his journey Romewards we are left to conjecture. When Polycarp, some months later, replied to the Philippians, he had not heard of the saint's death, though he supposes the Philippians, being nearer Rome, may have later news. Of this information we have unfortunately no record; but there is no question that he reached Rome, probably in October, and suffered death in the Flavian amphitheatre by the teeth of wild beasts, under the administration, and no doubt in the presence, of the humane emperor Trajan.

A tradition, which can be traced to the close of the fourth century, declared that his relics had been translated from Rome to Antioch, where his sepulchre was shown in the Christian cemetery outside the Daphnitic gate. In a later generation, under the younger Theodosius, his supposed remains were removed with great ceremony into the Tychæum, or Temple of Fortune, within the city, which was ever afterwards known as the Church of S. Ignatius, and the day of his commemoration (October 17) was altered to December 20, which, though really the anniversary of his translation to the Tychæum, became thenceforth regarded as the actual day of his martyrdom.

It should be remarked that his name, Ignatius or Egnatius (for both spellings occur), is the same as that of the two Samnite generals so well known in Roman history, and has nothing to do with *Ignis*, fire, but is derived, like Gnatius, from the root *gna*—seen in nascor, natus. Lightfoot gives instances of the occurrence of this name in the Eastern world in the early centuries after Christ. In all his letters, he calls himself by the additional name of Theophorus,[1] which is capable of being interpreted either as the God-borne or the God-bearer. From the former supposition a belief arose that he was the child whom Jesus took in His arms and held up to the disciples as the type of the Christian character; but this story, however attractive, is, on chronological grounds alone, evidently impossible. Moreover, it rests on a mistaken interpretation; for the word Theophorus is correctly taken in an active sense, meaning God-bearer, and was most likely given to or assumed by Ignatius at the time of his conversion or baptism. At any rate, it is used by him not as a title, but merely as a second name, just as Saul is also called Paul and Barsabas Justus in the New Testament.

Having thus mentioned at some length, on account of their special interest, the ascertained facts connected with the life and death of Ignatius, it remains to discuss briefly the (for us) more important subject of his literary remains. In this department we shall do little beyond recording the results of Lightfoot's monumental work. If we except the Gospel of S. John, it may be doubted whether any writings -have been the occasion of arguments so conflicting and learning so multifarious.

The first point we observe is that Eusebius, our chief authority, assigns to Ignatius seven epistles, which were extant in his day, and which he evidently regarded as genuine. He arranges them according to the order in which they were written, as follows:—(1) Written at Smyrna: Ephesians, Magnesians, Trallians, Romans; (2) written at Troas: Philadelphians, Smyrneans, Polycarp. These are called by Lightfoot the Epistles of the Middle Recension, and are the same which were discovered in 1646 by Isaac Voss, and are often called the Vossian Epistles. This, however, was not the form in which Ignatius was known to the mediæval and early modern world. Late in the fifteenth and beginning of the sixteenth century, thirteen epistles bearing the name of Ignatius were printed, first in Latin translations and then in the original

---

[1] Ἰγνάτιος ὁ καὶ Θεοφόρος.

Greek, together with a correspondence (manifestly spurious) with S. John and the Virgin, existing in Latin only. This latter was at once discredited. The thirteen letters which existed both in Greek and Latin are as follows: Mary of Cassobola to Ignatius, Ignatius to Mary; Trallians, Magnesians, Tarsians, Philippians, Philadelphians, Smyrneans, Polycarp, Antiochenes, Hero, Ephesians, and Romans. These documents are called by Lightfoot the Long Recension. They maintained their ground for some time, though doubts were entertained of their genuineness by several scholars, partly on account of certain anachronisms and other difficulties, and partly because they included six which did not appear in the catalogue of Eusebius, while the text of the other seven, where it could be compared with his quotations, differed from his. The opinion gradually gained ground that an earlier form of Ignatius was somewhere to be discovered, corresponding to the text which Eusebius possessed. The credit of making this conjecture a certainty is due to Archbishop Ussher, who, judging from quotations of Ignatius in Robert Grostête of Lincoln and other early English writers which differed from the received text, drew the conclusion that in England, if anywhere, the original of these quotations would be found. His sagacity was rewarded by the discovery in 1644 of a Latin translation of Ignatius among the MSS. of Caius College, Cambridge, which he affirmed to represent the genuine writings of the Father. His arguments were soon afterwards confirmed by the publication by Voss of the Medicean MS. of Florence, in which, though some of the leaves had perished, a considerable proportion of the seven epistles of Eusebius, together with the five others, were still decipherable, written in Greek, and with a text obviously representing the original of the Cambridge version.

This text differs from that of the Long Recension in being considerably shorter, and free from those obvious anachronisms which had raised suspicion against the latter, besides omitting several passages which betrayed an author writing in the interest of the Roman supremacy. It displayed, however, in all its fulness, that advocacy of the Episcopal form of govern-

ment, which had been from the first on the part of Protestant
critics the real obstacle of the reception of the Ignatian letters.
The genuineness of this text of the seven epistles, which
is called, as we have said, the Middle Recension, was assailed
by several writers, more especially by Daillé, but not very
successfully, and defended among others by Bishop Pearson.
The result of a long and somewhat bitter controversy was the
all but complete surrender of the longer recension, and the
somewhat hesitating and partial acceptance of the shorter.
Thus matters remained for a century and a half. But in 1847
the question entered on a new phase through the publication by
Canon Cureton, of Westminster, of the Syriac text of three
epistles, those to Polycarp, to the Ephesians and the Romans,
in a still shorter form, which he maintained was the true
original text of the saint, the Vossian letters, in his opinion,
representing an earlier, as the long recension represented a
later, development of the interpolator's art. This theory
found a warm advocate in Bunsen, and no doubt, could it
have been proved tenable, the great à priori obstacle to a
general acceptance of the letters as the genuine work of
Ignatius would have been removed, since the Syriac letters
contain few references to Episcopacy. But the criticism of
Zahn and Lightfoot has conclusively shown that the three
Curetonian letters, as was long ago affirmed by Wordsworth,
are merely an epitome of the Vossian; and that the absence
of the other four letters is due not to the epitomiser being
ignorant of their existence, but to the accidental fact of his
having come to the end of his parchment. The only questions, therefore, that call for solution are: firstly, the date
and author of the interpolated recension; and secondly, the
genuineness of the Vossian recension. Neither of these, perhaps, can be proved to demonstration. But, with regard to
the former, it is sufficiently probable that the author of the
five spurious epistles and the interpolator of the seven is one
and the same person, and that he wrote near the end of the
fourth century.

Zahn's conjecture that he was Acacius, the successor of
Eusebius at Cæsarea, is not an unlikely one; but the truth

will probably always remain in uncertainty. His date is inferred from three lines of argument—(1) an Armenian version from the Syriac, dating from the fifth century, already contains the spurious epistles of the long recension, together with the seven Eusebian; (2) the interpolator must have been familiar with Eusebius, on whose history he shows evident marks of dependence; he has also borrowed freely from the Apostolical Constitutions, which date probably from the fourth century; (3) the historical and ecclesiastical allusions in which he differs from the earlier recension point to the latter part of the same century.

With regard to the other and more important question, whether the Vossian Epistles are themselves genuine, we are justified in asserting that they undoubtedly represent the Ignatian text, as the Fathers from Eusebius to Severus of Antioch used it. It is hardly probable that these credentials will secure their complete acceptance with modern scholars; but even those who, like Rénan, regard the greater number of the letters as a forgery, are obliged to throw back the time of their composition to the second century. Lightfoot, representing the steady and judicial attitude traditional in English scholarship, sums up the evidence on which he decides in their favour in the following propositions, which are here given in an abbreviated form :—

1. No Christian writings of the second century, and few other writings of antiquity, are so well authenticated. If the Epistle of Polycarp be accepted as genuine, the authentication is perfect.

2. The chief objection to the Epistle of Polycarp is that it involves the acceptance of the Ignatian Epistles.

3. The Epistle of Polycarp is exceptionally well attested by the bishop's friend and pupil, Irenæus.

4. All attempts to explain the Epistle of Polycarp as a forgery have failed.

5. Consequently, as the external testimony is so high, only decidedly strong internal evidence (such as anachronisms) should shake our confidence in the epistles.

6. But all the supposed anachronisms have vanished under

the increasing light of criticism, *e.g.*, the alleged allusion to the Valentinian doctrine of Æons,[1] depends on a false reading. The word " leopard "[2] has been proved to have been in common use very shortly after Ignatius. The expression " Catholic Church," which seemed to Lipsius sufficient by itself to condemn the epistles, need create no difficulty at all, if we interpret it simply as " Universal " and not as " Orthodox," for the word Catholic is used again and again before the time of Ignatius in connection with various religious terms, though not actually with ἐκκλησία (Church).

7. Daillé denies the possibility of the prevalence of Episcopal government throughout Asia Minor at the beginning of the second century. But recent research has abundantly proved that he is in error.

8. Again, the circumstances of the saint's journey, as given in the letters and by tradition, did not appear incredible to people who lived within a few generations of his time. There is therefore no reason why they should appear incredible to us.

9. Objections have been taken to the type of character displayed in the epistles as having imperfections which we should not expect in an apostolic man. These objections it is scarcely necessary to answer.

10. The same applies to the imperfections of his style, his exaggerations, instances of false taste, and the like.

11. The careful student will perceive many indications of a very early date. The types of false doctrine condemned are substantially the same Judæo-Gnostic, mixed with Docetic, views which meet us in the New Testament, and not the later successors of these. The ecclesiastical developments are by no means those of the Irenæan age : the apostolic succession, the priestly functions of the clergy, are alike unknown to him. The mode of dealing with the evangelical and apostolic documents is wholly different from what we find in the next age.

12. Undesigned coincidences with regard to the route followed by the Martyr, the geography of the country through

---

[1] Magn. 8.   [2] Rom. 5.

which he passed, &c., have been collected, and shown to be consistent with the tradition.

13. The peculiarities of style, which are very striking, are just such as can be best explained on the supposition that the works are genuine.

14. No satisfactory account of the letters as a later forgery has ever been given. For it may be conclusively shown that they omit all those topics which would interest a later age.

Such are the grounds (briefly stated) on which Lightfoot decides to accept the seven Vossian Epistles. In these, therefore, we may safely conclude that we possess the genuine work of the saint, and the most important testimony extant to the state of Church government and doctrine in the East during the first quarter of the second century.

We now turn from the question of the authenticity of the letters, to that of their permanent interest and value as works of Church literature.

The long period of nearly a century which intervenes between the last of the New Testament writings and those of Irenæus, the first systematic ecclesiastical writer, was a period of rapid growth. At its commencement we are still among the *cunabula* of Christianity: Apostles linger here and there, giving that personal attestation to the Gospel message which was esteemed so much more weighty than written documents. Episcopacy, if it has been established at all, is still in its infancy; probably confined to a comparatively small area in Asia. The Old Testament alone is quoted under the name of Holy Scripture: such evangelistic writings as were circulated were not widely known: a few Epistles of S. Paul and others, and certain Gospels which were by no means yet reduced to their final form: far less was any canon yet fixed.

At the conclusion of this epoch, we see the organisation of the Church in all its essential parts complete. We see not only the same Church order prevailing in all parts of the Christian world, but a well-established system of intercommunication between the various churches, for the express purpose of maintaining the faith intact, and combating as it arises each new departure from primitive tradition. We see the term Catholic applied to the Church and the Faith no longer in its vague popular sense, but in the precise dogmatic one which it has ever since borne: we see a society, still unrecognised by law, still liable to bloody persecutions, increasing in numbers and confidence every day, thoroughly conscious of its strength and inspired by a sense of its destiny, not laying the foundations of its riper structure amid the existing ruins of ancient strongholds, but quarrying in the unbroken mountain-side with the full conviction that the future belongs to itself.

This long and eventful period is broken by but few voices. At its commencement we have the Apostolic Fathers, as they are called, Clement, Ignatius, Barnabas, Hermas, Papias, and a little later Polycarp; but scarce another writer who has left even a fragment behind. The heathen satirist Lucian, it is true, has in several of his treatises allusions to Christian customs, which, in the absence of better information, we are glad to examine, and learn from them what we can. But, on the whole, it may be questioned whether any period of equal importance for the human race has been left with so few authentic records, and that too at the very meridian height of the grandest civilisation the ancient world ever knew.

That this should have been so may well excite our wonder. The causes are various. In the first place, nearly all the early disciples confidently anticipated the speedy advent of Christ and the destruction of the Roman Empire. Even after the first eager hopes had faded away, there was, as we see from Ignatius, a settled conviction that the present state of things would not last long. Under such mental conditions, the practice of keeping written records for the benefit of future ages would not suggest itself, or, if adopted here and there, would not be general.

Moreover, the great majority of believers belonged to those nationalities and classes which were excluded from political and municipal life, to which, therefore, literary composition was unfamiliar, while anything in the shape of monumental or other permanent material records would, of course, be forbidden by the authorities. Indeed, even writings would be liable to seizure, and so become a source of peril to those who possessed them.

The apostolic letters and evangelical histories, which were now gradually making their way, and attaining to the position in which we find them in the time of Irenæus, as a body of authoritative documents, bearing a similar relation to the Christian religion that the Old Testament bore to the Jewish, no doubt satisfied for the present the spiritual needs of the churches, reinforced as they were by the oral testimony of persons who had conversed with Apostles, and faithfully repeated the substance and often the words of their teaching.

What may be called the Hebraic period of the Church's literature was still dominant. There is no sign in Clement or Ignatius, still less in the other sub-Apostolic Fathers, of any desire to incorporate with Christianity the ideas of classical culture or the truths of philosophy. There *may*, indeed there *must* have been a large number of letters and treatises written on different points of the faith as occasion arose, but these have perished, partly from confiscation by the authorities, instigated by hostile Jews, partly from their not having had sufficient general influence to secure their preservation. Hence the few fragments of this intermediate literature that remain have a peculiar interest for us, as forming practically the only landmarks for our guidance during a period when almost all the great institutions of early Christianity were matured. By far the most remarkable of these fragments are the seven letters which bear the name of Ignatius, both from their intrinsic value as evidencing the condition of the churches of Asia as to doctrine and discipline, and also as vivid portraits of a strikingly vigorous and original personality. It would be difficult for any one at all interested in Christian history to treat these letters with indifference. They are of the aggressive type that almost challenges criticism. No greater contrast to the calm, conciliatory and cultured tone of Clement can be imagined than these unskilful but impassioned utterances, which betray a nature ardent, affectionate, strong-willed, perhaps imperious, not moving easily amidst ideas, but deeply possessed with those it has acquired, and able to guard them against the assaults, insidious or violent, of all opposing influences. This strong grasp on ideas, in a mind evidently without literary training, shows itself in many short, pithy, sententious phrases, almost proverbial in their brevity. It is also accompanied naturally by a certain exaggeration of language and a frequent mixture of strained and often incongruous metaphors, which have been quoted as marks of spuriousness, but when candidly weighed tell quite the other way. If we compare the style of the letters of the Long Recension with that of the genuine Ignatius, we are conscious, even where the language is most nearly the same, of a subtle and pervading difference, none the less important because hard to define, which distinguishes the trained writer from the untrained. Simple the style of the letters is not, both thoughts and language requiring close attention before the reader can be sure he enters into them. But though written in haste, perhaps under the eye of an impatient soldier, the want of finish does not affect the thoughts, which are presented with singular power, and recur unmodified in nearly every epistle.

The cardinal conception on which all else turns is the reality of the life, death and passion of Christ as the Incarnate Son of God. It is opposed to the Docetic view so prevalent in early times, so unintelligible to ourselves, that the humanity and, above all, the sufferings of Christ were merely apparent. To Ignatius the passion of Christ is the quintessence of Christian doctrine. Properly understood, it includes the theory of His Divine Personality and His power to save mankind. Publicly confessed, it is the best safeguard against the innovations of heretical speculation.

The other idea, emphasised by Ignatius with continual and almost wearisome reiteration, is the great practical doctrine of the supremacy of the Bishop in each church, and the duty of implicit obedience to him. The prominence which is accorded to this doctrine has always been the great stumbling-block in the way of the acknowledgment of the letters.

The part it plays in them may be judged from the following passages :—

" ' Ye are attached to your Bishop as closely as the Church is to Christ, and as Christ is to God the Father' (Eph. 5). 'Every one whom the Master of the Household sendeth to be steward over His own house, we ought so to receive as Him that sent him. Plainly, therefore, we ought so to regard the Bishop as the Lord Himself' (Eph. 6). 'I advise you, be zealous to do all things in godly concord, the Bishop presiding after the likeness of God, and the presbyters after the likeness of the council of the Apostles, with the deacons also, who are most dear to me, having been entrusted with the diaconate of Jesus Christ' (Magn. 6). 'Be subject to your Bishop and to one another, as Jesus Christ to the Father, and the Apostles to Christ and the Father' (Magn. 13). 'It is therefore necessary that ye should do nothing without the Bishop: but be ye obedient also to the presbytery as to the Apostles of Jesus Christ; . . . and those who are deacons must please all men (i.e., the laity) in all ways' (Trall. 2). 'Let all men respect the deacons as Jesus Christ, even as they should respect the Bishop as being a type of the Father, and the presbyters as the council of God and as the college of Apostles' (Trall. 3). 'It is not lawful without the Bishop to baptize or hold a love-feast' (Sm. 8). 'It is well to know God and the Bishop. He that honoureth the Bishop is honoured of God. He that doeth ought without the knowledge of the Bishop serveth the devil' (Sm. 9). 'As many as are God's and Jesus Christ's, these are on the side of the Bishop. . . . Be not deceived. If any follow a maker of schism, he doth not inherit the kingdom of God'" (Phil. 3).

Passages like these, which are found in all the letters except that to the Romans, sufficiently prove the high conception the writer held of the Episcopal office. But, while we admit that to justify language like this Episcopacy must have been already fully established and its value been proved by experience, yet the references, when carefully considered, are almost as remarkable for what they omit as for what they contain. In the first place, there is no trace of the idea of apostolical succession, so dear to the Fathers of a later age. The Bishop is here in the place of God or Christ: the

presbyters occupy the place of the Apostles. This points
to a time when the memory of Christ and the Twelve was
sufficiently recent to make it the obvious parallel to the
position of the Bishop and presbytery. Again, the prohibition of baptism, except by the Bishop, implies a primitive
state of the Church; indeed, we know that this prohibition
was relaxed at an early period, a result which it is obvious
necessity would soon dictate. Moreover, there is no mention
of Episcopacy as a divine, nor even, if we except one doubtful
passage, as an apostolic ordinance.[1] We do not imply that
Ignatius had any doubt of this; on the contrary, his arguments
everywhere presuppose it; but it is not brought forward in his
letters as a cardinal point. To him the great value of Episcopacy is as a bond of union. As the Church has one faith, one
baptism, one confession, this oneness can only be practically
secured by having One Head, to whom all questions are referred, and all opinions bow. Not that the Bishop is absolute.
The council of the presbyters sit with him as assessors, and
often expressly share in the responsibility of his acts. Indeed,
he still remains a presbyter, and in a certain sense is only
primus inter pares, though the tendency towards monarchical
isolation grew rapidly. And this view throws light on the
omission, otherwise so hard to explain, of any salutation to the
Bishop of Rome. It was in the regions of Asia Minor that
the restless speculative temper of mind prevailed which refused to content itself with the limits imposed by the Gospel
doctrines. New ideas ever surging around and clamouring
for admittance, kept the guardians of the faith fully occupied
in holding their citadel. A central authority was clearly
needed, and thus the circumstances of time and place brought
out first in Asia Minor the inherent capabilities of that office,
which already in the New Testament shows promise of a fuller
development to come. But in other parts of the Empire
there was not the same intellectual ferment. In such cases,
the older constitution would continue, there being no such
call for a change. This we have good reason for believing

---

[1] Viz., "Hold fast to Jesus Christ, to your Bishop, and to the ordinances
of the Apostles" (Trall. 7).

was the case at Philippi, where Polycarp, writing at the time
of Ignatius' death, makes no allusion to a Bishop, but only to
the council of presbyters, as the supreme authority; and
such may well have been the case at Rome, a church which
in the early days was conspicuously free from heresy, and
the bishops of which, though we have their names, do not
appear to have been distinguished by any great difference of
rank or power from their brother-presbyters. The impro-
bability of a developed Episcopal government at so early a
date, then, becomes greatly lessened, if we adopt Lightfoot's
view, that this development was local, not universal; origi-
nating at or near Ephesus, where the last of the Apostles had
probably filled the office himself, and spreading rapidly from
its striking adaptability to the needs of the time; but not
for some time transcending the limits of Western Asia, the
European churches being either governed, like Philippi, by a
council of presbyters or by a bishop acting jointly with such
a council, but without separate prerogative. Where all is
so uncertain, we can at best estimate probabilities. But the
acceptance of the seven letters as genuine necessitates the
acceptance of Asiatic Episcopacy in the monarchical sense as
a form of polity existing already in the second century, and
dating at least from the closing years of the first.

Passing now to other points of interest in the Ignatian
epistles, let us note his theological position considered with
reference to the orthodoxy of a more dogmatic age. There
is no doubt that the spirit of his teaching is in complete
accordance with that of the Nicene Creed; but several expressions are used by him, which might be misunderstood by
those who were trained in a stricter phraseology. When
found in the inspired writings, such expressions are subjected
to canons of criticism which brings them into harmony with
what is believed to be the general sense of Scripture, but in
a few brief letters of a single writer this process is not so
easy to apply. Such are the expressions "generate and
ingenerate,"[1] applied to the Son; "the word (of the Father)

---

[1] γεννητὸς ἀγέννητος (Eph. 7.) These terms are not in strict accordance
with later dogma. Christ is always γεννητὸς never ἀγέννητος; always

proceeding from silence,"[1] which was so liable to misinterpretation that it was changed by the interpolator to "the eternal Word *not* proceeding from silence;" the absence of any distinct formulation of the doctrine of the Trinity, of the eternal generation of the Son, and of His consubstantiality with the Father. But this want of precision of language is in truth valuable testimony to an early date, and is compensated for by the very clear enunciation of those cardinal truths which contemporary heresies obscured. The early form of Docetism, which allied itself with Jewish notions of angelology, emanations and the like, and the inculcation of Jewish observances, is stated and combated with signal force; thus leading us to a time not far removed from the apostolic denunciations of similar views found in S. Paul and S. John.[2] It would be difficult for any theologian to have a greater horror of heretical teaching than Ignatius evinces in all his letters. He calls heretics the herbage of the devil, as contrasted with God's planting, which is the orthodox Church, and utters the strongest warnings to those churches which need them, against allowing themselves to be contaminated by heresy.

In conclusion, we will notice some of the more remarkable expressions used by this Father, as instances of his compression of thought and the quaintness of his imagery. Some of them are quoted by later writers, and have become well known. In the Ephesians we have the following: "Having been kindled into flame by the blood of God," *i.e.*, by the power of a true belief in the Passion, or perhaps by the gift of the Spirit in baptism:[3] "And hidden from the Prince of this world were the virginity of Mary, and her child-bearing, and likewise also the death of the Lord, three mysteries to be cried aloud, which were wrought in the silence of God."[4]

ἀγένητος (uncreated) never γενητός. But the gist of the distinction between these two words was probably not clearly seized by Ignatius.

[1] Magn. 8. Sige (silence) was the consort of Bythus, the Supreme Being of Valentinus.

[2] Allusions to these views occur in the Epistles to the Colossians, Timothy and Titus; in the Revelation, and probably in the first and second Epistles of S. John.   [3] Eph. 1.   [4] Eph. 19.

Again : "The fitly wreathed spiritual circlet of your presbytery." [1]   Again : "If ye be silent (and let me die), I shall be a
word of God ; but if ye love my flesh, I shall be but a voice." [2]
Here the interpolator, shrinking from the boldness of the
expression, has altered it to " I shall be of God."   "Nothing
visible is good," [3] quoted by Origen.   But the best known of
all his utterances is found in the Epistle to the Romans, " I
am the wheat of God, and am ground by the teeth of wild
beasts, that I may be found pure bread." [4]   This, again, is
quoted by several of the Fathers.

Another saying is often referred to for its beauty, " My
love has been crucified," [5] meaning Jesus ; but, although taken
in this sense as early as Origen, and accepted by many after
him, the word rendered love (ἐρώς) cannot be used in a
spiritual sense, but must refer to earthly passion.   The
sentence therefore should be translated, " My earthly desires
are crucified," evidently a reminiscence of S. Paul's " Crucify
the flesh with the affections and lusts."

A writer whose position led him to deal with heresies so
subtle as those of the Docetæ, must needs have acquired
some familiarity with philosophical terms.   Accordingly, we
are not surprised to find a few of them scattered here and
there ; [6] but these isolated instances in no way affect the
general tone of the writer, which is altogether spiritual, and
not in any sense philosophical.   Indeed, they were probably
the common property of educated people.   The same may be
said of the Latin words used, *exemplarium*, a pattern, *desertor*,
deposita, *accepta*, the last three technical military terms, with
which his military guard had no doubt made him very
familiar.

Much more interest gathers round those Christian expressions which we find in him for the first time.   We are indebted to Ignatius for no less than three of these, all of the

---

[1] Magn. 13.   [2] Rom. 2.
[3] Rom. 3.   The Greek words are οὐδὲν φαινόμενον καλόν, which reads like
a verse from a poet.
[4] Rom. 4.   See Is. xxviii. 28 : "Bread corn is bruised."   [5] Rom. 7.
[6] Such as φιλόϋλος, ἐνάρετος, φαινόμενον, τὸ ἀόργητον αὐτοῦ καὶ τὸ ἀκίνητον.

first importance. The word "Eucharist," in the undoubted sense of Holy Communion, occurs first in his Epistle to the Philadelphians.[1] Similarly the word "Christianity"[2] is first met with in him, and not only in its external meaning as a designation of belief, but in its spiritual meaning as a state of heart; in which sense also the word *Christian* occurs: "That I may not only be called a Christian, but also be found one."[3] The expression "Catholic Church" also is found for the first time in Ignatius: "Where Jesus Christ is, there is the Catholic Church."[4] The meaning here, as also in the Letter of the Church of Smyrna (written about A.D. 155), where it occurs three times, is not *Orthodox*, but *Universal*, implying extension, but not as yet doctrine or unity, thus bearing strong testimony to the writer's early date.

The spiritual value of these letters has always been highly esteemed. They form, indeed, no unworthy successors to the epistles of the New Testament. The fervent piety of the man, his transparent singleness of purpose, his unfeigned humility, his enthusiasm for the Lord he served, are indeed common to him with many another Christian writer. But the peculiar intensity of his style, cast in an Oriental mould, lavish in exaggeration, yet totally free from rhetorical artifice or mere word-painting, gives an almost weird power to his words which the more cultivated periods of a Chrysostom or a Basil cannot attain; while the calm strength of his convictions, the loftiness of his ideal, and his firm consciousness that the Divine Spirit is with him, lend a solemn grandeur to his witness for Christ, which is felt increasingly with every fresh perusal. That he was a clear-sighted ruler, may be inferred from his perception that Episcopacy was the surest safeguard against heresy; that he was a man of large practical grasp, may be gathered from his frequent recommendations to the various churches to confer with one another, and consult as to their various needs; that he was an acute judge of character, is proved by his selection of Polycarp as the

---

[1] Phil. 4. [2] Χριστιανισμός, Magn. 10, Rom. 3.
[3] Rom. 3. [4] Smyr. 8.

fittest man to withstand the disintegrating tendencies of the time. In all these points he stands out as the able states-man whose foreseeing genius has sketched out for all time the great lines of Church progress, viz., the threefold ministry, a right selection of the chief pastors, and the necessity of conference between the different dioceses. The subsequent development of ecclesiastical organisation, so far as it has been healthy and fruitful of good, has followed substantially on the lines indicated by him.

CHAPTER VII.

POLYCARP (A.D. 69-155 ?).

THE last of the Apostolic Fathers now claims our attention.[1] **Polycarp** the Elder, Bishop of Smyrna, like Ignatius, with whom he is so intimately associated, is known to us chiefly through information he has himself supplied. But he is more fortunate than his friend in having found a right worthy though unknown chronicler to record the circumstances of his death. In the case of such men as these, who not only belonged to the generation that had seen the Apostles, but held high positions in their respective churches, no authentic detail of their life, conversation, and death can ever lose its interest. Even half-visionary reminiscences of much inferior men are treasured by the pious with scrupulous care, simply because they date back to this sacred epoch; how much more precious are the reflections, precepts and counsels of those who were confessedly the first Christians of their time ?

All readers of Church history are aware that at the time of the siege of Jerusalem the Christian community, mindful of the Saviour's words,[2] had left the doomed city and established itself in Pella and the surrounding mountain strongholds. But these small towns were not fitted to be the headquarters of a new religion. The surviving Apostles and other leading members of the Church of Jerusalem sought a home in the populous cities of Proconsular Asia, and Ephesus virtually became for a time the centre of Christendom. S. John, S. Andrew, S. Philip, and two other disciples of

---

[1] In this chapter, as in the last, the writer expresses his indebtedness to the Bishop of Durham's researches, of which free use has been made.

[2] S. Matt. xxiv. 16.

Christ, Aristion and John the Elder, are the most celebrated names. These gathered around them a circle of reverential learners, of whom, when death had removed the other leaders, S. John became the venerated head. It was among this circle that Polycarp's youth was passed. If we accept as settled the date A.D. 155 or 156 for his martyrdom, then, arguing from his own testimony that he had been eighty-six years a follower of Christ, and interpreting it, as is most natural, to refer to his entire life, we may assign his birth with much confidence to the year A.D. 69 or 70. Irenæus declares that he was appointed Bishop of Smyrna by apostles,[1] and, if this statement be true, he must have held the office for upwards of fifty years. The supposition is not incredible in itself, nor inconsistent with the language either of Ignatius or Irenæus.

We know nothing of the circumstances of his early life. His name would seem to imply a servile birth, but this of course would prove nothing as to the nobility or meanness of his original extraction. From his intimate knowledge of the New Testament, and his almost unconscious reproduction of its language, we willingly infer that he was born of Christian parents, and this being so, he would naturally count his discipleship from his birth. At the same time, there is no certainty in the matter, and some have held that his eighty-six years' service of Christ dates from a conversion in early manhood.

Certain indications of familiarity with Clement's Epistle have led to the question whether he had any personal relations with the Roman Bishop. But to this no answer can be given. One of his early companions, as we know from Irenæus,[2] was Papias, afterwards Bishop of Hierapolis, a church which was in constant communication with that of Smyrna. With Ignatius he became acquainted on the occasion of the martyr's journey Romeward. The eagle eye of the saint, bright with the near rays of another world, detected at once in Polycarp a kindred spirit, and young though

---

[1] iii. 3, 4.

[2] Ver. 33, 4, Παπίας . . . Ἰωάννου μὲν ἀκουστής, Πολυκάρπου δὲ ἑταῖρος.

he was, discerned in him the man fittest of all he had met to be the bulwark of sound doctrine after he was gone. From Troas he thus writes to him, in words which have a prophetic ring :—

"I exhort thee in the grace wherewith thou art clothed to press forward in thy race. Vindicate thine office in all diligence of flesh and spirit. . . . Bear all men as the Lord also beareth thee. . . . Suffer all men in love, as also thou doest. . . . The season requireth thee, as pilots require wind, and a storm-tost mariner a haven, that it may attain unto God. Stand thou firm as an anvil when it is smitten. It is the part of a great athlete to receive blows and conquer. Be more diligent than thou art. Mark the seasons."

More than fifty years (says Lightfoot) elapsed before the athlete was crowned. But in the meantime he fulfilled the work for which he was thus singled out. His character was marked by modesty combined with tenacity of purpose. By an inflexible adherence to the doctrine which he had received from the Apostles, continued through long years, he kept at bay the many intrusive forms of heresy which clamoured for an entrance into the Church. A reverential disposition, which loved, above all things, to accept a trust from a superior and defend it, and an unambitious steadiness of mind, equally proof against the enticements of flattery or the jugglery of self-conceit, made it possible for him to hold a firm path himself and to exercise a steadying influence on the neighbouring churches. He himself was surrounded by a circle of disciples, who venerated him as he had venerated his teacher of old.[2] Of these, Irenæus is by far the most celebrated. Melito, Bishop of Sardis, Claudius Apollinaris and Polycrates, are also names of note. Probably Justin Martyr visited him, when he came to Ephesus. A tradition further asserts that Polycarp sent out Andochius, Benignus and Thyrsus to evangelise Gaul, but its trustworthiness is doubtful.

---

[1] Ign. ad Pol.

[2] See the interesting detail in the letter of the Smyrneans, chap. xiii.

In the closing years of his life he paid a visit to Rome, to consult with the Bishop Anicetus on the vexed question of the observance of the Paschal feast. Among the Asiatic churches, the custom had always obtained of celebrating the Passion of our Lord on the 14th Nisan, whatever the day of the week, in accordance with the Jewish Passover. Anicetus, however, alleged that since the time of Xystus (Bishop of Rome about A.D. 105) his predecessors had kept the Passion on a Friday and the feast of the Resurrection on a Sunday. The conference of the two bishops did not lead to any result, but that it was an amicable one is shown by the Roman Bishop asking Polycarp to celebrate the Eucharist for him, which he consented to do.

The date of this visit is not certain, but may with probability be referred to A.D. 154 or 155. Soon after the return of Polycarp to Smyrna, an outbreak of persecution occurred, to which several Christians fell victims, and Polycarp among the number. The story of his death is related in the beautiful letter of the Smyrnean Church, which will be noticed in the subsequent part of this chapter, and which there is good reason for regarding as an authentic narrative. We there learn that, as soon as the persecution broke out, Polycarp announced his intention of remaining at his post, but was prevailed upon by his friends to withdraw into a place of concealment. His retreat was discovered by a slave-boy under the application of torture, and he was brought back by an officer named Herodes to the stadium, where the people had assembled to witness the inhuman exhibitions of the amphitheatre. The proconsul who presided urged him to swear by the Genius of Cæsar, and say, "Away with the atheists." His reply is thus graphically described: Then Polycarp, with solemn countenance, looked upon the whole multitude of lawless heathen that were in the stadium, and waved his hand to them; and groaning and looking up to heaven, he said, "Away with the atheists." This mode of compliance, however, as may be supposed, was not considered satisfactory. On being further pressed to revile Christ, he made the memorable answer, "Fourscore and six years have I been His servant, and He hath done me no wrong. How, then, can I speak against my King who hath saved me?" Persuasion and threats being alike exhausted, the people shouted that he should be thrown to the beasts. The proconsul, however, explained that, the sports being ended, he could not comply with their wish. They then cried out that he should be burned alive, thus unwittingly bringing to pass a vision which the saint had seen three days before, and had then explained by predicting that he should suffer death by fire. A pyre was at once erected, and the sufferer, declining the kind offices of his friends, disrobed, and was bound to the stake. He raised his eyes to heaven and offered up a prayer. As soon as this was ended, the firemen lighted the fire, "and, a mighty flame flashing forth, we to whom it was given to see, saw a marvel; yea, and we were preserved that we might relate what happened to the rest. The fire, making the appearance of a vault, like the sail of a vessel filled by the wind, made a wall round about the body of the martyr, and it was there in the midst, not like flesh burning, but like a loaf in the oven, or like gold and silver refined in a furnace. . . . So at length the lawless men, seeing that his body could not be consumed by fire, ordered an executioner to go up and stab him with a dagger. And when he had done this, there came forth a quantity of blood, so that it extinguished the fire; and all the multitude marvelled that there should be so great a difference between the unbelievers and the elect." The Jews, who, according to their wont, had been busy inciting the malice of the crowd, persuaded the authorities to burn the body, on the plea, ridiculous in itself, but apparently credited by the proconsul, that it might otherwise receive divine honours; but the bones were collected by his faithful friends and deposited in a secure resting-place. The anniversary of his death was kept as a festival on February 23 in the Greek Church, and on January 26 in the Latin.

If the intrinsic merit of Polycarp's extant epistle were its sole passport to fame, we may safely assert that it would not have been now in our hands. As literature it does not rise

G

above the level of commonplace, and there is nothing in the arguments or exhortations that bespeaks a great mind. Nevertheless, this short letter has had more numerous and more careful readers than many a work of tenfold greater intellectual power, for it is confessedly the cardinal support of the Ignatian letters. If it be accepted, they cannot be rejected; if it be rejected, they lack their best and oldest witness. Thus it was the Ignatian controversy that first shook the credit of Polycarp, and still lies behind the adverse verdict of critics. But the authentication of his epistle is so good, resting as it does on the testimony of his own pupil Irenæus,[1] that nothing short of violent methods avails to discredit it.[2] There is good ground for believing that it was read in public in some parts of Asia as late as Jerome's day,[3] and that this practice had been long in existence when that Father wrote. The testimony of antiquity was wholly in its favour, and internal grounds alone would justify us in calling it in question. The only plausible argument of this kind is based on the expression, "whosoever perverteth the oracles of the Lord to (serve) his own lusts, and saith that there is neither resurrection nor judgment, is the firstborn of Satan." It appears that Polycarp used this very expression, "firstborn of Satan," when speaking of Marcion. If, therefore, the passage in question refers to Marcion, whom Polycarp saw at Rome certainly not earlier than A.D. 154, it is no doubt an anachronism. But Lightfoot proves conclusively that the charges made in the passage are quite inapplicable to Marcion, and are properly applied to the Antinomian Gnostics who taught in Asia Minor at the beginning of the second century. As to the opprobrious term of condemnation, a writer is not unlikely to have repeated it more than once if he felt the occasion called for it; and no more puerile

---

[1] Epist. ad Florinum, quoted by Eusebius, H. E. v. 20.

[2] Daillé supposes that the passage which refers to Ignatius (c. 13) alone is spurious. Bunsen followed him. Polycarp's complete silence as to Episcopacy seemed to these critics a sign of general genuineness ; but, as Lightfoot shows, the thirteenth chapter is actually better authenticated than the rest. This procedure, therefore, is rightly described as violent.

[3] Vir. Illustr. "usque hodie legitur," c. 17.

argument can be adduced than that a writer must be restricted to one use and no more of a pithy or sententious phrase. Every literary critic can recall among the later works of great poets reminiscences of their earlier expressions, sometimes exact, sometimes slightly varied, but cast in the mould of earlier days and easily recognisable. Many such instances are found even in the most careful writers, as Virgil and Milton; and Polycarp, who was hardly an author at all in the strict sense of the word, wrote for use and edification, not for literary fame.

The fact is, that neither expressions indicative of unauthenticity nor any suggestions of collusion between the writer of Polycarp's Epistle and those of Ignatius can be made good. With the exception of their identity of date and of certain contemporary allusions, there are no resemblances of thought or language, but many striking differences. Our conclusion is that the epistle may safely be accepted as what it professes to be, the genuine writing of Polycarp, and as such an invaluable witness to the genuineness of the more important letters of Ignatius.

Closely connected with the history of Polycarp is that of the letter from the Church of Smyrna already referred to, which professes to give from the hands of eye-witnesses the narrative of his martyrdom. It is addressed to the Church of Philomelium, a small town in the interior of the province of Asia, and was written shortly after Polycarp's death. Its genuineness has never until quite recently been called in question. The great scholar Lipsius is the most eminent of those who impugn it. He places its composition in the time of the Decian persecution, about a century later than its professed date. The chief argument he relies on is the occurrence of the expression " Catholic Church " four times in the letter. Three of the instances, however, use the word in its primitive sense of Universal, and one only in the later sense of Orthodox. And Lightfoot has shown that in this case the reading should, on the authority of the MS., be altered to ἀγία (holy), which thus meets the objection.

Among the more sceptical critics, Rénan holds it to be

genuine, and there can be little doubt that he is right. The earliest direct testimony to the letter is found in Eusebius, who quotes the greater part of it, and expressly intimates that it is the earliest history of a martyrdom with which he was acquainted. That it was widely popular within a few years of its composition is sufficiently clear from the traces of imitation which we find in the scarcely less celebrated Letter of the Gallican Churches attributed by many to Irenæus, and from the fact that Eusebius thought it worthy of a place in his "Collection of Ancient Martyrdoms."

If we ask to whom the authorship is to be referred, we must be content to confess our ignorance. At the conclusion of the letter there are three supplementary paragraphs which deal with some features of its literary history. (1) A chronological appendix giving particulars as to the time of the martyrdom, by which the date can be fixed with the same approximate precision as has been attained on independent grounds.[1] The appendix was almost certainly written by the same hand as the letter itself. (2) A commendatory postscript, also thought by Lightfoot to be genuine, and probably added by the Philomelian Church. (3) A history of the transmission of the document, which the same critic believes to be the work of the unknown author who wrote the spurious life of Polycarp ascribed to Pionius. If this conjecture be just, the present recension of the letter dates from the fourth century, and is therefore posterior to Eusebius. Pionius himself was martyred at Smyrna during the Decian persecution (about A.D. 250), and was celebrated, among other reasons, for his great reverence for Polycarp. And the writer who assumed his name in writing a life of Polycarp, though obviously an untrustworthy biographer, seems in this case to have been content with adding one or two interpolations to an otherwise faithfully preserved text.

"The Martyrdom of Polycarp" is well worthy to rank as the model on which such narratives should be based. Its deep earnestness, its transparent good faith, its touching

---

[1] See the most instructive argument in Lightfoot, vol. ii. p. 610 *sqq.*

simplicity of language—a little homely sometimes, but never wanting in refinement—have called forth from critics of widely different schools the warmest admiration. Not less striking than these is its moderation of tone, and, amid the general craving for marvels, the slightness of its appeal to the miraculous. It contrasts most favourably in all these respects with the "Acts of Ignatius," [1] and conveys, what few similar documents do, an irresistible impression of its truth. We may couple it with the Ignatian Epistle to the Romans, and consider them as forming together the most interesting memorial of the sub-apostolic age. The one, all fire and passion, seems in its impatience to devour the interval that delays the joys of martyrdom; the other, wistful and retrospective, scatters with tender hand sweet flowers over the grave of the martyr who has waited so long to win his crown. Those who are accustomed to treat this class of narratives as mere empty and untrustworthy panegyric, no doubt find many examples which justify their opinion; but if they begin the study of them by reading this, the first of the series, they will incline towards a more sympathetic criticism of documents emanating from zealous if uncritical disciples, who chronicled from time to time their teacher's or companion's "faithfulness unto death."

[1] Written probably in the fourth century.

CHAPTER VIII.

PAPIAS AND THE ASIATIC ELDERS (A.D. 70-150?).

IT has already been remarked that the centre of Christendom after the fall of Jerusalem shifted from Palestine to Asia Minor. Even before that event, if we accept the earlier of the two dates for the Apocalypse, the Asiatic churches had been S. John's special care. And if the later date under Domitian be preferred, it is still a fact worth remarking that this great prophetic forecast of the Church's final conflict was primarily addressed not to Hebrew nor to Roman Christians, but to the Seven Churches of Asia. At what time S. John fixed his home in Asia we know not. Probably it was not long after A.D. 70. Tradition speaks of a small band of disciples, including also Andrew and Philip, who settled at Ephesus. Of these S. John became the sole survivor, his life being prolonged until after the accession of Trajan (A.D. 98). In his later years he is represented as exercising a general supervision over Asiatic Christendom, and in particular as appointing bishops in the churches. The result of his unique and long-continued authority was the formation of what may fairly be called a school of theology, which flourished for more than a century, producing many famous names, from Polycarp to Polycrates.

Not the least distinguished member of this school was **Papias**, Bishop of Hierapolis, whose name is familiar to the readers of modern controversy from its intimate connection with the question of the New Testament canon. The name Papias is an uncommon one. It is recorded as one of the appellations of Zeus, the tutelary deity of Hierapolis, and so seems to point to a heathen origin ; but this is only conjecture, and the circumstances of the saint's conversion from heathenism, if conversion there was, are altogether unknown.

Irenæus tells us that he was "a hearer of John, and a comrade of Polycarp." [1] By John, Irenæus unquestionably means the Apostle, and by the term "comrade" he implies fellow-discipleship, and consequently near equality of age. From the position assigned to Papias in Eusebius' History, [2] we should infer that he was somewhat older than Polycarp, or at any rate, that his death preceded Polycarp's. He may thus have been born between 60 and 70 A.D. and have died about A.D. 135–150.

So far as his date goes, then, he might well have been a hearer of S. John. But, as in his existing fragments he makes no allusion to any such intercourse, and as Eusebius, in his notice of Papias, seems decidedly to dispute it, modern writers have generally done the same, though, as Lightfoot has shown, on inconclusive grounds. For Irenæus, with regard to a matter of fact within his own purview, is an authority of the highest order, and no doubt had access to sources of information denied to Eusebius. On the whole, it seems best to regard his discipleship of S. John as probable, though not fully proved.

Of his subsequent biography we know nothing. His appointment to the see of Hierapolis is evidence that he possessed a firm hold on Catholic doctrine and displayed administrative gifts. Accounts of his capacity differ. While Eusebius depreciates him as a man of very mean intellect, [3] Irenæus quotes him with high respect as an orthodox writer and trustworthy channel of apostolic tradition. This favourable judgment was adopted in the Church. The name of Papias has always stood high, in spite of the peculiarity of some of his views.

His literary monument was a work in five books, entitled, "Exposition of the Oracles of the Lord," or more exactly, "Of Dominical Oracles," [4] which was largely used by Irenæus, was known to Eusebius, was extant in the time of Jerome, and

---

[1] Ir. Hær. v. 33, 4.

[2] His notice of Papias occurs in the thirty-ninth chapter of his third book; that of Polycarp in his fourth book.

[3] σφόδρα μικρὸς τὸν νοῦν.   [4] Κυριακῶν λογίων ἐξήγησις or ἐξηγήσεις.

apparently was not lost until the beginning of the thirteenth century. The title of this work has been the subject of much discussion. The word ἐξήγησις has been explained by some to mean "narration," instead of "interpretation" or "exposition," and λόγια to mean "discourses," instead of "oracles." Lightfoot has conclusively shown that both these renderings are incorrect. Whatever matter Papias may have brought into the body of his book, he certainly intended its title to imply "an explanation or exposition of the sacred records concerning the Lord Jesus Christ." And the scanty fragments we possess correspond exactly with such a title. They are evidently parts not of a newly-constructed evangelical narrative, but of a commentary on one already existing. The scope of the work is in part also deducible from Papias' own words, contained in the preface or dedication. These form one of the many precious fragments of earlier literature preserved by Eusebius, and are as follows:—

"But I will not scruple also to give a place for you along with my interpretations to everything that I learnt carefully and remembered carefully in time past from the elders, guaranteeing their truth. For, unlike the many, I did not take pleasure in those who have so very much to say, but in those who teach the truth : nor in those who relate foreign commandments, but in those who record such as were given from the Lord to the Faith, and are derived from the Truth itself. And again, on any occasion when a person came in my way who had been a follower of the elders, I would inquire about the discourses of the elders—what was said by Andrew, or by Peter, or by Philip, or by Thomas or James, or by John or Matthew, or any other of the Lord's disciples, and what Aristion and the Elder John [1] the disciples of the Lord say. For I did not think that I could get so much profit from the contents of books as from the utterances of a living and abiding voice."

The advantage to the modern student of such a body of original tradition as Papias here implies that he had amassed

---

[1] On the highly interesting question first started by Eusebius, whether John the Elder and John the Apostle are different persons, the reader is referred to Lightfoot, Essays on Supernatural Religion. It is too complicated to be discussed here. The writer ventures to differ from Lightfoot's view, and believes that they were the same person.

would have been incalculable, quite independently of its
being (as it doubtless was) of unequal historical value. Even
supposing the compiler to have been, as Eusebius declares he
was, a man of limited intellect and poor judgment, nevertheless the possession of records drawn from the living voice
instead of from second-hand narratives would have more
than counterbalanced a good deal of garrulous pedantry.
Lightfoot has pointed out in his Essay on Papias[1] what a
multitude of interesting questions might be started even from
the few sentences of the procemium; how many facts, biographical and literary, about the Apostles, now unhappily
lost to us, are suggested by his enumeration of just those
seven whose names are connected with gospels canonical or
apocryphal. We may well deplore the unkindness of Fate,
or to speak more truly, the narrowness of dogmatic prejudice,
which has suffered such a work to perish, and preferred to
bequeath us the innumerable dry dissertations of a later erudition, which, however theologically unexceptionable, retain
little or nothing of that living voice which the simple Papias
had still the sense to value. As we have said, the object he
set before him was primarily to explain the existing evangelical narrative; but no doubt it also included the collection
of such additional authentic sayings or anecdotes of Christ
and His contemporaries as would be gathered from the "tradition of the elders." The term "elder," it may be remarked,
is applied by him to the Apostles as well as to their followers,
and denotes not office, but authority and antiquity. His personal intercourse with these elders was limited to his early
life, probably before he had any thought of writing his book ;
and the information he derived was in consequence fragmentary. When he set himself in his later years to collect a
systematic body of information, he found it necessary to
supplement his personal reminiscences by a free use of
secondary evidence.

The fragments of the Expositions of sufficient length to
enable us to judge of their quality are three in number.

[1] I have borrowed freely from Lightfoot, Essays on Supernatural Religion (5–7).

They are eminently characteristic, and their great interest will justify our insertion of them in full. The first is preserved by Irenæus,[1] and is a good example of the exegetical method of Papias, which was to give, first, the saying of Christ recorded in the written Gospels; secondly, the interpretation of the saying; thirdly, the illustrative story derived from oral tradition, to which the author gives a place along with his interpretation. It is founded on the saying of our Lord at the Last Supper,[2] " I will not drink henceforth of this fruit of the vine, until that day when I drink it new with you in My Father's Kingdom."

" As the elders relate, who saw John the disciple of the Lord, that they had heard from him how the Lord used to teach concerning those times, and to say, 'The days will come in which vines shall grow each having ten thousand shoots, and on each shoot ten thousand branches, and on each branch ten thousand twigs, and on each twig ten thousand clusters, and on each cluster ten thousand grapes, and each grape, when pressed, shall yield twenty-five measures of wine. And when any of the saints shall have taken hold of one of their clusters, another shall cry, " I am a better cluster; take me, bless the Lord through me." Likewise also a grain of wheat shall produce ten thousand heads, and each head shall produce ten thousand grains, and each grain shall yield ten pounds of fine white flour. And all the other fruits and seeds and grass shall follow the same proportion; and all the beasts that feed on those fruits that grow out of the ground shall become gentle and harmonious, being subject to mankind in all subjection.' And he added, saying, 'Now, these things are credible to them that believe.' And when Judas the traitor did not believe, and asked, 'How shall such growths be accomplished by the Lord?' the Lord replied, 'They shall see who shall come to those times.'"

One has only to read the above passage to understand why Eusebius disliked Papias, and only accords to him such space in his history as is consistent with the barest justice.[3] The

---

[1] Hær. v. 33, 1 sq.   [2] S. Matt. xxvi. 29.

[3] He uses the phrase ἀναγκαίως νῦν προσθήσομεν, implying that he feels bound in accordance with his plan to set down what he has, but that he will not weary his readers with more than he can help of such stuff.

critical and well-regulated intelligence of the courtier bishop
might well recoil from the coarse materialism and the scarcely
less culpable credulity of such exegesis as this. If some other
instances given by Eusebius are fair samples of the whole
work, it would seem to have been a good deal taken up with
stories of marvels, in which the mythical and the historical
were more or less confused. But it was not so much by
these that Eusebius was offended as by the decided millenarian views which Papias, in common, it must be confessed,
with a majority of the early Fathers, entertained. There is
reason to think that his whole interpretation of the New
Testament was coloured by this bias. And, however welcome
his traditional authentication of it might be to Irenæus, who
was himself similarly inclined, it would constitute a grave
blot on the book in an age when millenarian views were
utterly discredited; and no doubt this was one main ground
of the neglect into which it fell.

The second fragment, which, like the first, was taken from
the fourth book, is on the same subject, and is preserved in
the same book of Irenæus.

"As the elders say, at that time those who are counted
worthy of the dwelling in heaven, shall go thither; while others
shall enjoy the delights of paradise, and others shall obtain the
splendour of the city. For everywhere the Saviour shall be seen,
according as those who see Him shall be worthy. And this distinction of dwelling (they taught) exists between those who brought
forth a hundred-fold, and those who brought forth sixty-fold, and
those who brought forth thirty-fold: Of whom the first shall be
caught up into heaven, the second shall abide in paradise, and the
third shall inhabit the city: and it was for this reason the Lord
had said that in His Father's house are many mansions. For
all things are of God, who giveth to all their fitting dwelling-
place."

Here, again, though we may not think highly of a theology
which insists on defining exactly what the Divine Speaker
chose to leave undefined, and on materialising what is evidently
spiritual, yet we do not agree with Eusebius in regarding

such fragments of the Church's golden age as valueless, but rather as full of religious interest and historical significance.

The third fragment is of a wholly different character, and, as bearing on the question of the New Testament canon, is thought worthy of preservation by Eusebius. It refers to the origin of S. Mark's Gospel.

"And the Elder said this also: Mark, having become the interpreter of Peter, wrote down accurately everything that he remembered, without, however, recording in order what was either said or done by Christ. For neither did he hear the Lord, nor did he follow Him: but afterwards, as I said, attended Peter, who adapted his instructions to the needs of his hearers, but had no design of giving a connected account of the Lord's oracles. So then Mark made no mistake, while he thus wrote down some things as he remembered them; for he made it his one care not to omit anything that he heard or to set down any false statement therein. . . Matthew, indeed, composed his Oracles in the Hebrew dialect, and each translated them as he could."

As might be supposed, this passage has been the battle-ground of many opposing arguments. Scarce a line or a word in it that has not been subjected to a lynx-eyed scrutiny, not always benevolent. But on the whole it stands the for-midable test of modern criticism, and, in spite of its awkward style, supplies the most trustworthy account we possess of perhaps the oldest of the Gospels.

Besides these three consecutive fragments, there are a few very brief excerpts from the Expositions, amounting in all to some eight or ten lines, and all with one exception containing some valuable relic of information. It is obvious to any student of Scripture that the utility of a book like that of Papias is to a great extent independent of the ability of its author. Did we possess it entire, we should be well able to discriminate between apocryphal legends which imposed on Papias' credulity, and genuine traditions, such as the one just quoted, which carry us back to the apostolic period. We can hardly doubt, for instance, that in his emphatic declaration of S. Mark's perfect accuracy, Papias is drawing not on his own conviction, nor even on the general consensus of Church opinion, but is reporting the expressed judgment of an Apostle, and if so, who could that Apostle be but S. John himself, who alone would be competent from his age and dignity to criticise the work of a companion of S. Peter?

It is, perhaps, even now within the range of possibility that the entire Expositions may yet be brought to light; and if so, we may be sure that some of the burning questions as to the origin of the Gospels will be brought nearer solution, if not finally set at rest.

In spite of what he himself states in his preface, much misconception has prevailed as to the polemical object Papias had in view. While the author of "Supernatural Religion," following his German guides, regards him as intending to counteract unauthentic narratives by a more correct one, drawn from oral sources, Lightfoot, with infinitely greater probability, considers that he wrote against false inferences from the Evangelists' records made by the Gnostic heresiarchs. Any one who reads the *Philosophumena* of Hippolytus will at once appreciate the necessity for some such counterblast. Whatever may be thought of the intellectual originality of the Gnostic leaders, the unsoundness of their exegetical method is apparent, and Papias, living in the very time and place where these theories burst into life, could have chosen no better way of counteracting them than by insisting on the continuous stream of authentic interpretation, of which, though he might have selected it more carefully, he rightly estimated the value.

The fifth book of Irenæus is to a great extent occupied with such interpretations, and there is little doubt that many elements of Papias' work are embedded in it, though, in accordance with the custom of his age, he seldom acknowledges his obligations. As has been said, the early Church writers were far too full of their subject to trouble themselves about incurring the charge of plagiarism. Whatever commended itself to their judgment they inserted, sometimes with a reference to its source, sometimes without. It would not have occurred to them to think they were either defrauding a predecessor or themselves incurring the guilt of unfair appropriation.

Besides Papias, several other "elders" are referred to by Irenæus as "hearers of the Apostles and those who learned from them." One of these unnamed worthies composed a short metrical epigram, directed against the impostor Marcus, which the reader will find in the note.[1] Its poetical merits must be allowed to be a minus quantity; nevertheless, it is important as being the earliest attempt to embody party-criticism in verse, and thus evincing some desire to make it popular instead of confining it within a technical dialect accessible only to a few. The scanty fragments of this group of elders may be found in Routh's *Reliquiæ sacræ*, where the will find also much erudite and sensible criticism.

---

[1] In Iren. Hær. I. 15, p. 80.

εἰδωλοποιὲ Μάρκε καὶ τερατοσκόπε,
ἀστρολογικῆς ἔμπειρε καὶ μαγικῆς τέχνης,
δι᾽ ὧν κρατύνεις τῆς πλάνης τὰ διδάγματα,
σημεῖα δεικνὺς τοῖς ὑπὸ σοῦ πλανωμένοις,
ἀποστατικῆς δυνάμεως ἐγχειρήματα,
ἅ σοι χορηγεῖ σὸς πατὴρ Σατᾶν ἀεὶ
δι᾽ ἀγγελικῆς δυνάμεως Ἀζαζὴλ ποιεῖν,
ἔχων σε πρόδρομον ἀντιθέου πανουργίας.

The metre is crude and the epithets unparliamentary. The use of the term Azazel as a minister of the Evil One is remarkable.

CHAPTER IX.

THE "SHEPHERD OF HERMAS."

THE work that now comes before us differs widely in character from those we have already considered. They consist of letters, sermons or treatises, and belong to the ordinary types of religious literature. The "Shepherd of Hermas" is of a more ambitious scope. It professes to be the record of revelations made by an angel on many points of the Christian life, ranged under the several heads of Visions, Commandments, and Similitudes, and extending to considerable length. It was written in Rome in the Greek language, and speedily attained such reputation as to be translated into Latin for the use of the Roman Church, a version which dates almost certainly from the second century.[1] Later versions were also made.

This fact testifies to the high value set upon a book which formed almost, if not quite, the only example of prophetic literature in the early Church.[2] Not that the "Shepherd" is a prophecy in the narrow popular sense, for it contains no predictions. But it combines the assumption of direct supernatural teaching with general views on the mission of the Church and the way of salvation, directed towards the practical object of reforming certain abuses in the writer's own community. This gives it its main interest for us. As the Old Testament and Apocryphal Scriptures have their Daniel and Esdras respectively, as the New Testament has its

---

[1] The antiquity of the Latin version, which we fortunately possess entire, is shown by the translator thinking it necessary to explain the word *Episcopi* by *præsides Ecclesiæ*, and by other less striking marks of early date—*e.g.*, *nuntius* for *Angelus*, &c.

[2] The second Epistle of S. Peter and that of S. Jude are probably instances of what were known as prophetic writings in the apostolic age.

Apocalypse, so the Patristic records can point to Hermas as an example of the same spiritual illumination.

In order to give the reader some general idea of the book, which seems to be less appreciated than it deserves, we propose to give a short summary of its contents, omitting the homiletic portions, and confining ourselves to its peculiarly distinctive features.

Hermas, a slave of uncertain nationality, was sold at Rome to a lady named Rhoda. After an interval of some years, during which he doubtless obtained his freedom, he was admitted to her intimate companionship, and learned to love her as a sister. On one occasion he surprised her while bathing in the Tiber. Having assisted her out of the water, the thought came to him, " How happy I might have been if I had had such a woman as this for my wife ! " It should be remarked that Hermas was a married man of middle age, with grown-up children, and that his domestic relations were far from satisfactory. Some time after, while walking to Cumæ, meditating after his wont, he fell asleep on the road, and in a vision was transported by a precipitous path across a torrent into a level country, where he saw the heavens opened and Rhoda beckoning to him with the words, " Hail, Hermas ! " He asked her what she did there, and she answered, " I am brought hither to convict thee of sin before God." Hermas begged her to explain herself, whereupon she reminded him of the thought that had passed through his mind at the river-side, and advised him to pray for the Divine forgiveness. The heavens then closed, and Hermas lay trembling with fear, and almost in despair, when an aged lady appeared sitting on a throne as of white wool, clothed in shining raiment, holding a book in her hand. She asked him why he, who had been always cheerful, was now so sad. He told her the reason, and she assured him that though he had for the moment lapsed from his accustomed virtue, it was not on this account that the Divine displeasure was aroused, but rather because of his faulty management of his sons, who (it appears) had been guilty of disgraceful conduct, and brought on him the loss of a once thriving business.

She directed him to begin forthwith a stricter discipline, and offered, before departing, to read him a chapter from the book in her hand. Hermas listened with attention mingled with dread, but could not recall more than the last few words, which happily were such as to reassure him. The lady, having finished, rose from her chair, which was immediately lifted by four young men, and carried towards the sunrising. She then touched his bosom, and uttering a few words of comfort with a cheery smile, was transported by two men into the eastern quarter of heaven. Her last words rung in his ears ; they were, " Hermas, play the man ! "

The second vision appeared in the same place, not long after the first. The lady offered him her book, which he read, but for some time could not remember. Then its contents returned to him ; they were partly personal to himself, and partly referred to the rulers of the Church in Rome, to whom he was bidden to communicate its warnings. A handsome youth then appeared, who explained to him that the lady he had seen was not the Sibyl as he had fancied, but Ecclesia or the Church, who wore the form of an aged dame, because she is the eldest of created things, for whose sake, in fact, the world was made.

The third vision occurred in another locality, chosen at the lady's instance by Hermas himself. There he saw an ivory bench draped in white linen, to which the lady advanced attended by six youths. She bade him sit on her left hand, explaining that the right hand seat was reserved for such as suffered persecution for the cause of Christ. She then pointed out to him the six youths engaged in building a tower of many kinds of stones, which were brought from the pit by other young men. Some of these stones were wrought into the tower, others were in various ways rejected. She explained to him that this tower was the Church on earth ; the six youths were the six principal angels, the other young men the inferior angels, who were gathering the nations into it. The tower was built in water, to show that membership of the Church is obtained through baptism; and its foundations were cast in the rock, which is the Word of God. Hermas put many questions to her concerning the various sorts of stones, each of which was emblematic of some class of baptized Christians, whose judgment would be in accordance with the treatment of the stones in the vision. She next showed him seven women standing round the tower. These are the seven Christian graces, Faith the mother of them all; then Temperance, Simplicity, Innocence, Modesty, Knowledge, Love, all born successively one from another. Then followed other appearances, the explanation of which Hermas was bidden to seek by prayer and fasting. On complying with this condition, he was enlightened by a young man, evidently an angel, on all the points on which he sought information.

The fourth vision was seen twenty days after the third, in a retired spot near the Campanian road. A cloud of dust, as if from a large herd of cattle, appeared, but as it drew near, Hermas beheld a huge and uncouth monster, out of whose mouth proceeded a swarm of fiery locusts. Beside himself with terror, he cried for deliverance. A heavenly voice reassured him; he took courage, and passed it unscathed. Then he met a damsel fair of mien, but with silver locks, arrayed in gorgeous apparel, in whom, though changed, he recognised his friend Ecclesia. She explained to him that the beast was a type of the persecutions that shortly awaited the faithful, and entered into further details on the accessories of the vision.

The fifth and last vision is introductory to the *Commandments*, which form the second section of the book. A man of august demeanour, habited like a shepherd, visited Hermas in his own home, and offered to remain as a permanent guest. Suspecting some design of the Evil One, Hermas received him doubtfully; but his visitor, changing into another form, revealed a countenance which Hermas recognised at once as that of the Angel of Repentance, whom he now gladly welcomed as his own Guardian Spirit.

From this incident the book derives its title of *The Shepherd*. The second and third divisions are supposed to be spoken by the angel in this pastoral guise. The second division contains twelve commandments, the first of which is an important formulation of the central truth of theology, and may be taken as the basis of later authoritative pronouncements. The words are quoted as Scripture by Irenæus,[1] and referred to by Origen and Athanasius: "First of all believe that God is One, who created and set in order all things, and made all things to exist out of non-existence, who comprehends all things, being Himself incomprehensible. Believe in Him and fear Him, and believing in Him, be continent. Guard this doctrine, and thou shalt cast away from thee all wickedness, and put on all the virtue of righteousness, and thou shalt live unto God, if thou keep this commandment."

The second commandment speaks of simplicity, the third of truthfulness, in which Hermas admits himself in past times to have failed. The fourth treats of chastity, and, from its authoritative tone, seems to legislate for the Church. A decision is given by the angel on the difficult questions connected with unfaithfulness to the marriage vow: "A man may not without sin live with his wife, if he knows her to be unfaithful and unrepentant. He must separate from her and lead the single life; if he marries again, he sins. If the guilty one repents, the husband (or wife, for of course these rules are reciprocal) must accept such repentance, but only once."

The reason why marriage immediately after divorce for infidelity is forbidden is because it cuts off all chance of repentance from the offending party. By the sacrament of baptism all previous sins are washed away; after baptism there ought to be no lapse into sin: pardon, however, is allowed to one such lapse if followed by sincere repentance, but to no more than one. Further post-baptismal sin cuts off from salvation. Remarriage after widowhood is permissible, but not recommended.

It was this judgment of Hermas that so greatly scandalised Tertullian after he had accepted the rigid tenets of

[1] Ir. iv. 20, 2. καλῶς οὖν εἶπεν ἡ γραφὴ ἡ λέγουσα, Πρῶτον πάντων πίστευσον ὅτι εἷς ἐστιν ὁ θεὸς ὁ τὰ πάντα κτίσας καὶ καταρτίσας.

Montanism. He inveighs in no measured terms against the "Apocryphal Shepherd of adulterers," and declares that the book was adjudged spurious and apocryphal by the entire synod of the churches.[1] On the justice of this assertion something will be said hereafter. But it must be confessed that Hermas betrays a personal sense of relief at the lenity of the angel's views, which seems to suggest that "the wish was father to the thought."

The fifth commandment treats of longsuffering and command of temper. The cause and effects of anger are described at length, but without the power of analysis shown by Seneca or Epictetus. The sixth describes the two paths of justice and injustice, and attributes them to the influence of the angels who preside over each. This and the following sections afford frequent parallels with the Epistle of Barnabas and the Apostolic Teaching. No doubt the subject was a commonplace of the early Christian moralists.

The seventh and eighth commandments treat of the fear of God, and of abstinence; the ninth of faith and the necessity of a mind free from doubt; the tenth of cheerfulness and gloom. The eleventh begins with a vision of men seated on benches (*subsellia*), while another sat on a *cathedra*, or presidential chair. The former denote the faithful, the latter is the false prophet. By him we are probably to understand some influential teacher, who disseminated what soon came to be known as Gnostic views; but Hermas treats the Gnostics so gently that we may be sure they had not in his time revealed their full power of injury. Valentinus came to Rome before the middle of the second century; and as he set the Church ablaze with his teaching, it would be impossible to assign to Hermas a date posterior to his visit. The picture of the unstable Christian drawn different ways by the plausible arguments of unscrupulous pretenders to the prophetic office, and of the contrast between the false prophet

---

[1] De Pudic. cc. 10 and 20. Sed cederem tibi si scriptura pastoris, quae sola moechos amat, divino instrumento meruisset incidi, si non ab omni concilio Ecclesiarum, etiam vestrarum (the Catholic Church) inter apocrypha et falsa iudicaretur, &c.

and the true, are among the best portions of the whole book, and well deserve perusal not only from their vivid descriptiveness, but from the light they throw on the religious views of the time. There is little doubt that Hermas claimed for himself prophetic rank; and as we can detect a personal bias in most of his general observations, we may infer that the true prophet's method as here depicted is an idealised representation of that of Hermas himself.

The twelfth commandment treats of good and evil desire; after the exposition of which Hermas expresses a doubt whether human nature is capable of fulfilling the Divine requirements. The angel explains to him the power of grace, the longsuffering forgiveness of God, and the necessity of a renewal of heart. This closes the second part of the work.

The third, and by far the largest portion, is devoted to the ten *Parables* or *Similitudes*. The first of these is based on the well-known comparison of the Christian life to citizenship in the celestial city, so powerfully sketched by S. Paul and the writer to the Hebrews. The second is drawn from the mutual dependence of the elm and the vine, as illustrated by any of the vineyards of Italy. This comparison is familiar to classical students from the allusions in Virgil and Horace. It is here applied to the relationship of rich and poor in the Christian community, and to their divinely-appointed power of mutual help, the one by material, the other by spiritual charity. The third and fourth are drawn from the spectacle of a plantation of trees, some of which are quite leafless, some shooting forth tender leaves, others dry and dead. The points of comparison in this instance are far-fetched and not very instructive. The fifth similitude is more elaborate. Hermas had undertaken what was known as a *Station*, *i.e.*, a fast recurring at certain periods.[1] The Shepherd informed him of the usefulness of such discipline, explaining that the true and acceptable fast is to abstain

---

[1] From the use of this word Westcott infers the later of the suggested dates for the book. It is, however, possible that the word *Statio* came into use before we meet with it. Moreover, from the careful explanation given by Hermas, it is clear it was a new word in his day.

from all sin. He illustrates his doctrine by the following parable : [1] " A man owned an estate worked by his numerous servants, of whom he chose the most trustworthy to be the keeper of his vineyard. He directed him to hedge it round and stake it out, promising him his freedom when he returned if the work were well done. The servant did what was commanded, and, having time to spare, proceeded further to thoroughly clean the soil from weeds. The master returned, and great was his satisfaction at his servant's industry and goodwill. He called together his son and his friends, and proposed that as a reward for his extra work the servant should be admitted to joint-heirship with the son. To this they willingly agreed. In a few days the lord sent the man a present of choice meats from his own table. The servant at once summoned his fellow-servants and gave them all a share in his good things. This pleased the lord and his son still more." The drift of this parable, which is sufficiently obvious, is thought by some, though without reason, to involve the doctrine of works of supererogation, fasting being considered by Hermas to be one of such works. But this view, though plausible, is probably erroneous. The explanation of the several items is as follows : The estate is the world, the owner is God, his son is the Holy Spirit, his servant is the Son of God, the vines are his people whom he has planted, the fences are the angels; the weeds are the misdeeds of Christians, the dainty meats are the commandments given through the Son, the friends and counsellors are the first-created angels, the time of the owner's absence is the interval before the end of the world.

A point to notice in this interpretation is the apparent confusion of the Holy Spirit with the Eternal Son of God, an idea which has a Gnostic ring. The Christology of Hermas is somewhat undefined, and perhaps inconsistent : but Baur is certainly unjust in attributing to it an Ebionite significance. Dorner's masterly analysis shows that, though his

---

[1] The coherence of this parable with the sentence which introduces it is not very clear. But the general subject of fasting as an *extra* merit supplies the connection in the writer's mind.

language lacks precision, Hermas does *not* confuse the Holy
Spirit with the pre-existing Logos, nor represent Him as the
Divine Element in the historical Christ.

We now pass to the sixth similitude (to which the seventh
is an appendix), that of the two shepherds and the two flocks.
The sheep of the first flock are seen feeding abundantly,
frisking about, and ranging abroad at will; some, however,
are much less restive than others. These last are separated
and drafted off into the second flock, which is watched over
by a stern shepherd, armed with a rod and scourge, who
drives them over rough ground till they are worn out. The
two shepherds are the Angels[1] of Pleasure and Punishment.
The frisky sheep are the unrepentant wicked, the quieter
ones those that desire to repent and are by punishment
disciplined for a return to the Way of Life. The theory of
penitence given in this chapter is that which has prevailed
so largely at times in the Church, viz., that confession of sin
and change of life on the sinner's part are not sufficient, but
must be supplemented by voluntary humiliation and self-
inflicted suffering in order to be accepted by God.

The eighth similitude is that of a willow-tree, whose
branches are lopped by the sickle of the glorious angel,[2]
who distributes the small rods into which the branches are
divided to the different persons who take shelter under the
tree. After a time he returns to demand back the rods.
These are brought to him in various states of freshness or
decay. The angel, wishing to give them all a chance of
growth, has them planted in good soil and carefully watered.
The different results of the experiment are then described,
and explained with extreme minuteness, a graduated scale of
characters from the purest sainthood to the hopeless condition
of the reprobate being drawn, and adjusted to the award
given in each case by the Judge.

The ninth similitude is the most pretentious of all, and
occupies a full quarter of the entire book. It belongs more

---

[1] The word Angel in Hermas, as in the New Testament, is a neutral term.

[2] Called Michael. Probably the same as the Son of God in Sim. 5; not
ranked with the other angels.

accurately to the category of a vision; but Hermas draws
no very clear line between the three *media* of his revelations.
He is transported into Arcadia [1] into a wide plain out of
which a high mountain rises, surrounded by twelve hills,
each hill having a different aspect and different products.
In the midst of the plain stands a huge stony rock, having
a gateway which shines like the sun, guarded by twelve
virgins, with garments girt high, as if for some laborious
work. Then there enter on the scene six men of dignified
aspect, accompanied by a multitude of labourers. They call
up choice stones from the abyss, which come of their own
accord, and are delivered to the virgins to be carried through
the gate and handed on to the builders inside. Soon are
raised on the rock the foundations of a vast tower. The
labourers then go out to search for stones of all sizes and
colours, which they bring to the gate and hand over to the
virgins. These grew into a lofty tower, which, as it approaches completion, the Lord of the country comes to in-
spect. He tests all the stones, and those which will not bear
the test are taken out, and entrusted to the Shepherd to
dress and clean, so as to fit them, if possible, for reinsertion
into the tower. Then follows a long description of the various
defects in the stones, answering to the different faults of
character in their human parallels. The larger part are
finally trimmed up, and by the help of mortar and cement
present a fair appearance when wrought into the wall. Hermas is requested to assist the Shepherd in this work. The
Shepherd then leaves him for two days in the company of
the twelve virgins, who treat him with friendly familiarity,
insisting upon his passing the night in their company, and
even kissing him, but with all modesty, as sisters might kiss
their brother. On the Shepherd's return, Hermas applies
for an explanation of the numerous features of the parable,
which is granted. The rock and the gate both typify the
Son of God, the former representing His eternal pre-existence,

---

[1] Zahn for Ἀρκαδία would read Ἀρικία on the ground that Hermas had
never travelled out of Italy. But in this kind of literature accuracy of
time and place is not to be rigorously demanded.

the latter His mediatorial work. The Lord of the tower is also the Son of God; the six overseers are the six chief angels, the twelve virgins are the twelve divine graces, beloved of all faithful souls, and are contrasted with twelve other females, who are somewhat briefly alluded to as the desires of the flesh, and who lure unstable souls to their doom. The twelve graces are Faith, Continence, Power,[1] Longsuffering, Simplicity, Innocence, Purity, Cheerfulness, Truth, Intelligence, Concord, and Love. The twelve evil maidens are Unbelief, Incontinence, Disobedience, Deceit, Grief, Wickedness, Luxury, Anger, Falsehood, Folly, Evilspeaking, and Hatred. The different classes of selected stones typify the different lists of the righteous, viz., the patriarchs before and after the flood, the prophets, the apostles, and the later heroes of the Gospel. The depth from which all arise is baptism, even the patriarchs being supposed to have partaken of it in the abode of departed spirits. The twelve hills are the twelve nations of mankind, each with its own moral characteristics. The tower is the Church, and the renewal of the rejected stones is the discipline of repentance. The explanation is enforced with tedious minuteness, and interspersed with hortatory passages on the necessity of penitence and the terrors of the wrath to come.

The tenth similitude is preserved only in the Latin translation. It forms a kind of sequel to the last, and contains the final injunctions of the Shepherd to Hermas, and through him to all Christians, to persevere. It appears to be an afterthought, written when the book was already complete; and it contains no new ideas, except a warning that unless the Christians of his own day are quick to return to their Lord, the tower will be finished and they left out.

Such is a brief and imperfect analysis of this curious book, the high estimation of which by such authorities as Clement of Alexandria, Origen, and Athanasius, is in striking contrast to its comparative neglect by the modern reader. "Not very edifying and unquestionably dull," is, we fear, the common verdict. Nothing shows better the defective critical insight

---

[1] So the Greek. The Latin has *patientia*.

which accompanied the reverent and earnest spirit of those
times than the fact that the Shepherd was for some generations quoted as Scripture, and if not held to be inspired, at
any rate placed little below the Inspired Writings.

No doubt its claim to be a revelation stood it in good
stead; yet, if we compare it with the remains of Clement,
Polycarp, or Ignatius, its inferiority is at once manifest.
From beginning to end it rings the changes on a single idea,
the possibility and necessity of repentance. Important as
this is, and earnestly as it is enforced, it is hardly an adequate
presentation of the Gospel. The reader will in vain seek for
any intelligent appreciation of the great doctrines on which
Christianity is built, or for that wide view, that full and
varied spiritual insight that lends grandeur to the calm
tones of Clement; nor will he find any of that eager, trenchant force that makes the pages of Ignatius sound like the
march of a hero's tread. Yet the book has an enduring
value, partly as the unique remnant of quasi - prophetic
literature, partly as an earnest endeavour to concentrate
men's minds upon the paramount necessity of a holy life.

Notwithstanding this sacred object, doubts have been
raised as to the *bona fides* of the author. He is held by
some critics to have been no genuine seer, but to have
clothed his own lucubrations in an apocalyptic dress, the
better to accredit them with his contemporaries. On this
theory the direction to Clement in the third vision, requesting him to send the book to foreign churches, is an intentional anachronism, designed with the same object. It is
difficult to disprove this view; and the more so because
Hermas betrays more than one element of moral weakness.
He praises himself, he confesses to a lack of truthfulness,
he lingers too wistfully over incidents of female intercourse
for a man of chaste mind. Nevertheless, the broad fact that
the book so soon rose to reputation, in a community by no
means prejudiced in its favour, seems incompatible with the
theory that it is virtually a fraud. Donaldson's view is less
likely still. He regards it as an obvious fiction, issued as
such, and deceiving nobody. But here, again, the serious

use made of it by great Fathers of the Church stands in the way. It is impossible to believe that confessedly fictitious visions, even of higher merit than those of Hermas, would be cited as Scripture by men ready to die for their faith. The only tenable view is that which the book itself supports, viz., that Hermas really believed himself to be the recipient of angelic instruction, and, either in dreams or in abstracted moods of thought, saw the spectacles which he has described. The reader who comes to the book without prejudice will doubtless question the objective reality of the revelation claimed by Hermas; he will rank him with those whose claims to genius Time, the master-critic, has disallowed, while granting him the secondary distinction of an honourable place among pious writers.

The style of the Shepherd is simple and clear, though at times colloquial. His dialect is scarcely the Hellenistic of ecclesiastical authors. It has no Hebraic affinities, and shows no traces of the study of the LXX., in this differing remarkably from that of Clement, which is saturated with reminiscences of the Old Testament. Nor does Hermas display any greater knowledge of the New Testament. The only book with which affinities can be proved is the Epistle of James, to which indeed the resemblances are very marked. His theology also belongs to the same school, being practical and undogmatic. The Pauline doctrine of justifying faith is alluded to, but does not enter into his system, or affect his modes of thought. There are some correspondences with the teaching of S. Peter, and, as might be expected, occasional points of contact with the Apocalypse. But on the whole Hermas cannot be said to show much familiarity either with Scripture[1] or with the scheme of Christian theology, though there is nothing to show that he wandered away from either.

The materials for determining his personal history and position in the Roman Church are extremely scanty. The

---

[1] It is odd that the only book he quotes by name is the apocryphal one of Eldad and Modad, to which also the Pseudo-Clement is supposed to refer.

few notices of his life scattered in the book have been already referred to. His rank in the Church is indicated under the type of a bench (*subsellium*), as distinguished from a chair (*cathedra*); by which we are to understand that he was a layman. Moreover, that he disapproved of the strife for pre-eminence that existed among the Roman presbyterate, we gather from several allusions. Possibly he may have tried without success to obtain a place in its ranks.

As to his date, we can bring it within tolerably definite limits if we accept the authority of the Muratorian fragment on the canon as decisive. This fragment, which perhaps dates from about A.D. 170, and which Lightfoot believes to be a translation of an earlier Greek document in Iambic verse, contains an important sentence relating to the Shepherd. The words are :—

"But the Shepherd was written quite recently in our own day in Rome by Hermas, at the time when his brother Pius occupied the chair of the Roman Church; and for this reason, although it ought to be read, it cannot be set forth to the people in the Church either among the prophets whose number is complete, or among the apostles in the latter days." [1]

This passage is of importance on two accounts. First, for the chronology, with which we are now concerned; and, secondly, as bearing upon the reception given to the book. The assertion that Hermas, the writer of the "Pastor," was a brother of Pius, made as it is by a contemporary, carries such weight that nothing short of overwhelming counter-evidence can upset it. And no such evidence is forthcoming. It is true other considerations taken by themselves might suggest an earlier date, *e.g.*, the state of church government and discipline indicated, which belong to the Primitive Church, the mention of Clement as a contemporary, the early acceptance of the book by the Church. But none of these objections

---

[1] Vv. 73, 80. Pastorem vero nuperrime temporibus nostris in urbe Roma Herma conscripsit sedente cathedra urbis Romae ecclesiae Pio episcopo fratre ejus, et ideo legi quidem oportet, se publicare vero in ecclesia populo neque inter prophetas completum numero (numerum ?) neque inter Apostolos in fine temporum potest.

are sufficient to outweigh the express testimony of a credible witness. It is uncertain at what date Episcopacy proper was established in Rome. The mention of Clement need not imply that he was living at the time; possibly, as before noted, the name is an intentional anachronism. Or again, Hermas being perhaps an elder brother of Pius, may have lived almost if not quite as far back as Clement's time. The words *nuperrime temporibus nostris* do not suggest any very recent date, but rather the reverse. The term is used only as a contrast to a more remote period. It means little more than that he was a contemporary. On the whole, therefore, the balance of probability lies in assuming that Muratori's "author" was truly informed, and that Hermas had written his book soon after A.D. 139, if not a little before. Zahn, however, one of the ablest and most recent editors, claims for it a much earlier date (A.D. 96 or 97), and Salmon also seems to incline to the same view. This theory makes the acceptance of the work by so many churches easier to understand, and intrinsically would be probable enough, were not the evidence against it too strong to be set aside.

We shall now proceed to mention briefly the chief writers of the Church who allude to the Shepherd, with a view to showing the amount of authority accorded to it. To begin with the Greek Church. The earliest Father who refers to it is Clement of Alexandria. He quotes or alludes to it in some eight or nine passages [1] with much apparent reverence, though without explicitly asserting that he regards it as having the authority of Scripture. He is followed by Origen, who gives it as his opinion that the book is inspired, and ventures the conjecture (since uncritically adopted by numerous ecclesiastical writers) that the author is none other than the Hermas mentioned by S. Paul in his Epistle to the Romans. In the time of Eusebius we learn that the book was generally used in the preparation of catechumens, and found supporters for its insertion among the books of Scripture, chiefly on the ground of its conjectured authorship. To this claim, both for critical reasons and also from the

[1] Given in Harnack's Proleg. pp. liii.–liv.

general bent of his mind, Eusebius is decidedly opposed. But from the cautiousness of his language it is not very easy to decide what his judgment is. He seems inclined, however, to place it among the orthodox νοθὰ or spurious books.[1] Coming to the fourth century, we find that the celebrated *Codex Sinaiticus* gives it a place in the Appendix to the New Testament, after the Epistle of Barnabas. Since, however, several passages lent themselves to an Arian interpretation, the Shepherd must have gradually dropped out of use, or, at any rate, declined in authority. Accordingly, we find it omitted from the Alexandrian MS. at the beginning of the fifth century. Its further use in the Eastern Church is so slight as to amount to virtual non-recognition.

In the Western Church it had a longer currency. Without attaching any weight to the theory, which, from the undoubted resemblances between it and the so-called Second Epistle of Clement, would infer some connection between them, we may remark that both are the product of the same age and surroundings, and that therefore some similarity is to be expected. The first undoubted allusion is found in Irenæus, and has been already quoted.[2] This makes it probable that the book was read in his day in the Gallican churches, but not that it was ranked on a level with the Canonical Scriptures; for in that case it is inconceivable that Irenæus should not have made more frequent use of it. Somewhat later Tertullian, writing at Carthage, speaks of it in the same terms as Irenæus,[3] but also without implying that it was ranked on equal terms with the books of the Prophets or Apostles. Some years after, when he had become a Montanist, and changed his attitude of reverence for one of contemptuous hostility, he declares that the pretensions of Hermas to canonicity had been universally disallowed.[4] The

---

[1] Hist. Ecc. iii. 25, 4: ἐν τοῖς νόθοις κατατετάχθω . . . ὅ τε λεγόμενος Ποιμήν . . . ταῦτα δὲ πάντα τῶν ἀντιλεγομένων ἂν εἴη. It is not clear whether he regards it as merely pseudonymous, or whether he also denies its divine inspiration.

[2] See above, p. 115, *n.*

[3] De Orat. 16. Inimo contra *scripturam* fecerit, si quis, &c.

[4] De Pud. 10, before quoted.

index of verses of Scripture appended to the *Codex Claromontanus*, which probably belongs to the same period, refers to the "Pastor" after the books of the New Testament, classing it with the Revelation of Peter and the Acts of Paul, works which were never included within the canon. The Pseudo-Cyprianic treatise *de Aleatoribus*, also written in Africa, and probably in the third century, quotes a passage of Hermas as Divine Scripture. Later still, the author of the *Carmina adversus Marcionem* refers to Hermas as *Angelicus Pastor*, from which title Harnack draws the conclusion that in the fourth century, when the above work was almost certainly written, the "Pastor" had already ceased to be popularly known in the African Church.

In Rome itself, early in the second century, the fictitious letter of Pope Pius I. appeals to the authority of Hermas for the command to keep Easter on a Sunday. And in the "Liberian Chronicle" (A.D. 354) he is again referred to as a doctor of Angelic teaching, though the probability is that the compiler is here reproducing the words of Hippolytus, which go back a century earlier, when they would much more truly represent the current opinion of the Church. From this time onwards the notices of the "Pastor" are comparatively few, and seem to imply that the book had dropped almost entirely out of public use, though still employed for purposes of private edification. Throughout the Middle Ages, however, occasional attempts were made to rehabilitate its authority, until they were finally disposed of by a decision of the Council of Trent.

BOOK II.

THE HERETICAL SECTS.

CHAPTER I.

THE structure of Christianity was erected on the foundation of Christ's Messiahship. Detached from its Judaic antecedents, the coming of Christ would be a phenomenon impossible to explain. At the same time, His Messiahship was only the foundation of the Christian structure, not the structure itself. The effort to transcend the limitations of the Jewish conception was first made by S. Paul, and its striking success provoked the bitter jealousy of those Christians of the circumcision who had not freed themselves from their national prejudices. Even in the earliest age of the Church we find them making S. James their rallying-point, and, by a dishonest use of his influential name, undermining the authority of S. Paul. How fierce the contest was we see from many of S. Paul's Epistles; and it continued to rage after his removal from this earthly scene. S. Luke's conciliatory writings and S. John's labours in Asia were powerful factors in the mitigation of this rivalry; but, though mitigated, it was not wholly extinct, for in the time of Justin we still find among Christians of Jewish descent a party who insisted on the observance of the law by Gentile converts, as well as a party who, while continuing the Mosaic ordinances themselves, did not seek to impose them on others. These parties are the lineal representatives, the one of the Judaisers whom S. Paul combats, and the other of the genuine Church of the Circumcision, of whom S. James and S. Peter were the foremost leaders.

Now, both these classes are often spoken of under the common title of "**Ebionite.**" The exact meaning of this

term is uncertain. It is derived from a Hebrew word signi-
fying "poor," and may have been applied to the Hebrew
Christians on account of their poverty (of which we have
frequent evidence in the New Testament), or it may have
been assumed by them in token of the humility of their
condition and spiritual ideal. But among Gentile churches
the epithet suggested quite a different meaning; it implied
poverty, not of outward condition, but of Christological confession. An Ebionite was one who held inadequate views as
to the Person of our Lord. From this standpoint, however,
a distinction must be made between the two classes. The
more liberal party mentioned by Justin, who lingered on till
the end of the fourth century under the time-honoured name
of Nazarenes, are considered by S. Jerome to be only separated from the creeds and usages of Catholic Christendom
by their retention of the Mosaic Law. It is to this sect that
we must refer a very early work,[1] entitled "The Testaments
of the Twelve Patriarchs," which, in its liberal attitude towards Gentile Christians, and its honourable mention of S.
Paul, proclaims its connection with the teaching of the Church
of Jerusalem. Its most interesting feature is the conception
of our Lord as the Giver of the New Law, and as sprung,
not from the tribe of Judah, but from that of Levi.

To the second sect noticed by Justin more properly belongs
the name of Ebionite. These were a larger and more widely-
spread body than the Nazarenes. Their points of divergence
from the Church were mainly three: the imposition of the
Mosaic covenant upon all Christians; the rejection of the
authority and writings of S. Paul; and the denial of the
miraculous birth of Christ, whom they declared to have been
a mere man, justified solely by his perfect obedience to the
Mosaic law. The form of this doctrine, which is most prominent in early writers, is purely Pharisaic; but in the second
century we meet with a new type of it, agreeing with the
former up to a certain point, but introducing a foreign
element, half ascetic, half mystical. This element Lightfoot,

[1] Probably before the rebellion of Bar-cochba, but possibly a little later.
Edited by Sinker (Cambridge, 1869).

having regard to the original headquarters of the sect in the region of the Dead Sea, considers due to Essene influence in the first instance, though not excluding other influences more directly Gnostic and Oriental. The type of doctrine in this sect underwent various modifications; so that, according as the native or foreign elements preponderated, it may be more correctly designated Essene Ebionism or Gnostic Ebionism. The modifications referred to consisted in a difference of statements regarding the nature of the law, and the conception of Christ's Person; the Essene Ebionites inclining to regard Him as born in the course of nature, the Gnostic Ebionites admitting His supernatural origin, though always with unorthodox limitations.

This form of Judaic Christianity seems soon to have eclipsed the elder. It owed this prominence partly to its stronger missionary zeal, partly to its greater literary capacity. Two documents of considerable importance are known to have emanated from it. One of these, the well-known Clementine Homilies and Recognitions, we shall discuss at some length in the next chapter. The other, which is now lost, was even more influential. We allude to the Book of Elchasai or Elxai,[1] from which the sectaries are sometimes called Elchasaites. This word, which signifies *Hidden Power*, was no doubt the name of the angel who was said to have communicated the revelation contained in the book. It claimed to have arisen in the time of Trajan, but whether truly or not is matter of doubt. The greater part of its theological conceptions reappear in the Clementines, and will there be noticed; but a few are peculiar. It borrowed from Oriental sources the idea of a *Syzygy* or sexual duality in the emanations from the supreme Deity: also an exaggerated asceticism, especially in abstinence from wine and animal food, combined with constant lustral washings, though these may be rather taken from the Essene practice. From Christianity it borrowed the rite of baptism, which, however, it emptied of

---

[1] Our chief authority is Hippolytus, Hær. ix. 13. That writer's ignorance of Hebrew led him to regard Elchasai as the name of the founder of this sect, just as Ebion was held to have founded Ebionism.

all moral significance, making it a mere magical process of initiation and remission.

This sect inculcated the practice of magic and astrology, and seems to have laid great stress on the properties of numbers. It retained from Judaism the rite of circumcision and the recommendation of marriage, differing in this point from Essenism, which wholly rejected sexual intercourse. It seems to have regarded Christ as a man, though it admitted His birth of a virgin. His Messiahship was interpreted in connection with the Kabbalistic theory of an *adam kadmon*, or ideal man, who had reappeared several times in human history, first as Adam, then as Moses, and finally as Jesus of Nazareth.

Besides this work, other smaller productions must be attributed to this sect, notably the "Ascents of James," which will be referred to later on; the history of James the Lord's brother, from which Lightfoot thinks the curious details of his life and martyrdom given by Hegesippus[1] are derived; and a biography of S. Matthew, referred to by Clement of Alexandria,[2] which represented him as having abstained from animal food, and as having lived in the desert on seeds, berries and herbs.

In the first half of the third century these heretics seem to have attempted, though without much success, to propagate their views. We learn from Hippolytus that one Alcibiades of Apamea in Syria appeared in his time at Rome, and endeavoured to win over the Pope Callistus. This prelate, whose dogmatic convictions, if he had any, underwent several changes, and were always made subservient to his personal interests, seemed inclined to lend a favourable ear to the tempter. But Hippolytus so completely exposed the falsehood of the system that the danger was removed, and we hear no more of any further hesitation on the part of the Pope. The proselytising zeal of the Elchasaites, however, died hard; for, some years later, a fresh emissary propagated their doctrines in Cæsarea, where he was confuted by Origen. The importance of this sect has been unduly exaggerated

---

[1] See Book III., ch. 7.　　[2] Pædag. ii. 1 (p. 174, Potter).

by the Church historians of the Tubingen school. Not content with dividing the Apostolic Church into two hostile camps of Petrines and Paulines, they carry the antagonism far into the second century, and represent Papias, Hegesippus, as well as a strong party in the Palestinian, African, and Roman churches, as Ebionite and anti-Pauline. This theory has been thoroughly dealt with by Lightfoot in his essay " On S. Paul and the Three," and its baselessness clearly demonstrated.[1] No doubt Ebionites existed even as late as the close of the fourth century, not only in the east of Palestine, but in many of the great cities of the Empire. But within a short period after this they seem to have been absorbed either into the Catholic Church or into the Jewish Synagogue; most probably into the latter.

---

[1] In his edition of the Epistle to the Galatians. The writer has freely used this essay, among other authorities. While admitting the conclusiveness of the bishop's argument, he thinks that it hardly lays sufficient stress on the signs of sympathy shown by S. James towards those who misunderstood S. Paul (Acts xxi. 18 *sqq.*; cf. Gal. ii. 12 *sqq.*). The treatment of the antithesis of faith and works in James ii. 14 *sqq.* points in the same direction. It is clear that from an early period in S. Paul's career the so-called " party of James " confused or identified his vindication of Gentile liberty with a claim for the immunity of Jewish converts from the observance of the Law. This latter is certainly taught by the Apostle, but it is not in question in the Acts. No doubt it was the suspicion of this doctrine which led to the calumny that Paul was no true Pharisee, but a Gentile proselyte. This explains his emphatic and reiterated assertion of his Jewish extraction and antecedents. See Acts xxii. 2, xxiii. 6, xxvi. 5.

CHAPTER II.

THE CLEMENTINE LITERATURE.

THE great name and high authority of S. Clement were used in the century succeeding his death to give currency to various theories and legends, which appeared in numerous forms, externally differing, but animated by a tolerably uniform spirit, and which had sufficient plausibility to pass for genuine in the uncritical ages of the Church. They are now universally admitted to be wholly devoid of historical accuracy, though of the greatest possible interest and importance to the student of the early development of Catholic doctrine. They are known by the general name of **"The Clementines,"** and include two long treatises, the *Homilies* and *Recognitions*, the *Epistle to James*, the *Epitome of the Acts of S. Peter* in two forms, and the *Martyrdom of S. Clement*, both which last are much later and entirely untrustworthy documents.[1]

. The method in which the subjects are treated is in substance biographical. Clement is introduced as the narrator; and he interweaves with the story of his own life an exposition of the Christian faith, clothed with the authority of S. Peter, whose intimate companion he is represented to have been. In the earliest form of the work, which scholars are almost unanimous in thinking is now lost, the element of doctrinal exposition and polemics was predominant, the narrative portions being only the framework in which the former was set. But, as time went on, the story grew more popular, and the somewhat dry disquisitions gradually came to occupy

---

[1] To these may be added a short Epistle of S. Peter to S. James of Jerusalem, and a *testimonium* or authentication of the same attached. The Epistle of Clement to James is prefixed as a kind of introduction to the Homilies.

the second place, until in the Epitome they are to a great extent sacrificed, and the whole interest centres in the story.

The two fuller accounts (the Recognitions and Homilies respectively) agree in their main features and in most of the historical details. But their differences are almost as pronounced as their agreement. The twenty Homilies, which we possess in the original Greek, represent with considerable fidelity the theological views of that Ebionitic sect from which the work emanated. The Recognitions, of which only the translation by Rufinus is extant, is a production of greater literary merit, and has softened down many of the most unpalatable aberrations from doctrinal orthodoxy. This may be partly due to Rufinus, who is generally as a translator more careful to guard the orthodoxy of his original than to render the exact words. But since he assures us in this case that he has been content to act as a faithful translator, we may assume that the wide demand for the work had produced a revised edition free from the gravest objections of the earlier production. As to the comparative priority of the two recensions, opinions are equally divided ; but on the whole it seems preferable to decide with Lightfoot that the Homilies are the earlier. It is true, no doubt, that their narrative portions contain some inconsistencies which do not appear in the Recognitions, but these may be explained by the feebler interest felt in them by the writer as compared with the polemical discussions.

Before criticising the origin, merits and date of these compositions, it will be well to give our readers an outline of the story, which may fitly be described as the earliest precursor of the modern religious romance.

The Autobiography of Clement of Rome.

Clement, the hero of this picturesque story, informs his correspondent, S. James, of the main events in his life. He states that he was born of a noble Roman family, closely connected with that of the Emperor. From his earliest youth he had devoted himself to the pursuit of virtue, and more

especially, of chastity. He had sought counsel from the leading professors of wisdom, and had plunged deep into the
most abstruse sciences, but only to find his higher aspirations
still unsatisfied and a gloomy despair settling upon his soul.
A report had reached his ears of a Great Preacher of truth
who had appeared in Galilee ; and rumour declared that one
of His disciples, named Barnabas, was actually teaching in
Rome. Clement sought him out, and heard him address
one of his missionary discourses to a large crowd; this so
touched the young inquirer's heart that he offered the Apostle
his friendship, which was graciously accepted. In a few
days Barnabas left Rome for Palestine, whither Clement,
unable to rest without a fuller knowledge of the truth,
determined to follow him.[1] At Cæsarea he was introduced
to S. Peter, and this introduction was the turning-point of.
Clement's life.

It so happened that the most persistent enemy of the
Gospel, Simon the magician, was also at Cæsarea. This
gave occasion for arranging a public discussion between the
true and the false apostle. Peter occupies the interval of preparation in teaching Clement the chief mysteries of the faith,
and bidding him transmit a written account of his instruction
to James of Jerusalem, to whom Peter himself was required
to send an annual report of his mission work.[2] Meanwhile,
Peter's controversial armoury is strongly reinforced by the

[1] In the Homilies, Clement first meets Barnabas at Alexandria, from
whence he sails for Judea. Both accounts agree in making Clement meet
Peter at Cæsarea.

[2] It has been pointed out that there are several discrepancies in this
account, which seem to indicate it as a recension of some earlier document.
This may have been the "Ascents of James" (ἀναβαθμοὶ Ἰακώβου), which
contained a narrative of the conflicts between the Apostles and the Jewish
leaders on the Temple steps (whence the name) ; when an enemy who is
not named, but is undoubtedly Saul of Tarsus, raises a tumult and hurls
James down the steps, leaving him for dead. The Apostles flee to Jericho,
carrying James with them. While here, James, who has the chief authority in the Jerusalem Church, hears of the mischief done by Simon at
Cæsarea, and sends Peter down to confute him. The dates in the Recognitions are confused. Clement first speaks of our Lord as still preaching when he first met Barnabas ; but afterwards he fixes the date of
his meeting with Peter as seven years after the crucifixion.

desertion to him of two of Simon's most trusted disciples, Nicetas and Aquila, who, by revealing the secret villanies by which the magician's fame is purchased, supply the Apostle with information of the most damaging kind. The discussion takes place before a large audience, and lasts three days. Simon is vanquished in argument, and put to shame by an exposure of his necromantic arts. Full of malice, he departs for Rome, and traduces the character of Peter at every halting-place on the road. Peter finds it necessary to follow him from city to city, but before he leaves he ordains the ex-publican Zacchæus as Bishop, and baptizes over ten thousand converts. Clement is selected as Peter's personal attendant and confidential secretary, evidently as a set-off to the position assigned by S. Paul to S. Luke.

After stoppages at Dora, Tyre, Sidon, and Berytus, a halt is made at Tripolis in Phœnicia, where, among other noteworthy events, Clement receives baptism, and is then for the first time allowed to join the Apostle at meals.[1] While at Aradus, Clement, encouraged by the paternal kindness of S. Peter, confides to him the story of the family troubles. He relates that his father, Faustinianus, whose wife was the high-born and virtuous Matthidia, had three sons, Faustus and Faustinus, twins, and Clement, who was several years younger. When Clement was about five years old, he remembered that his mother had a dream, warning her of some impending calamity, which could only be avoided by her leaving Rome. Her husband consented to the separation, and sent her with the twins to Athens. At the expiration of a year a messenger was despatched to inquire after their welfare, but he never returned. Other messengers were sent, but all that could be learnt was that the ship in which Matthidia sailed had never arrived at Athens. Unable to endure the continued suspense, Faustinianus left Clement under the care of guardians, and set out to seek for the lost ones. This happened in Clement's early boyhood, and since

---

[1] Observe the importance attached to this mark of comradeship; and compare it with S. Paul's account of S. Peter's conduct in the second chapter of the Galatians.

then he had heard nothing of his father or mother, and had given them both up for dead.

The Apostle listened to this story with affectionate interest, and an expedition being proposed to the neighbouring isle of Antaradus, he consented to join the party. While seated on the steps of a temple, he fell into conversation with a beggar-woman, who related the story of her life, which exactly corresponded with Clement's narrative of what had befallen his mother. It was no other than Matthidia herself, who was thus happily restored to her youngest son; and shortly afterwards, at Laodicea, she found in Nicetas and Aquila the two twins whom she believed to have been lost in the shipwreck. The story is gracefully interwoven with references to many New Testament characters, among whom is Justa, the Syrophenician woman. Matthidia, after due preparation, is baptized by Peter in the sea.

On the following day the Apostle, while praying on the shore, was addressed by an old man, meanly dressed but of refined bearing, who expostulated with him on the uselessness of prayer. Peter asked the reason of this unbelief. The old man replied that all things were governed by astrological necessity or fate (*Genesis*). Peter, being unversed in the subtleties of the schools, proposed that his three young friends should discuss the subject with the old man, and, if possible, convince him of error. A long debate follows, in which Nicetas treats the objections of philosophy, Aquila those of physical science, and Clement those of mathematics and astrology. The old man was unable to answer their arguments, but he maintained the truth of his own views as resting not upon theory, but on the irrefragable evidence of his life's experience. He stated that his wife's birth had taken place under a conjunction of the stars that foreboded conjugal infidelity and great subsequent misfortunes. In spite of her naturally virtuous disposition, she had been guilty of adultery with a slave (a fact which he had learned from the evidence of his brother), and had feigned to have received a divine communication bidding her leave Rome, as a cloak for carrying out her designs. The ship in which she and her two sons, together with her paramour, sailed for Athens had been lost, and he himself, wearied with the miseries of life, had determined to drag out the wretched remnant of his days as an unknown outcast. Peter at once perceived that the old man was he whose death they had all mourned, the long-lost Faustinianus. He not only had the happiness of reuniting him to his family, but was able to convince him of his wife's innocence, and of the consequent falsity of the astrological prediction. The old man's prejudices at last gave way, and, fully satisfied of his own grievous mistakes, he professed himself willing to be taught the truth.

Meanwhile Simon had not been idle. Full of bitter hatred against Peter, he had gone to Antioch and denounced him as an impostor and a magician. But Peter had despatched some Christian envoys to watch his movements, one of whom hit on the expedient of applying to Cornelius (the Centurion of the Acts), who was then at Cæsarea, to set in motion the edict of the Emperor, by which all sorcerers were ordered to be seized and sent to punishment. Simon in alarm fled to Laodicea, where Faustinianus met him at the residence of some common friends, Apion (or Appion), the celebrated grammarian, and Anubion, a Syrian rhetorician. Having heard of the relations between Faustinianus and Peter, Simon determined to revenge himself on both of them. He invited Faustinianus to a banquet, and gave him a drugged potion which had the effect of transforming his features into those of the magician. Meanwhile Simon escaped, and left Faustinianus to be apprehended in his stead. The old man, ignorant of his change of form, rejoined the Apostle and his companions. The latter turned from him with horror; but Peter was not to be deceived by Simon's arts. Instantly recognising what had taken place, he turned it to Simon's disadvantage by sending Faustinianus to Antioch, and instructing him, while still wearing Simon's features, to appear in public and make a full confession of his villanies. This he did to such good purpose that the populace, fickle in love as in hate, turned against him, and would have slain him, had he not been assisted to escape by some Christian brethren who were in the secret. · When Simon appeared shortly afterwards, he was received with derision, and Peter, on his arrival at Antioch, was welcomed as the bearer of a divine message. Faustinianus was restored to his true shape, and received baptism at the Apostle's hands.

This incident concludes the original story. A Letter from Clement to James of Jerusalem, purporting to be written from Rome shortly before Peter's martyrdom, gives an account of Clement's consecration as Bishop of Rome by Peter. The Apostle, who is described in exalted terms as having carried the light of the Gospel into the whole Western World, knowing that his end was near, called together the elders of the Church, and announced that he had chosen Clement to be his successor. Clement earnestly deprecated the unwelcome honour; but Peter was firm, and, in the presence of the whole Church, ordained him Bishop, giving him instructions how to behave in his office, and enjoining upon the priests and deacons implicit obedience to their superior. The expression "Eye of the Bishop"[1] is applied to the Diaconate in this letter, in which also occurs the beautiful comparison of the Church to a ship, of which so much use has been made by succeeding writers. The passage, which is worth transcribing as a specimen of the style of the Clementines, is as follows:—

"The whole framework of the Church is like to a great ship, which carries through a mighty storm men of different lands, all desiring to dwell in the city of a good kingdom. The owner of the ship is GOD Almighty: Christ is the Pilot, the man at the look-out is the Bishop, the able seamen are the Presbyters, the overseers of the rowers are the Deacons, the collectors of passage-money are the catechists, the entire multitude of the brethren are the passengers; the world is the sea, the adverse winds are temptations, the billows are persecutions: the words of seducers and false prophets are the squalls coming down from the mountain gorges: the headlands and rough places are the magistrates who threaten death; the shallows and counter-currents are those

---

[1] Now applied only to the Archdeacon.

who are irrational and doubtful of the promises : hypocrites are like to pirates, whirlpools and eddies and mortal accidents and capsizings may fitly be compared to sins."

The Epitome, as has already been mentioned, gives in an abridged form the points of the foregoing history. The original portion of it ends with the 147th chapter, where the full title of the work, " Clement's Epitome of the travels and preaching of Peter,"[1] is given. To this an appendix is added, carrying on the biography of the Bishop to his martyrdom, and relating the wonders that were wrought at his tomb. Eloquent testimony is given to the liberal and generous character of Clement, whose intellectual culture enabled him to sympathise alike with Jews and Gentiles in their difficulties. His episcopate was eminently successful in conciliating opposition, and his munificence endeared him to the poor. But his virtues did not shield him from the malice of enemies. A friend of the Emperor Nerva, named Sisinnius, enraged at the influence of Clement's teaching over his wife Theodora, determined to put her to shame and to annoy Clement in the very act of public worship. Entering the church with some of his attendants, he looked about for his wife, intending to carry her off by force. But while Clement was offering the opening prayer, Sisinnius was suddenly smitten with deafness and blindness. Neither he nor his attendants could find the door, and they were fain to accept the guidance of Theodora, who escorted them home. Clement visited the unhappy man, in the hope of softening his anger, but was repulsed with insults and threats. Owing to his prayers, however, Sisinnius next day came to a better mind, and confessed his injustice. His repentance was accepted, and a complete reconciliation took place. But the magistrates, terrified at the Bishop's influence, preferred against him a charge of magic and sedition, and prevailed on the prefect Mamertinus to report him to the Emperor. Trajan, who was now on the imperial throne, gave orders that Clement should either sacrifice to the gods or be banished

---

[1] Κλήμεντος τοῦ Πέτρου ἐπιδημιῶν τε καὶ κηρυγμάτων ἐπιτομή.

immediately to the Crimea. The Bishop's constancy over-
came Mamertinus, who grieved bitterly for his own injustice
in procuring his condemnation. It was, however, too late to
save him. He was exiled to the barren shores of the Cher-
sonese, and by his gentleness so wrought upon the inhabitants
that nearly all were converted to the faith. On learning this,
Trajan sent a bigoted heathen named Aufidianus to assume
the government of the territory. After many acts of cruel
persecution, this Aufidianus determined to destroy Clement
as the only means of checking the growth of the Church, and
threw him into the sea with an anchor tied round his neck,
to prevent the faithful from gaining possession of his relics.

But, at the prayer of two of Clement's disciples, the sea
receded and left the body exposed. It was revealed to these
two men that the corpse must be left where it was, and a
small shrine erected over it in the sea. This was done, and
the miraculous retirement of the water took place every year,
lasting for seven days, when an annual festival was held in
honour of the saint. On one of these occasions a man of
good family, who had entered the shrine with his wife and
little son, by some accident left the boy behind, and when
the waters advanced, he was found to be missing. Over-
whelmed with grief, the parents came to the spot the following year, expecting to find the corpse of their son; but,
wondrous to relate, they had no sooner entered the shrine
than the boy met them, alive and well, God having provided
this striking testimony to the sanctity of the holy bishop,
who, even in death, was permitted to minister comfort to the
sorrowing, and to strengthen the faith of believers.

Such is the celebrated romance of the Clementines, a
romance which for ages was regarded as historically true,
and which, though now deservedly discredited, must, from
its beauty, always hold a high place in the literature of the
Church, where dogmatic rigorism does not step in to blind
our judgment to the many excellences, religious and artistic,
which adorn it.

We now proceed to offer a few remarks on the difficult
questions that surround the origin of the work. Though

decidedly Christian in tone, it is obviously far from orthodox.   Three important departures from the true standpoint
of Catholic doctrine mar its religious usefulness.   These are—
(1) the assumption of metaphysical rather than spiritual first
principles, which necessitates a false criticism of the Old
Testament; (2) an incorrect theory of the law, and inadequate
views of the Person of Jesus Christ; (3) a falsification of historical justice in ignoring the work of S. Paul and substitut-
ing for it a fictitious apostleship to the Gentiles of S. Peter.

As to the first defect, it is shared by many teachers of the
Church, such as Tatian, Clement, and Origen.   But while
these restrain their speculations within the limits of revelation,
the Gnostic thinkers, from whom our author has evidently
borrowed, acknowledged no such necessity.   They no doubt
felt it incumbent on them to make their views appear to tally
with the words of Scripture, but this was invariably done by
wresting the sense of Scripture into conformity with their
views.   In a sense, therefore, they deserve the name of Biblical
critics; but their criticism is arbitrary and *à priori*, and supported by an utterly perverted exegesis.   From the Scripture
texts quoted as misapplied by them in Irenæus, Hippolytus
and Tertullian, we can understand the fallacy of their method.
Intolerant of authority, impatient of verification, they found
it easiest to strike out as an interpolation whatever they did
not approve.   And this is the critical method applied by
Marcion to the New Testament, and by the Clementine
writer to the Old.

The second defect is the one which touches most closely
the relation of this book to the Catholic Church.   It is no
mere accident in the system, but implies a carefully con-
structed and ambitious attempt to reconcile three divergent
points of view, that of the Jew-Christian, that of the Gnostic-
Ebionite, and that of the Gentile-Christian.

The fundamental conciliatory idea is that of a simple and
original religion, divinely revealed, as the common source of
Judaism and Christianity.   And, inasmuch as the primal man,
or *Protoplast*, was the ancestor of Gentiles also, this original
religion explains all that is true in the Gentile faiths.   There is

a distinct trace of Platonism in the theory of the heavenly man
or Divine Idea of humanity, of whom the earthly Adam was
an adumbration; and in general, the relation of the Divine
to the material is conceived in a semi-Platonic sense. Thus
the writer, holding the threads of many discordant points of
view, twists them together at their source, and out of the
mass of doctrines educes his conception of a True Prophet,
manifested at intervals throughout the history of the world,
whom Jews and Gentiles alike can recognise as speaking
with the authority of God.

The first embodiment of this prophetic power was Adam,
the story of whose fall must be regarded as an unauthorised
interpolation of the Scripture record. Had his posterity only
kept true to his primeval doctrine, the Jews would have had
no need of Moses, nor the world of Christ. It was the de-
scendants of Adam who fell away, not Adam himself. The
writer admits the Pentateuch to be the nearest approach to
an authentic deposit of revelation, but he strongly contests
the common view of its genuineness, affirming that it was
subjected to many recensions, and that the original revelation
was often falsified or overlaid.

The tests of True Prophecy are first clearness, then consistency, then spirituality. All that fails to fulfil these conditions he ruthlessly casts away. All oracles that are obscure,
veiled, or mystical, must be false. All oracles that contradict
the distinct assertions of the Pentateuch must be differently
explained or rejected. All carnal or outward delineations of
Messiah's Kingdom, especially those Chiliastic dreams so dear
to the Hebrew-Christian, must be sternly suppressed. He is
unable to rise to the modern conception of a progressive revelation, with successive steps of ascending spirituality. Hence
his hard, unsympathetic treatment of many parts of Scripture.
He thinks the written books were given to men as a test of
their spiritual discernment, so that the spirit that is truly
Christian can by an instinctive insight tell what to accept
and what to reject. The spiritual man will refuse to accept
anything that contradicts the metaphysical idea of God. The
godly nature is the medium in which the inward revelation

of the Divine is effected. This inward revelation is superior to that by visions, angelic appearances, or dreams, which are external, and presuppose estrangement from God.

The highest prophetic type is Moses. To him the Almighty spoke face to face, as a man speaks to his friend. The doctrine of Christ is at bottom but a restatement of that of Moses, which had been lost sight of by all but a few Jews, and by the whole mass of the Gentile world. Hence it was necessary that the Supreme Father should manifest Himself in the person of Jesus of Nazareth, to recall His faithful ones to the original form of their religion. He came to extend the blessing of a true Law, once confined to Israel, to all mankind. In Jesus the spiritual Jew witnessed a new manifestation of that first Adam, whom he had constantly revered as the source of all that was noble in humanity.

The question might be asked—In what respect, then, is the Christian position an advance upon the Jewish? What need is there for a believer in Moses to change his faith at all? And the Clementine writer does not shrink from asserting that such a change is wholly unnecessary. The work of Christ is mainly to shed fresh light upon misapprehended truth, and to extend the plan of salvation from Jew to Gentile. It does not in any way affect those who have understood and accepted the Mosaic law in its purity. He who possesses the true faith of Moses must not, indeed he cannot, blaspheme Christ; on the other hand, a Christian need not submit to the Mosaic ordinances, though he must not slight or condemn them.

This view of Christ as the True Prophet and second Lawgiver, the resuscitator of lost truths, harmonises with the general position of the Essenes, though the Clementine author goes far beyond them in his unsparing excision of Pentateuchal precepts.

The third defect that we noticed in this book was the unjust estimate of S. Paul and his work. In defiance of history, S. Peter is pourtrayed not only as the Apostle of the Gentiles, but as the mouthpiece of abstruse metaphysical theories. Great care is taken to emphasise his strict observance of lustral washings, of vegetable diet, of the custom of greeting the sunrise, and other Essene practices; while his conciliatory attitude towards the rival Judaic and Gentile forms of Christianity, though founded on a historical basis, is grossly perverted.

In the same spirit, we trace throughout an overdrawn picture of the character and position of S. James. Not only is he the supreme ruler of the Church in Jerusalem, but he is the bishop of bishops, the president of the apostolic college, and the highest authority in the Church Catholic throughout the world. He directs S. Peter in his missionary enterprises, commands him to send in a full annual report of his doings, as well as a shorter summary every seven years. Clement's narrative is addressed to him, and he himself is declared to have derived his unique position directly from the hands of Christ.

On the other hand, S. Paul and his labours are never once mentioned, and to the reader who can read between the lines there is not only an ignoring of his work, but a constant undercurrent of disparagement of it. The theory of Baur that this disparagement is the main purpose of the treatise, and that S. Paul is intended throughout by Simon Magus, is indeed not without plausibility; but his idea that it emanated from the Petrine faction within the Church is devoid of foundation. For, if it was necessary for a churchman to veil the personality of the Apostle under a pseudonym so unrecognisable as Simon Magus, it follows that the public for whom he wrote was not the powerful section of Christendom which on any showing the Petrine party must have been. A distinction, however, must be made between the Homilies and the Recognitions. The former, which we possess in the Greek, shows far more evident traces of an anti-Pauline spirit than the latter, which we possess only in the Latin version. Yet even in the Homilies it seems more probable that the historical Simon is kept in the foreground, and that the masked allusions to S. Paul arise from time to time when the situation seems to suggest them. There can be no doubt, for instance, of the applicability to S. Paul of the following remonstrance of Peter, professedly addressed to Simon :—

"If then our Jesus was made known to thee and also conversed with thee in a vision, He was angry with thee as an adversary, and therefore He spake with thee by visions and dreams, or even by outward revelations. Can any one be made wise unto doctrine by visions? If thou sayest he can, then why did the Teacher abide and converse with us a whole year when we were awake? And how shall we ever believe that He was seen of thee, when thy thoughts are contrary to His teaching? If having been seen and instructed of Him for a single hour, thou wast made an Apostle, then preach His words, expound His teaching, love His Apostles, do not fight against me, His companion. For thou hast withstood and opposed me, the firm rock, the foundation of the Church. If thou hadst not been an adversary, thou would'st not have reviled and calumniated my preaching, that I might not be believed when I told what I had heard myself in person from the Lord, as though, forsooth, I were condemned and thou wert highly regarded. Nay, if thou callest me condemned, thou accusest God, who revealed Christ in me, and assailest Him that called me blessed in my revelation." [1]

This is by far the most explicit allusion in the whole work. Yet even this, unquestionable as it is, may well have passed undetected by the untheological reader. Everything points to an uneasy consciousness on the writer's part that he is not in harmony with the general mind of the Church : consequently he does not venture beyond the region of innuendo and negative misrepresentation. There can be no doubt that, in spite of its currency among Catholics, the drift of the Recognitions, and still more of the Homilies, is wholly Ebionite and heretical. The charm of the story made it generally popular, and induced orthodox writers, such as Rufinus, to recast it in a more or less expurgated form. This is clearly indicated by the increasing prominence of the narrative portion in the successive editions. In the lost original, critics are of opinion that the doctrinal disputations held the chief place : in the Homilies they are, at least, equal in amount to

[1] Hom. xvii. 19. Compare Galatians ii. 11. See Lightfoot, Galat. p. 315, 1st ed.

the biographical sections; in the Recognitions, the story begins to assume the prominence, and in the Epitome,[1] it almost monopolises it.

The date of the Clementines has been much discussed, but cannot be determined with accuracy. The earliest recension may perhaps be placed as far back as the middle of the second century, and the form in which they at present exist as somewhat later. The place of their composition is also uncertain. Milman follows the majority of German authorities in affirming their Roman origin. And there is this much in favour of the opinion, that they evidently desire to represent themselves as such: as well as the general consideration that Rome was the meeting-point of all heretical philosophies and creeds. But the local colouring of both works is so decidedly Eastern that we consider Lightfoot's view far more probable, that they originated in Syria or the adjoining regions, very possibly in Cæsarea.

Space forbids us to discuss more fully the many other interesting topics brought forward in these works, such as the doctrine of successive incarnations, which savours of Indian thought; the theory of human depravity as the work of fallen angels; the catalogue of contradictory moralities prevailing among different tribes, which was borrowed from the Greek topographers and moral theorists; the fancy speeches of Apion and Anubion, after the style of Plato's Symposium; the satire on the degradation of philosophers; the varied picture of social life. A translator who would treat the existing Recognitions as Rufinus probably treated his original, omitting the more tedious and objectionable discussions, might produce a book even now quite readable, and of a more popular type than most of the treatises that have come down to us from the great Church age.

---

[1] Besides this a book is mentioned by Jerome, called the "Circuits of Peter" (περίοδοι Πέτρου), from which numerous details are quoted which reappear in the Clementines, e.g., Nicetas and Aquila, Clement's attendance on Peter, Peter's attack on heathenism, and the discourses of Apion and Anubion; but apparently it said nothing about the restoration of Clement to his family.

CHAPTER III.

THE EARLY APOCRYPHAL LITERATURE—GOSPELS AND ACTS.

OUR familiar division of the New Testament into two parts, adopted for convenience of reading in church, corresponds to a real difference in the books themselves. The four Gospels, Acts, and Apocalypse, are simple in style and appeal to the mass of mankind ; the Epistles are hortatory or argumentative, and appeal to the educated.

Now it is to this latter category that nearly all the extant literature of the early Church belongs. It is emphatically a literature of teachers, and rulers, and dialecticians, and learned men ; it is as emphatically not a popular literature. There are indeed some exceptions. The *Didaché*, the Shepherd of Hermas, the works of Papias and Hegesippus, and in a different way the Clementine writings, contain a large popular element. But they are the exceptions that prove the rule. Their credit did not stand high with theologians proper. Considerable authority was no doubt awarded them, but it was awarded grudgingly and without enthusiasm. They were out of harmony with the ruling tendency of Christian thought, which was towards exposition and metaphysical argument. And this tendency increased with each succeeding generation. The writings of the Apostolic Fathers, it is true, put no severe strain upon the reader's attention. They are far less difficult to follow than the Epistles of S. Paul. Nevertheless they undoubtedly appeal to an educated circle of believers, not to the uneducated multitude. The writer to Diognetus, Justin and Irenæus, represent a stage still further removed from that of the popular consciousness. Philosophic ideas and dialectical methods mingle

with their expositions of Christian doctrine, and are pursued
for the most part through long and elaborate discussions,
which even the well-trained student finds it no slight tax
upon his powers to follow.   This process reaches its culmina-
tion in the works of Clement and Origen, which demand
from the reader not only the closest attention, but familiarity
with a wide extent of heathen as well as Christian learning,
and the power to grasp conceptions at once recondite and
profound.

In the African school, the thoughts are somewhat less
difficult, but the ambitious rhetoric in which they are conveyed places them beyond the reach of the undisciplined
mind.   Even granting an average of intelligence fully equal
to that of the present day, it is impossible to believe that
such works as those of Justin, Origen, or Tertullian could
have been appreciated or even understood by the ordinary
Christian of humble life.

Are we then to suppose that the rank and file of believers
were entirely without a popular religious literature ?   Were
they content with the Gospels and such oral explanations of
doctrine as their preachers and catechists supplied ?   Or did
any writers come forward and endeavour to provide a religious
pabulum suited to the average capacity ?

This question, so natural, so easy to ask, is by no means
easy to answer.   The preface to S. Luke's Gospel implies
clearly enough that evangelical narratives were already
numerous in his day ; but what they were, and in what
respects they differed from the existing Gospels, we have
unfortunately no means of knowing.   Every one of these
early records has perished, and except a few doubtful names
and a score or two of almost equally doubtful fragments, we
have no data on which to build conjecture.

But early in the second century, when the Church was
growing in numbers, and divergences from the orthodox
faith arose, it seems to have occurred to various heretical
teachers that the surest method of spreading their views was
to compose simple narratives on the plan of the Gospels and
endeavour to pass them off as genuine apostolic literature.

In this respect, as in others, they showed considerable sagacity. An age, uncritical in temper and willing to bow before the authority of great names, might easily be induced to accept such documents on very slender evidence. A predilection for plain religious reading, especially of the biographical sort, has always been a characteristic of the mass of mankind. Besides, there was a wide, and, as it appeared, legitimate field of curiosity in the gaps left by the sacred narrative. Quite apart from the question of orthodoxy, every Christian would be glad to think he knew something of those periods in the life of our Lord and His Apostles on which the Gospels are silent.

The information given in the Scriptures is indeed extremely full as regards the birth, ministry, death and resurrection of Christ, and tolerably so as to the movements of S. Peter and S. Paul. But the intervals between Christ's birth and baptism, death and resurrection, resurrection and ascension, to say nothing of the careers of the other Apostles, are so cursorily sketched or so obscurely hinted at as to afford the most natural ground of curiosity, and almost to challenge the invention of the pious.

To these causes we may trace the chief motive of Christian apocryphal literature. There was, however, another motive, which has recently been brought into unexpected prominence by the discovery of the lost Apocalypse of Peter, namely, the desire to furnish Christendom with a clear conception of the portion of believers and unbelievers after death, a subject already partially revealed in the Apocalypse of S. John, but needing, as it seemed, a fuller and more comprehensive statement.

In criticising this literature, we propose, for the sake of clearness, to consider it under three heads, Apocalypses, Apocryphal Gospels, and Apocryphal Acts. The origin of them all is in the main heretical. But while in one set of documents the heretical idea was prominent, and sought to accredit itself by the fictitious claim to an apostolic guarantee, in another it was merged in the simple desire to supply food for the popular imagination, in which it was so successful as to win for its productions not only widespread popularity, but the acceptance of the Church itself, in whose authorised teaching they were gradually and permanently incorporated.

It is impossible, at least in the primitive period, to keep these two channels distinct. For in the case of those legends that were most generally accepted, there can be little doubt that the original documents were touched and retouched by orthodox hands, all uncatholic elements being by this process eliminated; so that the works which have come down to us are in scarcely any instance preserved in their original form.

It is remarkable how scrupulously the earliest orthodox writers resisted the temptation to invent legend, or even to give literary shape to legends already current. Nearly all the specimens of this literature betray, by tendencies inconsistent with the primitive faith, an origin outside the orthodox circle. The only exceptions are the various Acts of Martyrdom. These undoubtedly represent a type of literature at once popular and orthodox. But these, again, are exceptions which prove the rule. For they are entirely concerned with the saints of the post-apostolic age, and never profess to invest with a legendary halo any features in the life of our Lord or of the Twelve Apostles.[1]

1. Apocalyptic Books—The Apocalypse of Peter.

Historians have remarked that under stress of persecution or extreme spiritual trial the religious consciousness tends to express itself in that symbolic and imaginative style which we call Apocalyptic. This was specially the case with the Jews during the great war of liberation under the Maccabees. And after the destruction of Jerusalem by Titus, and again by Hadrian, the same tendency reappeared, and was even more prolific of results. Nor was it wholly unknown in the Christian Church. An example of it stands imbedded in the New Testament, the most mysterious and disputed of

---

[1] It is possible that the correspondence between Christ and King Abgarus of Edessa may be an exception. Eusebius at any rate seems to accept it as orthodox.

the writings of the canon. The Revelation of S. John has ever been the favourite study of a certain class of theologians, to whom the enigmatical is more attractive than the evident, and historic anticipation more congenial than inductive research.

To us this wondrous book stands apart like a cloud-capped peak, in isolated grandeur. But in early times its solitude was shared by a companion somewhat less inscrutable, if somewhat less authoritative, bearing on its title-page the honoured name of Peter.

Until last year this work was known only by a few paltry fragments and some scattered allusions. But quite recently the French Archæological Mission at Cairo have published three early documents of first-rate interest, though unfortunately incomplete, viz., parts of the Book of Enoch, of the Gospel of S. Peter, and of what is universally admitted to be his Apocalypse. Nearly half of the latter is preserved, sufficient, that is, to form a fair estimate of its value, and to enable us to indicate its influence on succeeding literature.

We begin by mentioning the chief early notices of this supposed Petrine work. The first occurs in the Muratorian fragment on the canon[1] (A.D. 170–200), where, according to the received reading, it is placed among the Canonical Scriptures along with the Apocalypse of S. John, though with the qualifying remark that some members of the Church objected to its being publicly read.[2]

The next writer who mentions it is Clement, who, according to Eusebius, commented on it in his *Hypotyposes*, and this statement is confirmed by three quotations in an existing fragment of that work, one of which speaks of it as Scripture.

S. Methodius of Olympus, in Lycia (A.D. 300), also quotes one of these passages, and says that it comes from "divinely inspired writings."

---

[1] See Book III., ch. 10.

[2] "Apocalypses etiam Iohannis et Petri tantum recipimus, *quam* quidam ex nostris legi in ecclesia nolunt." Zahn imagines a *lacuna* after "Petri" of the following sort: "Unam epistolam, quam tantum recipimus; altera extat epistola," &c. But this is a somewhat arbitrary change.

Eusebius, a little later, includes it in a list of the Petrine writings with these cautious words, "The book (so-called) of his Acts, and the (so-called) Gospel according to Peter, and what is known as his Preaching, and what is called his Apocalypse, these we know not at all as having been handed down among Catholic Scriptures, for no ancient Church writer nor contemporary of our own has made use of testimonies taken from them."[1] In the face of the citations from Clement and Methodius this last statement cannot be called correct, nor can the former be reconciled with the present text of the Muratorian fragment. In another passage Eusebins classes it with those spurious books which, though pseudonymous, are not of heretical tendencies and were considered by more indulgent critics as only *disputed*, *i.e.*, of doubtful authenticity.[1]

About a century later Macarius Magnes, refuting the objections of a heathen adversary, refers to his use of this book as a standard Christian work. Macarius evidently disbelieves its genuineness, but accepts its teaching as orthodox.

Sozomen (about A.D. 450) testifies to its public use once a year on Good Friday by the churches of Palestine in his day, though he admits that the ancients generally considered it spurious.

Nicephorus (about A.D. 850), in drawing up a classified list of inspired writings for practical use, places this book among them, though in an inferior position, and assigns it a length of three hundred lines, or a little shorter than the Epistle to the Galatians.

On looking back upon this record, we find that the Apocalypse of Peter held an honourable but precarious position among deutero-canonical writings, being in all probability accepted in Rome in the second century, and certainly in Egypt, Lycia, and Palestine, while it continued to be transcribed

[1] H. E. iii. 3, 2.

[2] H. E. iii. 25, 4. The universally accepted books are ὁμολογούμενα: the undoubtedly spurious, νοθά: those of an intermediate character are ἀντιλεγόμενα (disputed) of which some are of such very doubtful authenticity as to approximate to spuriousness: and in this last category Eusebius no doubt rightly places the Apocalypse of Peter.

as late as the ninth century in Jerusalem, and no doubt also in Egypt.

It is further probable that Hippolytus of Portus (A.D. 220) made use of it: and clear traces of its employment are found in several later documents, such as the "First Book of Clement, or Testament of our Lord Jesus Christ" (a work proceeding from the same source as the Clementine Recognitions), the Second Book of the Sibylline Oracles, and the History of Barlaam and Josaphat.

The language of the newly-discovered fragment shows moreover such evident connection with that of the second Epistle of S. Peter that, though it is without a title, there can be no question that it belongs to the Petrine cycle, and may be confidently accepted as part of the long-lost Apocalypse. Its date cannot be certainly determined: but the opinion of scholars seems to be in favour of a very early origin, going back to quite the beginning of the second, or possibly even to the last years of the first century. It will thus be among the most ancient relics of Christian literature, and this antiquity is rendered more probable by its qualified canonical recognition in spite of the peculiar nature of its contents. The existing portion is divisible into three parts, a prophetic discourse of Christ with His Apostles, a description of Paradise, and an *Inferno* or account of the punishment of the wicked. There is little to indicate any particular tendency in the work. It is built on the strong instincts of the religious imagination, and has evidently influenced the popular belief of Christianity in no slight degree. Its interest is so great, that we think our readers will prefer to have some specimens put before them rather than any general criticism of its contents : [1]—

THE VISION OF PARADISE.

"And the Lord said furthermore, Let us go unto the mountain and pray. And as we the twelve disciples went with Him, we besought Him that He would show us one of our righteous

[1] The translation is that of Professor James of King's College, 1st edit.

brethren that had departed from the world that we might see of what form they were, and so take courage, and encourage them also that should hear us.

"And as we were praying, there suddenly appeared two men standing before the Lord towards the East, whom we could not look upon: for there was light, such as never eye of man beheld nor mouth can describe, nor heart conceive the glory wherewith they were clad and the beauty of their countenance.

"And when we saw them we were amazed: for their bodies were whiter than any snow and redder than any rose, and the red thereof was mingled with the white, and, in a word, I cannot describe the beauty of them: for their hair was thick and curling and bright, and beautiful upon their face and their shoulders, like a wreath woven of spikenard and bright flowers, or like a rainbow in the sky, such was their beauty.

"When therefore we saw their beauty, we were all amazement at them, for they had appeared suddenly: and I came near to the Lord and said, 'Who are these?' He saith to me, 'These are your brethren the righteous, whose forms ye wished to behold.' And I saith to Him, 'And where are all the righteous, or of what sort is the world wherein they are and possess their glory?'

"And the Lord showed me a very great place outside this world, shining excessively with light, and the air that was there illuminated with the rays of the sun, and the earth itself blooming with unfading flowers, and full of spices and fair-flowering plants, incorruptible, and bearing a blessed fruit: and so strong was the perfume that it was borne even to us from thence.

"And the dwellers in that place were clad in the raiment of angels of light, and their raiment was like their land: and angels encircled them there. And the glory of the dwellers there was equal, and with one voice they praised the Lord God rejoicing in that place."

FROM THE INFERNO.

"And I saw also another place over against that other, very squalid, and it was a place of chastisement; and those that were being chastised and the angels that were chastising had their raiment dark, according to the atmosphere of the place.

"And there were some there hanging by their tongues; and these were they that blaspheme the way of righteousness: and there was beneath them fire flaming and tormenting them.

"And there was a certain great lake full of flaming mire, wherein were certain men that pervert righteousness; and tormenting angels were set upon them.

"And there were also others, women, hung by their hair over that mire that bubbled up : and these were they that had adorned themselves for adultery : and the men that had been joined with them in the defilement of adultery were hanging by their feet, and had their heads in the mire, and all were saying, 'We believed not that we should come to this place.'"

These extracts are sufficient to show the character of the work. Coming as it did with the supposed authority of the chief Apostle, and satisfying as it did some of the deepest instincts of the religious heart, we cannot wonder that its influence was great and permanent, not so much among theologians as in the popular imagination, where its ideas reigned supreme for more than a millennium, culminating in Dante's poem; and even now, amid colder spirits and a more rational faith, they still retain much of their power to terrify or to console.

In connection with this Apocalypse, a few words may be added with regard to the **Sibylline Oracles,** one book of which shows clear traces of acquaintance with it. The collection, as we have it, consists of fourteen books of very various ages and of mixed authorship, partly Jewish, partly Judæo-Christian, and in some cases an originally Jewish document has been interpolated by Christian hands. The series extends from the period of the Ptolemies (circ. B.C. 150) to the closing half of the third century A.D., or even later. The subjects of all are similar, prophetic denunciations of judgment upon the various nations, mingled with apocalyptic visions of the last days. The language is that of the Alexandrian Epos, a pseudo-Homeric dialect, the laws of rhythm and scansion being often imperfectly understood. The first and second books, the sixth, and parts of the third and eighth, and possibly the procemium, are generally held to be of Christian origin. Their language is for the most part too vague to be of any great importance for historical purposes. But they are of interest as indicating the presence of a prophetical impulse in the Christian Church, and a desire to blend the formal excellence of Gentile poetry with the spiritual enthusiasm of Judæa. Though reflecting the popular as distinct from the patristic element in Christian literature, and proceeding from Judæo-Christian rather than orthodox circles, these oracles gained considerable currency among the Apologists, and such writers as Theophilus, Justin and Clement, evidently value them highly. At the same time, they belong more strictly to the history of Jewish than of Christian literature.

A few obscure Gnostic apocalypses are also occasionally referred to. Epiphanius speaks of an *Ascent of Paul*[1] (*i.e.,* when caught up in ecstasy into heaven), and the *Decretum Gelasii* mentions apocalypses of Thomas and Stephen. The celebrated "Apocalypse of Paul," together with other similar productions, belongs to the post-Nicene age.

2. Apocryphal Gospels (1ST CLASS).

The Apocryphal Gospels are of two widely distinct kinds. They may be considered either as competitors of the Canonical Gospels, or as supplements to them. The former are the more ancient. They are, with perhaps one exception, of heretical origin, and until lately were known only by a few short fragments. The others have to a considerable extent survived, being considered less objectionable, and susceptible of an orthodox redaction.

Of the first class, we shall mention first a work that stands by itself, and is referred, not without hesitation, to the apocryphal category. This is the "*Gospel according to the Hebrews,*" identified by some, but without good reason, with the "Gospel according to the Twelve Apostles," mentioned by Origen and others. It is referred to by Clement as Scripture.[2] Origen, though with some reservation, speaks of it

---

[1] ἀναβατικὸν Παύλου.

[2] Strom. ii. 9, where the word γέγραπται (*It is written*) introduces the quotation.

as authoritative.[1] Eusebius reckons it among the disputed books, though he allows that some accept it as canonical. There is no doubt that it was written in Aramaic, and was very generally identified or, more strictly, confused with the lost Hebrew Gospel of S. Matthew. Jerome speaks of it as used by the Nazarenes and Ebionites, and appears to endorse the attribution of it to S. Matthew, though his opinion is not very consistent. That Hegesippus, the Jewish Christian, employed it we learn from Eusebius. According to Irenæus, the sect of the Ebionites used only S. Matthew's Gospel, by which is probably meant the Aramaic Gospel commonly confused with the original S. Matthew—in other words, the Gospel according to the Hebrews.

The fragments that remain sufficiently attest its close relation to S. Matthew, though there are also some remarkable affinities with S. Luke. Jerome, who had seen and read it, attributes to it very high authority, though he does not go so far as to call it Scripture. It is very likely that the original text was preserved in the small and all-but orthodox community of the Nazarenes, and that the Ebionites who separated from them tampered with it considerably to suit their views of the Person of Christ. Thus their Gospel, as we know, suppressed S. Matthew's account of the miraculous birth, while the Nazarene Gospel retained it. Then again it introduced our Lord as calling the Holy Spirit His Mother, a phrase which has a Gnostic ring.[2] Moreover, at the institution of the Lord's Supper, Christ is made to express His unwillingness to eat the flesh of the Passover lamb,[3] in language which is a distorted reminiscence of S. Luke. In another place He condemns sacrifice. On the occasion of His baptism He utters these remarkable words, "Wherein have I sinned that I should be baptized by John, except perhaps this

---

[1] Jerome affirms that Origen often used it. In the extant passages Origen implies that it was not universally accepted.

[2] This was probably in the account of Christ's temptation. The words are "Just now My Mother the Holy Spirit took Me by one of My hairs and bore Me up to the great mountain Tabor."

[3] "Have I desired with desire to eat this flesh of the Passover with you?" Cf. Luke xxii. 15.

very thing that I have said is ignorance ? " words which imply His possible peccability. Many other divergences, more or less slight, from the Canonical Gospels can be detected in the thirty-three fragments we possess. One of its most striking features was the inclusion of a paragraph concerning a woman accused of many sins, which has been held with great probability to be the section on the woman taken in adultery, which doubtless belonged to the synoptic tradition, but is now embedded in the eighth chapter of S. John.

The problems connected with this lost Gospel are of the deepest interest, but it is impossible to pursue them here. The reader is referred to the learned and thoughtful work of Mr. Nicholson,[1] which gives all the authorities and ably summarises the evidence. His estimate may be inferred from the following quotation : " The Fathers of the Church, while the Gospel according to the Hebrews was yet extant in its entirety, referred to it always with respect, often with reverence ; some of them unhesitatingly accepted it as being what tradition affirmed it to be—the work of Matthew—and even those who have not put on record their expression of this opinion have not questioned it. Is such an attitude (he asks) consistent with the supposition that this Gospel was a work of heretical tendencies ? "

Our own answer will on the whole agree with Mr. Nicholson's. As retouched by the Ebionites it doubtless did convey heretical ideas, but in its original form this can hardly have been the case. The evidence seems to point to a very ancient origin almost within the apostolic age, and to a nucleus of authentic narrative, the immense value of which was unhappily discredited by Ebionite insertions and omissions, these being rendered possible by the restriction of the book within the limits of a little known language and a comparatively narrow section of Christendom.[2]

---

[1] " Gospel according to the Hebrews," by E. B. Nicholson, Bodley's Librarian, Oxford.

[2] One very interesting addition to the canonical narrative was its account of the Risen Lord's appearing to James, which is alluded to by S. Paul in the fifteenth chapter of the first Epistle to the Corinthians. James, the Lord's brother, is related to have sworn that he would not eat bread from

We now proceed to discuss the Apocryphal Gospels, properly so called. The first is the "*Gospel according to the Egyptians*," written as the title implies in Egypt, some time during the first half of the second century, by an author strongly imbued with Gnostic views. It claimed to be considered an inspired document, and as such was received by the Encratites,[1] and perhaps by the Naassenes and Sabellians. It was never acknowledged by any orthodox church, but we find it quoted as a reliable source of Christ's sayings in Pseudo-Clement, as already stated.[2] Lipsius characterises it as a product of that pantheistic gnosis which we meet with among the Naassenes of the *Philosophumena*,[3] according to which the soul is of pneumatic nature, and comes into this lower world to undergo manifold changes till finally purified and redeemed by Gnosis. This alone can teach men to apprehend the unity underlying the apparent contradictions of sense, such as male and female, one and many, body and soul. The practical result of this theory is asceticism, and in particular, celibacy; and this Encratite tendency is exemplified in a conversation with Salome attributed to Christ. She asks, "How long shall death reign?" and receives the answer, "So long as ye women give birth." She replies, "Then have I well done that I bare not," and receives the further admonition, "Eat of every herb, but the bitter one eat not." By this expression the intercourse of the sexes is intended.

Another apocryphal Gospel was that "*according to Peter*," of which, until last year, we knew scarcely anything except that it affirmed our Lord's brethren to be sons of Joseph by a former wife, and that Serapion, Bishop of Antioch before A.D. 200, found it in ecclesiastical use at Rhossus in Cilicia,

---

that hour wherein he had drunk the cup of the Lord until he saw Him risen from the dead. On the day of the resurrection, James having kept his vow, the Lord appeared to him and said to them that were by, "Set a table and bread;" then, taking the bread, He blessed and gave to James the Just, saying, "Rise, My brother, eat thy bread, for the Son of Man is risen from the dead."

[1] Clem. Al. Str. iii. ch. 9.
[2] See page 42, where quotations are given.
[3] As described by Hippolytus (A.D. 225).

and was so much displeased with its Docetic tendency that he suppressed it. There was a theory, founded on a questionable reading, that Justin had used it,[1] and Eusebius mentions that Clement, whose judgment was not equal to his learning, had quoted it, though in another place he expressly states that no early Church teacher had regarded it as genuine. The great discovery already referred to[2] has enabled us to judge of this celebrated Gospel for ourselves. An important fragment, containing the account of the Crucifixion and Resurrection, has come to light, and fully confirms the judgment of Serapion. As its first English commentator observes, it is a good instance of what the Germans call a "tendency-writing," i.e., a history told with a purpose, and modified to suit that purpose. The purpose in this case is to deny the actual sufferings of our Lord, and to convey the doctrine of a heavenly Christ, who came upon the earthly Christ at His baptism, and left Him at the moment of His death. This theory belongs to the early Docetism, combated by Ignatius, of which Cerinthus is the first example, and must not be confounded with the later Docetism, which gave to our Saviour only an apparent body, and arose from the Gnostic unwillingness to allow the Divine any contact with gross matter.

For purposes of theological controversy the fragment is highly important. It reveals an acquaintance with all our four Gospels, apparently without any misgivings as to their equal authority ; it gives no countenance to the once popular theory of an *Ur-evangelium*, or original Gospel on which the synoptics were founded, nor does it show any sign of acquaintance with any other Gospel besides the canonical four. The further its date is thrown back, the more telling does this testimony become. Some points of coincidence with the Leucian Acts and with Justin's works, as well as its use by Clement, all point to an early origin, probably well within the first half of the second century. It belonged to the cycle

---

[1] Dial. § 106. The reading ἀπομνημονεύματα αὐτοῦ (sc. Πέτρου) should almost certainly be changed to αὐτῶν (sc. τῶν ἀποστόλων). Justin never refers to any such isolated apostolic testimony.　　　　[2] See p. 155.

of anti-Jewish documents, of which we have other examples in the *Wanderings* or *Circuits of the Apostles*, and the later *Paradosis Pilati*. In its hostility to the Jews it may also be compared with the Apology of Aristides, and of the writer to Diognetus.

We think our readers will be glad to have the whole of this interesting fragment before them. We avail ourselves of Mr. Robinson's kind permission to use his translation (first edition) :—

"But of the Jews none washed his hands, neither Herod nor any one of His judges. And when they wished to wash them, Pilate rose up. And then Herod the king commandeth that the Lord be taken, saying to them, What things soever I commanded you to do unto Him, do. And there was come there Joseph, the friend of Pilate and of the Lord ; and knowing that they were about to crucify Him, he came to Pilate and asked the body of the Lord for burial. And Pilate sent to Herod and asked His body. And Herod said, Brother Pilate, even if no one had asked Him, we should have buried Him ; since indeed the sabbath draweth on ; for it is written in the law that the sun go not down on him that is put to death, on the day before the unleavened bread.[1]

"And they took the Lord and pushed Him as they ran, and said, Let us drag away the Son of God, having obtained power over Him. And they clothed Him with purple, and set Him on the seat of judgment, saying, Judge righteously, O King of Israel.[2]

"And one of them brought a crown of thorns and put it on the head of the Lord. And others stood and spat in His eyes, and others smote His cheeks : others pricked Him with a reed ; and some scourged Him, saying, With this honour let us honour the Son of God.

"And they brought two malefactors, and they crucified the Lord between them. But He held His peace, as having no pain.

[1] We see here the author's correct estimate of Jewish scrupulosity. The regularity rather than the justice of the sentence is the object of their concern, while the idea of a criminal surviving till after sundown would disturb their consciences greatly.

[2] Here, as in other points, there is a coincidence with Justin's account which makes it quite possible that Justin had read this book.

And when they had raised the cross they wrote upon it, This is the King of Israel. And having set His garments before Him they parted them among them and cast a lot for them.

"And one of those malefactors reproached them saying, We have suffered thus for the evils that we have done, but this man, having become the Saviour of men, what wrong hath He done to you? And they, being angry with him, commanded that his legs should not be broken, that he might die in torment.

"And it was noon, and darkness covered all Judæa: and they were troubled and distressed, lest the sun had gone down, since He yet lived: for it was written for them, that the sun go not down on Him that is put to death. And one of them said, Give Him to drink gall with vinegar. And they mixed and gave Him to drink, and fulfilled all things, and accomplished their sins against their own head.

"And many went about with lamps, supposing that it was night, and fell down. And the Lord cried out, saying, My power, My power, hast thou forsaken Me? And when He had said it, He was taken up.[1] And in that hour the vail of the temple of Jerusalem was rent in twain.

"And then they drew out the nails from the hands of the Lord, and laid Him upon the earth, and the earth all quaked, and great fear arose. Then the sun shone, and it was found the ninth hour: and the Jews rejoiced, and gave His body to Joseph that he might bury it, since he had seen what good things He had done. And he took the Lord and washed Him, and rolled Him in a linen cloth, and brought Him into his own tomb, which was called the Garden of Joseph. Then the Jews and the elders and the priests, seeing what evil they had done to themselves, began to lament and to say, Woe for our sins: for the judgment and the end of Jerusalem hath drawn nigh. And I with my companions was grieved; and being wounded in mind we hid ourselves: for we were being sought for by them as malefactors, and as wishing to set fire to the temple. And upon all these things we fasted and sat mourning and weeping night and day until the sabbath.

"But the Scribes and Pharisees and elders being gathered together one with another, when they heard that all the people

---

[1] This is the form of Docetism condemned by Irenæus. The Hebrew word, we are told, was translated thus by other authorities. It makes for the reading 'Ηλί as against 'Ελωί.

murmured and beat their breasts, saying, 'If by His death these most mighty things have come to pass, see how just He is;' the elders were afraid and came to Pilate, beseeching him and saying, Give us soldiers, that they may watch His sepulchre for three days, lest His disciples come and steal Him away, and the people suppose that He is risen from the dead and do us evil. And Pilate gave them Petronius the centurion with soldiers to watch the tomb. And the elders and Scribes came with them to the sepulchre, and having rolled a great stone together with the centurion and the soldiers, they all together who were there set it at the door of the sepulchre; and they put upon it seven seals, and they pitched a tent there, and kept watch.

"And early in the morning as the sabbath was drawing on, there came a multitude from Jerusalem and the region round about, that they might see the sepulchre that was sealed. And in the night in which the Lord's day was drawing on, as the soldiers kept watch two by two on guard, there was a great voice in the heaven; and they saw the heavens opened, and two men descending thence with great light and approaching the tomb. And that stone which was put at the door rolled away of itself and departed to one side; and the tomb was opened and both the young men entered in. When, therefore, the soldiers saw it, they awakened the centurion and the elders, for they, too, were hard by keeping watch; and, as they declared what things they had seen, again they see coming forth from the tomb three men, and the two supporting the one, and a cross following them. And of the two the head reached unto heaven, but the head of Him that was led by them overpassed the heavens. And they heard a voice from the heavens saying, 'Hast thou preached to them that sleep?' And an answer was heard from the cross, Yea.

"They therefore considered with one another whether to go away and show these things unto Pilate. And while they yet thought thereon, the heavens again appear opened and a certain man descending and entering into the sepulchre. When the centurion and they that were with him saw these things, they hastened by night to Pilate, leaving the tomb which they were watching, and declared all things which they had seen, being distressed, and saying, Truly He was the Son of God. Pilate answered and said, I am pure from the blood of the Son of God; but ye determined this.

"Then they all drew near and besought him and entreated him

to command the centurion and the soldiers to say nothing of the things which they had seen : For it is better, say they, for us to owe the greatest debt of sin before God, and not to fall into the hand of the people of the Jews and be stoned.   Pilate therefore commanded the centurion and the soldiers to say nothing.

"And at dawn upon the Lord's day Mary Magdalen, a disciple of the Lord, who, fearing because of the Jews, since they were burning with wrath, had not done at the Lord's sepulchre the things which the women are wont to do for those that die and that are beloved by them, took her friends with her and came to the sepulchre where He was laid.   And they feared lest the Jews should see them, and they said, Even if on that day on which He was crucified we could not weep and lament, yet now let us do these things at His sepulchre.   But who shall roll away for us the stone that is laid at the door of the sepulchre, that we may enter in and sit by Him, and do the things that are due ?   For the stone was great, and we fear lest some one see us.   And even if we cannot, yet let us set at the door the things which we bring for a memorial of Him ; let us weep and lament, until we come to our home.

" And they went away and found the tomb opened, and coming near they looked in there ; and they see a certain young man sitting in the midst of the tomb, beautiful and clothed in a very bright robe, who said to them, Why are ye come ?   Whom seek ye ?   Is it that crucified One ?   He is risen and gone away.   But if ye believe not, look in and see the place where He lay, that He is not here ; for He is risen and gone away thither, whence He was sent.   Then the women feared and fled.

"Now it was the last day of the unleavened bread, and many went forth from returning to their homes, as the feast was ended.   But we, the twelve disciples of the Lord, mourned and were grieved ; and each one grieving for that which was come to pass departed to his home.   But I, Simon Peter, and Andrew my brother, took our nets and went away to the sea : and there was with us Levi the son of Alphæus, whom the Lord . . . ." (The rest is lost.)

The questions suggested by this fragment are so numerous and important that we may be sure they will excite keen attention, not only among scholars, but among the religious public.   The most reassuring result of its discovery is the confirmation it gives to the original authority of the four Gospels.   And if, as seems likely, its date be thrown back to the commencement of the second century, it will prove one of the most effective champions of that church tradition which has been so fiercely attacked, but has shown itself so impregnable.

The *Diatessaron*, or Composite Gospel of Tatian, is also classed among the apocryphal writings. A somewhat full account of it will be found in the chapter on Tatian. It is not truly parallel to those we have been considering, being a distorted picture of the Canonical Gospels rather than an independent work.

To the same class belongs the celebrated *Gospel of Marcion*, the greater portion of which can be recovered from the fourth book of Tertullian *Against Marcion*, and from the forty-second chapter of Epiphanius' work on Heresies. It was a Gnosticising recast of S. Luke, and omitted everything which would not agree with Marcion's *à priori* theory of Gospel truth. It had no critical value, but was only useful as embodying what he acknowledged as the source of his teaching. Its date may be given as about A.D. 145.

This passion for revising and rewriting the Gospels in accordance with their own views was widely spread among the Gnostics. Origen speaks of a *Gospel of Basilides*, which may have been founded on one or more of the Canonical Gospels, with additions drawn from the supposed "Traditions of Matthias," on which he greatly relied. Indeed, a Gospel of Matthias is mentioned in another place by Origen, which consisted of secret discourses received by Matthias from our Lord. If this be the same as the Gospel of Basilides, we may infer, from the short fragments given by Clement, that its tendency was severely ascetic, and therefore favourable to the Gnostic views taught by Basilides.

One main difference between the Gnostics and the Orthodox was the invariable preference of the former for the revelations of some particular Apostle, whereas the Church always held fast to the consentient tradition of the whole college. All the Apologists emphasise the unity of apostolic teaching, and no suspicion of any particular revelation is ever discernible. On the contrary, the Gnostic Gospels usually bear some one name.   For instance, we hear of a Gospel of Andrew, a Gospel of Barnabas, a Gospel of Bartholomew, a Gospel of Philip, a Gospel of Thaddeus ; and last, but not least, a Gospel of Judas Iscariot, in use among the Cainite sect, who made it their boast to reverence all those characters whom the Church and the Scriptures condemn.   Besides these works, there were others of a more general character, embodying doctrinal dissertations in the garb of narratives, as the *Gospel of the Four Corners ;* the *Gospel of Truth*, used by the followers of Valentinus ; the *Gospel of Perfection*, and the *Gospel of Eve*, both probably composed under the influence of Ophite Gnostics, and of doubtful moral tendencies.

Gospels of the Second Class.

The next class of Gospels to be considered contains those which aim at supplementing the canonical ones by filling up the gaps in their record.   They are concerned chiefly with the events preceding our Saviour's birth, the parental ante-cedents of Mary, the infancy of Jesus, His trial before Pilate, His descent into the under-world.   Whatever their original source, they soon became popular with the mass of Latin Christians, and in their turn reacted upon dogmatic theology, which has incorporated several of their ideas.   Thus the perpetual Virginity and Assumption of the Blessed Virgin Mary, possibly also the Immaculate Conception, are due to this source.   Only a few of these writings belong to the period surveyed in our book ; but the instinct which gave them birth undoubtedly had full play in the second century, and though the existing documents may be two or three hundred years later, yet the nucleus of the legend is in most cases early.

The first in order of time and interest is the *Gospel of James*, commonly known as the *Protevangelium*.   This work was thought by Tischendorf to have existed in its present form as early as Justin.   But when scrutinised, its patch-work character betrays an editor's hand.   Moreover, the citations in the Fathers appear to come from a different and earlier recension.   This is the case with some of those in

Justin.[1] Probably there were several recastings before it assumed its present shape. The archetype which Justin and Origen probably used, was no doubt a Judæo-Christian writing, which was subsequently amplified by a Gnostic hand. It was attributed (on no historical grounds) to James the Lord's brother. The Gnostic redaction may be rightly ascribed by S. Jerome (in his letter prefixed to the Pseudo-Matthew) to Leucius Charinus. Dating this writer about A.D. 250, we shall bring our existing Protevangel down to A.D. 280 or even later.

Its author, besides S. Matthew and S. Luke, used portions of the Old Testament and Apocrypha, as well as Jewish and Christian legends. We find in it for the first time the names of Joachim and Anna as parents of the Virgin, but it is uncertain whether traditional or invented. The book abounds in mistakes and inconsistencies, as well as marvellous legends,[1] but says little about those of the infancy. It is extant in several Greek MSS., also in Arabic and Coptic. The name *Protevangelium* was given to it by Postel, who brought it to Europe, and soon after (1552) it was printed in Latin and Greek.

SUMMARY OF THE PROTEVANGELIUM.

Joachim, a wealthy Israelite, came to present his gifts before the Lord : but the High Priest would not receive them, because Joachim had raised up no seed in Israel : therefore he withdrew to the wilderness and fasted forty days and forty nights, praying for seed. His wife Anna also prayed to the Lord : and the Lord sent His angel to comfort her with promise of a child. And at the appointed time she bore a beautiful girl and called her name Mary, and vowed that the child should be given to the Lord. So when Mary was three years old, her parents brought her to the Temple, and left her there. And Mary was like a dove brought up in the Temple of the Lord, and received food from the hand of an angel. And when she was twelve years old, it was revealed

---

[1] Justin mentions Christ's birth in a cave ; so does this Gospel, but with significant differences, which throws doubt on their connection. Again, Justin brings the wise men from Arabia, the Protevangelium does not.— *Trypho*, 78.

[2] Particularly the opening of the rock to hide Elizabeth and her son from Herod's wrath.

to the high priest that he should summon the widowers of the people and assign her to him whom the Lord should choose for her guardian. Joseph was the widower selected : but he wished to decline the charge. In this, however, he was overruled, and Mary was taken to his house, but not as his wife. One day, when she was sixteen years old, as she was drawing water, the Angelic Salutation came to her. She accepted it, and went to tell her cousin Elizabeth, who was also with child. On her return Joseph was greatly troubled, and kept away from his place at the council. But the thing became known, and Annas the Scribe induced the priest to try Joseph and Mary by the ordeal of the Water of Jealousy. They passed it without reproof, and shortly afterwards Mary brought forth her Son in a cave at Bethlehem. The whole creation is represented as spell-bound at the heavenly birth-throes.[1] Salome, who was passing by, ventured to doubt the miracle, but immediately her hand was withered. Then follows the episode of Herod and the Magi. Jesus having been conveyed into Egypt, the king's rage vents itself upon Zacharias the father of John the Baptist, whom he murders at the altar, having in vain attempted to seize the child and his mother, who are wondrously preserved by God.

An inferior dressing-up of this interesting story is preserved under the title of the *Pseudo-Matthew*, or the *Gospel of the Infancy of Mary*, belonging probably to the fifth century. The work is compiled from at least three sources—chapters 1–17 from the Protevangelium, chapters 18–25 from some unknown document, and chapters 26–42 chiefly from the Pseudo-Thomas. The middle portion especially is full of marvels, but as the whole document is late, we need not stop to

---

[1] The passage (ch. 18) is very curious, and points to a Gnostic source. "And I Joseph walked and I walked not : and I looked up into the air, and saw the air violently agitated, and I looked up at the pole of heaven, and I saw it stationary and the fowls of heaven still; and I looked at the earth, and saw a vessel lie, and workmen reclining by it, and their hands in the vessel, and those who handled it did not handle it, and those who took did not lift, and those who presented it to their mouth did not present it, but the faces of all were looking upward: and I saw the sheep scattered, and the sheep stood, and the shepherd lifted up his hand to strike them, and his hand remained up ; and I looked at the stream of the river, and I saw that the mouths of the kids were down, and not drinking; and everything which was being impelled forward was intercepted in its course."

consider it. The *Gospel of the Nativity of Mary* is a less pretentious composition, and though in its present form belonging to the fifth or sixth century, it is no doubt based on early popular legends.

The only other apocryphal Gospel that can lay claim to an early date is that of *Thomas*, or the *Gospel of the Infancy*.[1] We possess this remarkable work in three forms, but none of them is the original; this mounts back to the middle of the second century, or even earlier. It covers a definite period in our Saviour's life, from his fifth to his twelfth year, and represents Him as a captious and wayward Being, fully conscious of His supernatural powers, and using them sometimes in mercy, but oftener in wrath, proving an intolerable scourge to His neighbourhood. One mark of His divine knowledge is His insight into the hidden properties of the letters of the alphabet, in which He puts His teachers to shame, and apparently gives inspired sanction to the wild dreams of Marcus and his school.[2]

This Gospel was in use among the Naassenes and Marcosians, and is cited by several Fathers from Origen downwards. Its character was Docetic, and its hypothesis of the consciousness of Deity on the part of the infant Christ is against the Church tradition. In spite, however, of its objectionable features, it responded so acceptably to the popular craving for the marvellous that it was thought worth dressing up by a succession of orthodox redactors. The same remark applies to another document of uncertain age, *The Passing of Mary*,[3] attributed to the Apostle John, but most probably the work of Leucius Charinus of Antioch, an inventive heretic, to whose unscrupulous pen a multitude of falsifications are ascribed.

Decidedly the most orthodox of all these forgeries are the *Gospels of the Passion*, of *Nicodemus*, or *The Acts of Pilate*.[4] Readers of Justin will remember that that Father appeals

---

[1] τὰ παιδικὰ τοῦ Κυρίου.

[2] See the reference to Marcus in the chapter on Irenæus.

[3] Κοίμησις τῆς Μαρίας. Transitus Mariæ.

[4] I call it "Gospels" rather than "Gospel," because I think the two parts are by different hands. See Cowper's Apocryphal Gospels, p. lxxxv.

with confidence to Pilate's Acts as laid up in the Imperial Archives, and accessible to all who wish to test the truth of the Gospel history.[1] From another passage in his Apology it was inferred that Pilate may have been convinced of the Divinity of Christ. Hence the idea spread that Pilate bore public testimony to this as well as to His innocence, which last fact we learn from S. Matthew. As regards the present form of the work, together with all the Pilate and Herod literature connected with it, the majority of critics believe them all to be later than Eusebius, Tischendorf being almost alone in suggesting a pre-Nicene date.[2] Several of the stories told in the second part of Nicodemus are certainly drawn from early sources, among which may be the Apocalypse of Moses.

Before quitting this part of the subject, we may briefly notice the correspondence between King Abgar of Edessa and Jesus Christ, which has acquired a fictitious celebrity from being included in the history of Eusebius. How so cautious a writer could have imagined these letters genuine, or even worthy of serious consideration, is hard to understand. They were probably first issued in Syriac by some Christian of Edessa in the third century, and this Syriac origin may have imposed upon the historian.

3. Apocryphal Acts.

We now leave the Gospels and pass to a brief review of the Apocryphal Apostolic Acts. It may be noted that the strong repugnance felt by the Catholic Church to any tampering with the biography of Christ did not extend equally to those of the Apostles. It is indeed a surprising thing

---

[1] There is nothing improbable, quite the contrary, in the idea that Pilate sent in a formal statement of the condemnation of Christ. But it was probably contained in a few lines, and it is doubtful whether any of the Fathers who speak of it had seen it.

[2] Justin and Tertullian, in speaking of the Acts of Pilate, refer to an official document, not to a history. The fact is that the title *Acts of Pilate* is a misnomer, and calculated to mislead. There need be no connection whatever between the two documents.

that so little authentic information about the Apostles exists. In the dearth of knowledge a rich crop of legend sprang up, chiefly circulated by the Gnostics, but soon appropriated and highly esteemed by the Church.[1]

The earliest nucleus of the legend is found in the separation of the apostolic band from Jerusalem. It was traditionally reported that the Twelve arranged for their respective missionary provinces, after the manner of the Roman proconsuls, by casting lots. This story afterwards crystallised into a work called the *Sortes Apostolorum*. Out of it grew, as early as the second century, the *Apostolic Ordinances*,[2] of which there are traces of three separate collections in the existing Apostolical Constitutions. The idea that underlies these works is that the Apostles, before parting, agreed to deliver certain ordinances under separate names but with joint responsibility, and these of course were to be binding on the whole of Christendom. Such were the *Judgment of Peter*[3] and the *Circuits of Peter*,[4] and probably the still older *Preachings of Peter*,[5] a Jewish-Christian writing, modified by Catholic hands into the *Preaching of Peter and Paul*,[6] which had a harmonising tendency. The *Traditions of Matthias*[7] and the *Ascents of James*[8] have already been referred to; they probably represent a similar motive among the Gnostics and the Ebionites respectively.

The Acts of Apostles, strictly so called, were at first mainly Judæo-Christian. They provided missionary enterprises for all the Twelve, though some were more fully dealt with than others. S. Paul's name is conspicuous by its absence. The Catholic party, in adopting these fictitious Acts, seem to have had no suspicion of the Judaising fabrications that underlay them, chief of which is the world-wide activity and double episcopate of S. Peter, first at Antioch, then at Rome.

[1] The writer is indebted for most of these details to the article in Smith's Dictionary of Christian Biography.

[2] Διατάξεις τῶν ἀποστόλων, or διδαχαὶ τῶν ἀποστόλων.

[3] Κρῖμα Πέτρου, *Judicium Petri*, or *Duæ Viæ*, known to Clement of Alexandria.   [4] The basis of the Clementine Recognitions.

[5] κηρύγματα Πέτρου.   [6] κήρυγμα Πέτρου καὶ Παύλου.

[7] παραδόσεις Ματθίου.   [8] ἀναβαθμοὶ Ἰακώβου.

The original sources of this romantic literature are four-fold—(1) Ebionite; (2) Gnostic; (3) Catholic; (4) Gnostic-Ebionite, Catholically revised.

Of the Ebionite documents we possess little more than the names, and of these most have been already given. The one of most interest for us is the Circuits of Peter, which has been recast and amplified in the Clementine writings. The *Acts of Peter in Rome* was also an Ebionite work. It contained a dramatic account of the death of Simon Magus at Rome and S. Peter's crucifixion, including the exquisite legend of the *Domine, quo vadis?* This was incorporated into the Catholic Acts of SS. Peter and Paul, which, in their present form, are not earlier than the fifth century, but in more primitive recensions (*Acts of Paul*) are referred to by Origen.

The Gnostic Acts were generally supposed to have emanated from the pen or the school of Leucius Charinus. Who Leucins was, or whether he existed at all, it is impossible to say. He was said to have been a younger contemporary, perhaps a disciple, of S. John at Ephesus, and to have vexed the Apostle by promulgating error. But the testimonies to his personality are not earlier than the fourth century, when he sometimes appears as a Manichæan, sometimes as an inspirer (real or supposed) of the Montanists. It is best to regard his name as a convenient peg on which to hang the anonymous apocryphal Acts. These Acts are certainly early, and may go back as far as the supposed age of Leucins. The Leucian legends are generally of an Encratite character, and were widely circulated. In one of them S. John is said to have been miraculously cured of the desire for marriage, in another to have been immersed in boiling oil, but rendered invulnerable by his purity. It is possible also that the beautiful story of S. John's unwillingness to compose a Gospel, and how this unwillingness was overcome by a revelation, and how in the presence of the brethren he burst forth with the inspired words of the Prologue, may be due to the same source.

There was an immense number of such stories current, some exquisitely beautiful, some grotesque, others superstitious and childish; but all so suited to the popular taste that the Church, being unable to compete with them, adopted the sagacious course of recasting, expurgating, and adopting them.

The following passage from Lipsius [1] expresses with such admirable clearness the attractive features of these writings, that for the reader's benefit we transcribe it in full :—"That this process of purification was not always complete need not surprise us when we consider how changeable and uncertain on some points was the boundary-line between Gnostic and Catholic doctrines. In general, however, these Gnostic productions betray their origin by the over-growths of a luxuriant imagination, by their highly-coloured pictures, and by their passionate love for mythical additions and adornments, in excess even of the popular belief in signs and wonders. The favourite critical canon, ' The more romantic the more recent in origin,' does not hold good as against this branch of literature, in which exorcisings of demons, raisings of the dead, and other miracles of healing or of punishment, are multiplied endlessly. The incessant repetition of like wonders baffles the efforts of the most lively imagination to avoid a certain monotony, interrupted, however, by dialogues and prayers, which not seldom afford a pleasant relief, and are sometimes of a genuinely poetical character. There is withal a rich apparatus of the supernatural, consisting of visions, angelic appearances, voices from heaven, speaking animals and demons, who with shame confess their impotence against the champions of the truth; unearthly streams of light descend, or mysterious signs appear, from heaven; earthquakes, thunders and lightnings terrify the ungodly; the elements of wind, and fire, and water minister to the righteous; wild beasts, dogs and serpents, lions, bears and tigers are tamed by a single word from the mouth of the Apostles, or turn their rage against the persecutors; dying martyrs are encompassed by wreaths of light or heavenly roses and lilies and enchanting odours, while the abyss opens to devour their enemies. The devil himself is often introduced into these stories in the form of a black Ethiopian, and

[1] Article on the Apocryphal Acts in the Biographical Dictionary.

M

plays a considerable part. But the visionary element is the favourite one. Our Lord often appears to His servants, now as a beautiful youth, and again as a seaman, or in the form of an Apostle ; holy martyrs return to life to manifest themselves, at one time to their disciples, at another to their persecutors. Dreams and visions announce beforehand to Apostles their approaching martyrdom, or to longing souls among the heathen the fulfilment of their desires. All this fantastic scenery has been left, for the most part, untouched by Catholic revisers, and remains therefore in works which in other respects have been most thoroughly recast. Yet it was only in very rare cases that these romantic creations of fancy were themselves the original object in view with the writers who produced them. That object was either some dogmatic interest, or, where such retired into the background, an ascetic purpose. Many of these narratives were simply invented to extol the meritoriousness of the celibate life, or to commend the severest abstinence in the estate of matrimony. On this point Catholic revisers have throughout been careful to make regular systematic altera- tions, now degrading legitimate wives to the condition of concubines, and now introducing objections connected with the nearness of kin or other circumstances which might justify the refusal or repudiation of a given marriage. But where merely the praise of virginity was concerned, the views of Catholics and Gnostics were nearly identical, except that the former refused to regard the maintenance of that estate as an absolute or universal moral obligation."

The titles of the Gnostic Acts were numerous. There were *Acts of Peter* attributed to Linus, the disciple of Apostles and first bishop of Rome ; *Acts of Paul*, also ascribed to Linus (both these were superseded by orthodox redactions, the *Passio Petri* and *Passio Pauli*); *Acts of Andrew, Philip*, and *Barnabas*, all forming detached portions of what we may call the Christian Epic Cycle, the extent of which must have been simply enormous. The *Acts of Thomas, John*, and *Thaddeus* are also known. The last is probably the authority for the letters of Abgarus and Christ.

The *Acts of Paul and Thecla* have been so recast as to lose their heretical colouring. They go back to the second century, are cited by Tertullian, and form a sort of romance of asceticism. Paul, accompanied by the traitor Demas, arrives at Iconium, where he preaches a gospel of continence, and wins over Thecla, the daughter of his host. He is brought before the tribunals as a Christian, and seeks safety in flight. Thecla follows him from place to place, and becomes an ardent disciple. She is seized and condemned to be burnt, but the flames will not touch her. Paul then baptizes her. At Antioch her resolve of chastity again exposes her to persecution, but she is protected by an old woman whose daughter's spirit appears in a dream and craves the prayers of the virgin Thecla to help her to heaven. This is the first appearance of the intercession of the saints. She is represented as the pearl of monachal virginity.

Besides these Acts, there are a few anomalous apocryphal works belonging to the first three centuries, to which we may just allude. Such are the *Apocalypse of Moses*, possibly a fragment of some larger work. This contained the account of Adam and Eve's death, and the story of Seth's discovery of the Oil of Comfort. The grandeur of thought and poetical cast of the language made this legend widely popular. It represented Adam and Eve in truly noble proportions, and invested their history with lofty pathos. It is noticeable that while dogmatic writers generally insist upon the sin and imperfection of Adam, the popular mythology invariably dwells on his higher attributes as the protoplast, created in the Divine image. Other documents referring to him were the *Apocalypse of Adam* and the *Testament of Adam*, which are said to betray traces of Persian influence.

The tendency of all this literature which we have thus cursorily reviewed is primarily to give a concrete form to the ideas of Christianity. From a literary point of view it may be likened to the mass of Epic poetry which clustered round the name of Homer. The pre-eminent glory of the Iliad and Odyssey eclipsed, but did not extinguish, the fainter brightness of many another ancient bard. Though unmarked by creative genius, these cyclic poems were treasured by later ages as belonging to the true birthtime of imagination, and thus renewed their life, reviving after a long sleep to gain a second currency in the Alexandrine period.   Just so the Apocryphal Gospels and Acts, though obscured by the excess of light that radiated from the inspired Gospels of the canon, nevertheless partook in some slight degree of the same mysterious vitality ; and after a period of depression and neglect were able to reassert their claims to a hearing, and to secure no inconsiderable recognition both in the dogma and in the hagiological literature of the Church.   As has been acutely remarked, oral tradition is a kind of universal suffrage, which, as soon as it finds articulate expression, rests not until it is in a position to dictate its will, when it compels the official authority, not merely to recognise, but to consecrate it.

CHAPTER IV.

ON GNOSTICISM IN GENERAL.

HARDLY had the last apostolic voice died away when the Church was confronted with a sudden influx of strange doctrines and speculations, which, by explaining away her creed, threatened her very existence. Yet they did not enter her camp in the guise of enemies. They professed to afford either a purer statement of essential Christianity than that of the orthodox, or a fuller explanation of its place in the universe, and so far from abjuring the Christian profession, they claimed alone to retain it in perfection.

The Church, however, refused to admit this claim. She resisted the intrusion of all elements which disagreed with the apostolic tradition, and her writers vindicated the wisdom of this course by a thorough exposition of the essential principles of the faith. For more than a century the struggle was carried on with varying fortunes, till in the end orthodox belief triumphed, and the heretics of the second century, if not extinguished, were at least put to silence.

The order of time requires that we should first consider the aberrations from Christian belief, and then the orthodox statement of it, the former being in fact the exciting cause of the latter. It would be impossible to appreciate the position of the great Apologists without some knowledge of the external ideas they combated, as well as of those they adopted. Hence the necessity of a brief survey of the leading heretical sects.

On the Rise of Heresy.

Now, the first point to make clear is, why heretics should have arisen ? What was it that prevented these men from

accepting the orthodox faith? Was it simply the pride of
the human intellect that led them astray, or was it moral
laxity, or was it a genuine search for truth? The answer
will depend on the evidence, and this varies in different cases.
But in the case of Basilides, Valentinus, and Marcion, at any
rate, the evidence points to a very high earnestness of purpose; and our unfavourable judgment on their orthodoxy
must be balanced by a due respect for their good points.

When the Christian religion was preached to the world, it
was inevitable that men's minds should reason upon it. It
could not be accepted blindly. It must be made to fit in
with the system of things. It was announced as being at
once a fulfilment of Jewish prophecy and a new world-embracing religion. To the Gentile thinker, the Christ of the
Jews could not, primarily and as such, be conceived of as the
Son of God and Lord of the human race. To occupy such a
position He must be regarded in the wider light of a Being
universal as humanity itself, and so brought into an intelligible
relation with the past of the Gentile world. The Scriptures
of the New Testament offer no scientific definition of Christ's
Person or work. Such a definition can indeed, by a logical
process, be evolved from their statements; but neither they
nor the Fathers of the succeeding age indicate what the process is. Hence, when men of acute intelligence, dialectically
trained, having adopted the Christian system, began to ask
themselves for a reasonable account of their belief, they were
to a large extent left to their own methods, and those methods
were the product of heathen philosophy. Now, nothing is
more difficult than to break one's mental continuity. Moral
continuity is far more easily broken than intellectual. In
cases where a new intellectual system is adopted, the habits
and methods of the old are continually cropping up. Now
the great bulk of converts was made at first from the less
educated classes, who had no fixed system of belief. But
in time, as the Gospel spread, an increasing number of cultured minds submitted to it. And many of these, whether
Jews or Gentiles, retained, under an apparent acceptance of
Christian teaching, the root-ideas of their former faiths, from

which they were not, and perhaps hardly desired to be, emancipated.

Hence two leading types of heresy arose, the Jewish or Ebionite, and the semi-heathen or Gnostic. The latter, which was decidedly the more powerful, exercised no small influence on the former, and produced a sort of compound heresy which we may call Gnostic-Ebionite.[1] As the Ebionite Gnostic systems made little impression on the Catholic Church, being confined to small and narrow communities, they need not enter into our consideration here. We shall confine our present remarks to the leading ideas of the Gentile Gnostic systems.

To revert to our question, why heresies arose? we must acknowledge that in the Church of the second century considerable freedom of thought was permitted. When the entire Christian world agreed in accepting a certain body of doctrine, we may be sure that the grounds for accepting it were very strong. When the entire Christian world agreed in rejecting certain ideas as subversive of its faith, we may be equally sure that it did not do this without good ground. We may refuse to accept the bulk of the charges against the lives of the heretics; we may give them full credit for believing their views to be compatible with revelation; we may even admit their superiority in personal gifts to their opponents: but we have no hesitation in endorsing the unanimous verdict of the Church that Gnosticism in all its forms is subversive of Christianity, and that the Gnostics were utterly mistaken in thinking the two could be combined.

Errors of Gnosticism.

(a.) RELATION BETWEEN FAITH AND KNOWLEDGE.

Their main point of view was the presentation of Christianity as a theosophy or scheme of divine knowledge

---

[1] Lightfoot, in his essay on *Essenism*, prefixed to his Epistle to the Colossians, shows that Gnosticism was a system of thought existing before Christianity, and that it had already influenced Judaism before the rise of Jewish Christianity. Hence the true analysis of Gnostic Ebionism would be (Gnostic-Judaism × Jewish-Christianity).

(γνῶσις), not as a system of faith. The Apostle bids Christians " add to their faith knowledge ; " and no doubt this knowledge is what we should call theology. But it is recommended as an adjunct to faith, not as the foundation of it or the substitute for it. Christianity is primarily an intervention of God in history, a fact and not a theory. This the Gnostics failed to perceive ; and, accordingly, they identified the highest Christianity with a speculative system of thought, and left only a lower practical form of it to the sphere of faith. At the same time, they did good service by revealing the need of a true Christian gnosis, restricted according to the Apostle's words, and this the Alexandrian theologians strove not unsuccessfully to supply.

But the whole difference lies in the subordination of the one element to the other. In the orthodox gnosis, the license of speculation is strictly limited by the data of revelation : in the heretical gnosis, revelation is forced to express itself in the categories of speculative thought. Moreover, if theology be in the true sense *a science*, its sphere, like that of all other sciences, is that of necessity and not of freedom. Its conceptions and generalisations are beyond the grasp of the uninitiated, and salvation, achieved through the intelligence, becomes open only to a few. This is exactly the position of Gnosticism. It regards the difference between the spiritual and carnal natures as inherent in the constitution of things, and provides no bridge from one to the other : hence it propounds two doctrines, an esoteric for the elect, an exoteric for the multitude ; and two redemptions, an eternal union with the Deity for the spiritual, and a lower beatitude for the carnal.

It practically adopts the proud motto of the Academy, " Let no one ignorant of science enter here," [1] thus placing itself in direct contradiction to the position laid down by Christ, "I thank Thee, Father, Lord of heaven and earth, because Thou hast hid these things from the wise and prudent, and hast revealed them unto babes." [2] The essence of Christian doctrine lies in its openness to all. There is not

---

[1] μηδεὶς ἀγεωμέτρητος εἰσίτω.   [2] S. Matt. xi. 25.

one teaching for the poor, another for the rich : one revelation for the wise, another for the ignorant. What Christ taught His apostles, that they taught their disciples—that, and nothing else, they embodied in their writings. Such is the first and most fatal error of Gnosticism.

(b.) DUALISM.

Its second error is its inability to disengage itself from the conceptions of Paganism, and more especially of oriental Dualism. It never really adopted the Christian idea of God, as at once the Eternal Spirit and Source of Being, and also the Personal Father and Governor of the universe that He has made. Substantially this idea is drawn from the Old Testament, reaffirmed and filled up by Jesus Christ. But Christian thought has incorporated with it the conception of Deity as the One Absolute Existence and the Ultimate First Cause, which belongs to Greek philosophy. This compound conception, which is enshrined in our first Article of Religion,[1] is a legitimate fusion of two modes of thought, which, combined in the first instance by Philo, have ever since mutually co-operated to form the body of Catholic dogma.

But the pure metaphysical notion, which sufficed for the best thinkers of Greece, had, in the times we speak of, suffered grievous deterioration. The abstract thought of the Eastern world, though professedly Greek in character, invariably sought to embody itself in symbolic intuitions, which it proceeded immediately to clothe with a vague spiritual personality. Unable to maintain itself on the level of truly abstract thought, it projected its fundamental conceptions in the form of a hierarchy of mysterious beings or powers, called Æons, which in their origin are nothing but hypostatised attributes of the inscrutable Source of Being, but which came to be regarded either as inferior deities, or angels, or dæmons, to whom were assigned the various domains of

---

[1] "There is but one living and true God, everlasting, without body, parts, or passions, of infinite power, wisdom and goodness, the maker and preserver of all things, both visible and invisible."

creative, redemptive, or administrative agency. On some Jewish minds these ideas exercised a strong attractive power from their contrast with the bare, stern monotheism of later Judaism, and from the facility with which they seemed reconcilable with the angelology of the Old Testament. To the strictly Hellenic mode of thought they were far less conformable, though there is one aspect of Plato's teaching that finds room for them. Moreover, we must remember that the Hellenism of this epoch was mixed with alien elements,[1] and many of its most distinguished exponents were born in climes far removed from the sober and clear-thinking influences of European Greece.

But there was another element in oriental philosophy even less capable of harmonisation with Christianity than its mythological spiritualism. We allude to its fundamental Dualism, viz., the eternal antagonism between the supreme God and some other force or power which confronted him on a footing of equality, at any rate in the present world. In theory, no doubt, all Gnostics admitted the Unity of the Divine Essence. But in order to maintain its purity un-sullied, they refused to allow the possibility of any direct contact between the incommunicable Godhead and the visible world. To them the first source of created being was derived from an original self-consciousness, involving a *necessary* self-limitation, on the part of God. This was the first passing of the hidden essence into manifestation, first to itself, then, by various intermediate acts not so much of volition as of a kind of organic development,[2] to the emanations from itself, which, in successive degrees of declining purity, it threw forth. This obscure and difficult theory need only be noticed here in so far as it affects the Christian doctrines of Creation and the nature of the principle of evil. As it bore directly upon these, a few words on these two points may

---

[1] This is pre-eminently true of Plutarch, who, though born in Greece proper, shows a strong leaning to the corrupted orientalised forms of Platonic doctrine.

[2] Or "pullulation" (προβολή). The process may be compared to the repro-duction of the zoophyte, with the addition of self-consciousness.

not be out of place. To take the latter first. On the emanation hypothesis above given, it is evident that the ultimate
source of evil must be God Himself. But this, which is the
doctrine of *Monism*, would, if logically worked out, involve
the inconsistency of a double nature in the Deity, at once
bad and good. But this was too repulsive. It was therefore
softened down by the conception of evil as the negative, the
unreal, the non-existent, the realm of darkness, the privation
of light. But, as a rule, a more pronounced dualism was
held. The origin of evil was sought either in the remoteness
of the stage of emanation from the primal deity, or in an act
of individual volition [1] on the part of one of the æons, or in
the essential nature of matter howsoever formed ; or else it
was held to be the characteristic operation of a secondary or
antagonistic deity, according as the Alexandrian or Syrian
type of Gnosticism prevailed. To Plato evil had no place in
the world of ideas, but was inextricably interwoven with the
world of sense as a necessary condition of the manifestation
of good ; hence to rise above the world of sense altogether
and contemplate the idea in its purity was the only escape
from earthly imperfection.[2] But this being impossible to a
composite nature, the idea of a *redemption* of the sensible
world was logically involved in his system. And in this
way the Christian Platonists of Alexandria [3] may be said
to have bridged a path from Plato to Christ. But the
Gnostics carried out their theory of redemption on lines
fundamentally different from those of the Catholic thinkers.
Just as Philo in reconciling Plato with Moses had abandoned
the true view of Creation as an act of the Divine Will, and
fitted it into his system as a cosmological fact or process,
exactly so did the Gnostic teachers deny the essential character of redemption as an act of free grace, and relegate it
to the sphere of cosmological necessity.

---

[1] More correctly "desire" or "dissatisfaction." In this view we can
trace the influence of the Buddhist philosophy, which practically identifies
evil not with the material world, but with the desire which in that philosophy is regarded as the source of the material world.

[2] Theætetus, p. 176 A.   [3] Clement and Origen.

Thus they were inexorably led by their logic to explain away the reality of Christ's manhood, and to adopt the strange theory known as Docetism, which denied to the Redeemer not only the possession of true human nature, but any direct contact with the limited and contingent. They thus cut at the root of all true Christianity, and amply justified the Church in her incessant polemic against them. Moreover, by confining the work of redemption to the spiritual enlightenment of such natures as were already spiritually constituted, they drifted away from the Christian doctrine of its universality, and from its vital application to the moral regeneration of mankind. And the erroneous conclusions they drew, not only in theory but in practice, formed one of the strongest arguments advanced by the Church against them.

(c.) Effect on Morals.

It is true we must receive these pictures of moral corruption with caution, for the method of discrediting people's opinions by condemning their practice is too familiar to students of theology to be much regarded except in cases where it can be established by something better than mere assertion. Making, however, every allowance for the prejudices of their opponents, we believe there is good ground for concluding that the ultra-dualistic schools at any rate, misled by their false views of matter, put forward a radically erroneons moral ideal, either recommending asceticism, i.e., a complete subjugation of the body, as the essential condition of spiritual freedom, or else permitting unbridled indulgence in fleshly desires, to secure the undisturbed tranquillity of the immaterial part. We see in these different views a counterpart of the Greek philosophic schools, in which those who held pleasure to be the supreme good (Cyrenaics and Epicureans), gradually came to recommend instead of it an apathetic indifference to everything; while those which held up a sterner and more ascetic ideal (Cynics) at last permitted the grossest forms of vice, if mental immobility could be attained in no other way.

(d.) Theories of Creation.

Next, as to the question of Creation. Here the divergence between the two systems is traceable to the same fundamental difficulty, viz., how to connect the incommunicable essence on the one hand, with matter on the other. It seemed inconceivable to the Gnostic that this world, with all its imperfection, should have been created directly by God. They therefore account for it by a theory which combines the fancies of the Timæus with the doctrine of the Old Testament.[1] The Creator of the world is to them not the Supreme Deity but the Demiurge, a limited secondary god, who receives his power from the Supreme, but is ignorant of his limitation. This Being revealed himself to the Jews as the Creator, which in truth he was; as the God of righteousness, which, in the narrow sense of retributive justice, he was also; and, finally, as the supreme and only Deity, which he was not. No small part of their theory is taken up with defining the relation of the Demiurge to the Eternal God, some thinkers regarding it as one of obedient inferiority, others as one of hostility. None of them accept in their obvious sense the words of Genesis, that "God saw all that He had made, and behold it was very good." The majority, on the contrary, regard it as evil; and whether they attribute it to an automatic process, to a Demiurge, or an angel, they all agree in holding that its final goal of perfection consists in some form of reabsorption into the primal essence, or in the annihilation of such elements as are incapable of absorption.

Effects of Gnosticism.

Before proceeding to give a brief sketch of the most influential Gnostic teachers, we may add a few words on the general position of Gnosticism in the evolution of Christian thought.

[1] We need not particularise the different shapes this theory took. On the principle of the amount of evil being determined by the remoteness of the emanation, it is generally held that the Creator of this visible world held but a low place in the hierarchy of spirits.

Its great service at once to the Church and to humanity consisted in this, that it compelled the Christian conscious-ness to define its position accurately, both to itself and in the eyes of the thinking world. So long as Christianity and Paganism were two rival systems, each promulgating its own views without any point of contact, it might well seem at first sight that Paganism had a fair chance of survival; but, so soon as a party arose claiming to represent the genuine spiritual doctrine of Christ, and yet willing to explain and justify those very mythological ideas that the Church so emphatically repudiated, it was evident that a crisis had come. If a philosopher could embrace Christianity without sacrificing his philosophy, the Church obviously did not un-derstand her mission. Hence the struggle with Gnosticism, as afterwards with Arianism, was really a vital one; and the effect of Gnostic teaching upon morals, upon discipline, and upon worship, was a legitimate subject for the Christian controversialist, in which he was not slow to perceive his great advantage.

Another involuntary service of Gnosticism to the cause of true religion was the obligation it brought upon the Church of distinctly asserting the paramount importance of faith. The Gnostics allowed the sufficiency of faith for the *psychici* or carnally-minded multitude; but the *pneumatici* or spiritual believers lived in a higher state of immediate knowledge, which raised them into what was virtually a different world. Now this opposition between knowledge and faith was by no means unknown to Judaism; and with other elements of Judaism it might well have crept into the Church, had it not been for the salutary manifestation of its results displayed in the Gnostic doctrines. The Church was forcibly recalled to the exposition of the nature of faith given by S. Paul; and the great principle was re-established that faith is the organ whereby revealed truth is received, consisting primarily not in a state of the intelligence, but in a disposition of the heart, whereby the will is subordinated to the revealed will of God, in such wise that the intelligence is illumined by the Divine Spirit in and through the obedience of faith. The vain

figment of an exoteric and esoteric doctrine, founded on misinterpretation of Christ's parables and of certain passages of
S. Paul, was clearly met and once for all refuted. And the
universal applicability of the Gospel of Christ to all orders of
intelligence, wherein consists its true catholicity and its promise of regenerating mankind, was triumphantly vindicated.

It must be said, in justice to the Gnostics, that in one
important respect they showed themselves able to appreciate
the system which in other respects they perverted. In their
recognition of the coming of Christ as the turning-point in
the world's history, they do not yield to the most orthodox
of their opponents. It was indeed impossible to state this
idea in more emphatic terms, though their apprehension of
it was confined to a single aspect. "When the Gnostic
systems (we quote from Neander) describe the amazement
which was produced in the kingdom of the Demiurge by
the appearance of Christ as the manifestation of a new and
mighty principle which had entered the precincts of this
lower world, they give us to understand how powerful was
the impression which the contemplation of the life of Christ,
and of his influence on humanity, had left on the minds of
the founders of these systems, making all earlier institutions
seem to them as nothing in comparison with Christianity.
It appeared to them as the commencement of *the great*
revolution in the history of mankind. The ideas of the
adjustment of the disturbed harmony of the universe; of
the restoration of a fallen creation to its original source;
of the reunion of earth with heaven; of a revelation to
man of an ineffable Godlike life transcending the limits of
mere human nature; of a new process of development
having entered into the whole system of the terrestrial
world—such were the ideas which henceforth formed the
centre of these systems. The distinctive aim of the Gnostics
was to apprehend the appearance of Christ, and the new
creation proceeding from Him, in their connection with the
evolution of the whole universe. In a theogonical and cosmogonical process, remounting to the original ground of all
existence, everything is referred backwards and forwards to

the fact of Christ's appearance. What S. Paul says respecting the connection of redemption with creation, they made the centre of a speculative system, and endeavoured to understand it speculatively."

It is this speculative pretension that constitutes at once their glory and their shame. If the speculative intellect could have penetrated the mysteries of redemption, those inner secrets of the Divine Counsel which the angels desire to look into, we may well believe that these subtle, bold, and truly earnest inquirers would have arrived at results, if not absolutely, at least partially true, and most useful to Christian theology. But they had misread the fundamental lesson of the Incarnation, and the character of Christ; they drew their inspiration from the Pagan idea of the human spirit rising by abstraction into the Divine, not from the Christian teaching of the coming down of God to tabernacle with men, and the indwelling of the Divine Spirit as the source of wisdom in the contrite and humble soul. Hence the interest of their theories is for us mainly historical. Though it would be unjust not to acknowledge the ability with which they approached such questions as the canon of Holy Scripture, the doctrine of Inspiration, and the relation of the Old Testament to the New; yet their repudiation of the first principle of Christian gnosis, viz., the submission of the intellect to the revelation as given in Holy Scripture, is enough to vitiate their entire method, and to render them conspicuous examples of what a true religious philosophy, if it is to be Christian, must avoid.

Finally, we must not omit to mention an indirect but very real service rendered by the Gnostics to the Christian Church, viz., the bringing into prominence the importance of a written canon of inspired doctrine. They professed themselves anxious to harmonise their views with the accepted documents of the Church. Now, in those early times, the canon of the New Testament was by no means settled. No doubt the great majority of its writings were in circulation, and received with general reverence. But other writings of a different level of excellence were also current, and in some quarters received as Scripture. Moreover, apocryphal books were in circulation purporting to proceed from apostles and their followers, which, as containing heretical teaching, it was imperatively necessary for the Church to reject. This led to a thorough investigation of the question what writings were to be considered as genuine and what were to be disregarded or repudiated. The investigation was not conducted by the whole Church in common, nor was any authoritative stamp put upon any set of writings by any synodical act. But the general consciousness of Christendom agreed, by a sort of tacit understanding, to accept only those which had come down to it properly accredited. The Gnostics, though from mixed motives, were really the pioneers in this movement. The bold and unscrupulous way in which they interpreted the Gospels and Epistles in accordance with their views, and rejected what they could not force into conformity, compelled the Church both to examine the claims of its ancient documents and to arrive at some understanding how they should be interpreted. It is well known that some heretics, notably Marcion, used the utmost freedom in mutilating or rejecting the sacred texts; while others endeavoured to gain currency for works composed by themselves under the pseudonym of an apostle. The remarkable unanimity with which the different churches, uncompelled by any central authority, accepted the greater part of the New Testament, is a most significant proof of the adequacy of its attestation. The laborious process by which this grand result was established is almost lost; nevertheless we can form some idea of its thoroughness when we observe that in the time of Irenæus (180 A.D.) the New Testament, with one or two small exceptions, was not only accepted in its entirety, but had secured a position of authority as undisputed as it now enjoys.

CHAPTER V.

Simon Magus, the opponent of S. Peter and traditional founder of heresy, appears for a moment in the Acts of the Apostles, but his historical character is so overlaid with romance and legend that it is difficult to speak of him with much confidence. It is to Hippolytus that we are indebted for most of the details of his system. He was a native of Gitteh in Samaria, and was well versed in the arts of magic and theurgy. His great ambition was to be considered a manifestation of the Deity, and no doubt this fact explains his attempt to traffic with the Apostles for the possession of what he regarded as a secret which they might be expected to offer for sale on reasonable terms.

If anything is certain about his life, it is the fact that he united himself to a courtesan named Helena, whom he purchased at Tyre, and declared to be his first Thought (ἔννοια), who had emanated from him in a supramundane stage of existence, and whom he identified with the lost sheep of our Lord's parable. His chief work was called the "Great Annunciation,"[1] and was known to Hippolytus and Justin. It contained a confused mixture of Old Testament and Gnostic doctrines, chiefly cosmogonical and quasi-mystic. He seems also to have incorporated some ill-understood elements of the Stoic philosophy. He professed to dispense salvation through his gnosis, which had for its primary object the setting right of the mismanagement of which the angel who had been entrusted with the care of the world had been guilty. Though in human form, he was not a man, but an incarnation of the

---

[1] μεγαλὴ ἀπόφασις. This word admits also the meaning "denial."

Divine Being, manifesting himself to Samaria as the Father, to the Jews as the Son, and to the Gentiles as the Holy Spirit.

It is only by applying force to language that his system can be called an aberration of Christianity. It is rather a rival theory, bitterly opposed in every point to the Christian spirit.

There can be no doubt that a sect of Simonians existed in Samaria in Justin's time, and probably in Rome also. And it was probably from the misrepresentations of these latter that Justin was led to believe that Simon was worshipped at Rome as a god. Origen [1] informs us that this sect (the members of which were also called Helenians) was almost extinct in his day. It has been conjectured, not without probability, that there were really two Simons—the magician mentioned in the Acts, and another Simon of Gitteh, separated from the former by about two generations, to whom the heretical system should properly be referred. One Dositheus is mentioned in the Clementines as an adherent of his views, and Justin speaks of another Samaritan named Menander, who continued the same heretical teaching, probably about thirty years before Justin's own time.

The doubts that hang over the historical character of Simon do not exist in the case of his contemporary **Cerinthus**.

This teacher lies on the border-land between the Ebionites and the Gnostics, having affinities with both systems. He was of Egyptian origin, and educated, no doubt, at Alexandria, in the Philonic school of thought. He is said to have travelled widely, visiting among other places Jerusalem, Cæsarea and Antioch. His date goes back to apostolic times, and tradition is busy with his relations to the Apostles. The following is a summary of them:—He is said while in Palestine to have been one of those who contended with Peter because he had eaten with Gentiles, one of those who went out from James and troubled the brethren at Antioch, one of those who raised the tumult against S. Paul for introducing Trophimus into the temple, and one of those who are

[1] Cels. v. 57.

stigmatised by S. Paul as false apostles and false brethren.
The well-known story of his meeting S. John in the bath at
Ephesus is of value as an indication of the strong feeling of
repulsion with which the Church of that age regarded him.
He is also reported to have rejected the Acts of the Apostles
and all the Gospels except S. Matthew, and from that he
exscinded the miraculous birth. He further maintained the
necessity of circumcision for all believers in Christ.

Our knowledge of his doctrines is derived from the notices
in Irenæus, Hippolytus, and Epiphanius. He is to be regarded
as the true originator of Judæo-Christian Gnosticism. The
great problem that presented itself to his mind was the
co-existence of good and evil, which he identified with spirit
and matter. The opposition between these he described as
that between the essentially perfect and that form of passive
imperfection which yet was ultimately dependent upon God.
The world, in his opinion, was created not directly by God,
but by angels of an inferior grade of emanation. He held
the God of the Jews to be identical with the Angel who
delivered the Law, but not with the limited and inferior
Creator of the world as conceived by the Gnostics. His
instinctive reverence for the Old Testament, in which he
contrasts with later theorisers, kept his speculations within
bounds.

On the Person of our Saviour he entertained peculiar
views, approaching in some respects to those of Ebionism.
He seems, however, to have allowed the truth of the Resurrection.[1] But the evidence for his views is somewhat conflicting, and includes many elements of a more fully developed
Gnosticism. It seems certain that he held strongly Chiliastic
beliefs, of a sensuous and material character, borrowed from
the current Judaism. He is reported to have prescribed that
in case a person died unbaptized, another should be baptized
in his stead. His name gained a certain notoriety in the
Church from the tradition, apparently not unfounded, that
S. John's writings were directed against his views. Oddly
enough, this tradition is counterbalanced by another to the

---

[1] This is, however, denied by Epiphanius.

effect that Cerinthus himself was the author of both the
Apocalypse and Gospel of S. John.   The Chiliastic images
of the former book might have afforded some specious grounds
for this assertion; while it was thought that Cerinthus might
have endeavoured to gain credit for his Christological doctrine
by putting it forth under the venerated name of the Apostle.

Whether Cerinthus taught that peculiar doctrine of Christ's
personality which is known as Docetic is very doubtful.   If
the Gospel and Epistle of S. John are really directed against
him, we must suppose that he did.   But Irenæus does not
mention his name in this connection.   He speaks of Simon
Magus as the first and Saturninus as the second, who taught
this heresy.   The title *Docetic* is given to that view by which
the body of Christ was supposed to be like ours in appearance only, but in reality to be impassible and immaterial.
It was founded on the prevailing philosophical idea that
matter contained the original principle of evil, and that
therefore the real union of the divine and human natures in
one Person was impossible.   It is a remarkable testimony to
the early prevalence in the Church of the ideas of Christ's
pre-existence and superhuman nature, that in the Gnostic
sects which arose every teacher, with the insignificant exceptions of Justinus and Carpocrates, while refusing to admit the
union of both natures, denied the reality not of the divine
but of the human part.   Saturninus broached his Docetic
theories at Antioch quite early in the second century.   And
this fact is important as throwing light on the strongly anti-
Docetic passages in the Ignatian Epistles, which used to be
thought inconsistent with their assumed early date, especially as they are absent from the Syriac recension.   It is,
however, by no means necessary to reject them, inasmuch as
Antioch, where Ignatius dwelt, was in his time an undoubted
seat of this heretical tendency.   The first assumption of the
name *Docetæ* as the title of a sect dates from **Julius Cassianus,** an Egyptian, who lived probably towards the close of
the second century, and is chiefly known by the references
in Clement to a work of his called *Exegetica*, on the comparative antiquity of the Jewish and Pagan systems.

In one sense all Gnostics were Docetics, because they all thought that the real work of redemption was done by the spiritual Christ and not by the man Jesus. But this is not the ordinary sense of the term, which means rather that He who appeared to be true man was not in reality such. The Docetic theories of Valentinus and Marcion will be discussed under their respective headings.

CHAPTER VI.

Basilides (flor. A.D. 117–138 ?), the subtle thinker, who shares with Valentinus the distinction of being selected by opponents as the representative of Gnosticism, called himself the disciple of Glaucias, interpreter of S. Peter. Whoever Glaucias may have been, if he ever existed, we need not suppose that Basilides learnt his Christianity anywhere else than at Alexandria, where such elements of Syrian gnosis as we find in his system were well known, and where it is almost certain that he flourished and taught during the reign of Hadrian. His chief treatise was called *Exegetica*, a commentary on the Gospel in twenty-four books, which was answered by Agrippa Castor.[1] Origen further attributes to him an apocryphal gospel which he calls "The Gospel according to Basilides;" but as to the reality of this work there is considerable doubt.[2]

Our main authorities for his teaching are Irenæus, the anonymous supplement to Tertullian's *Præscriptio adversus Hæreticos*, the lost *Compendium* of Hippolytus preserved in part by Epiphanius, the *Stromateis* of Clement, and the *Refutation of Heresies* of Hippolytus.

Of these the two latter are the most important. Both in point of date, and of ability to weigh the evidence before them, they are entitled to high consideration. At first sight they seem to disagree, and this disagreement has given occasion for regarding both with suspicion; but it can be explained by the fact that the two authors are dealing with different portions of Basilides' system. Clement is criticising

---

[1] Cf. Eus. H. E. iv. 7.   [2] See Book III. ch. 3.

his moral theory, Hippolytus his cosmogony. Allowing for this, their testimony is by no means so inconsistent as at first sight it appears. If we possessed the Hypotyposes of Clement, which dealt with the cosmical theories of Basilides, we should doubtless find many points of coincidence with Hippolytus. Clement and Hippolytus are both accurate writers, and it is impossible lightly to disregard their testimony. We therefore follow Dr. Hort in accepting the portion of Hippolytus (Bk. vii. ch. 20–27) as an imperfect, but so far as it goes tolerably correct, reproduction of the speculations of the *Exegetica*.[1] We use this guarded language owing to the extreme difficulty of apprehending the subtle ontology of Basilides.

His Philosophy.

This commences with an affirmation, arrived at by so thoroughgoing a process of abstraction as to be indistinguishable from pure negation. The Supreme Fountain of all that exists is conceived of as the *non-existent* God,[2] all positive predicates being withdrawn from the conception. This Deity, wholly inconceivable to us, and apparently to Himself, willed (if such a term can be used) to create a not-being world out of not-being things. This archetypal world was a kind of germ-potency, containing within it the seed-mass of the existing world, the origin of all subsequent growths. Basilides does not allow of an antecedent existing matter. He recognises the words of Genesis, " God said, Let there be light, and there was light," to be the nearest approach that human language can make to the hidden truth.

He conceives that this original seed had within it a tripartite principle of development, to which, in order to emphasise its spiritual character, he gives the name of sonship.

---

[1] Abridged from Dr. Hort's article in Smith's Dictionary.

[2] Perhaps more correctly " *non-existent god.*" οὐκ ὢν θεός (without the article). Compare Hegel's dictum, " Pure Being is Pure Nothing." Others have connected this conception of his with the Aristotelian theory of δύναμις and ἐνέργεια—qs. a potentially-existent Being.

Part of this was subtile or pure, part coarse, and part such as to be capable of purification. The subtile sonship mounted aloft till it reached the supreme God; the coarse sonship raised itself to a certain degree of nearness to God by the aid of the Holy Spirit, who, when unable to carry his companion further, remained as a kind of limiting firmament between the supramundane sphere and the world.[1] The third sonship still continued within the seed-mass, out of which burst a Being called the Great Archon,[2] who raised himself as far as the firmament, supposing it to be the highest heaven, where he fixed his seat, and became superior to all things except the third sonship, which, though he knew it not, was in reality better than himself. He then turned to create the world, but before doing so, begat out of the things below a Son, wiser and better than himself, whom, in admiration of his excellence, he placed at his own right hand. This is the *Ogdoad*. Then the Great Archon, inspired by his Son, proceeded with the heavenly creation as far as the moon. At this stage another Archon arose out of the seed-mass, inferior to the first Archon, but superior to all things else, with the exception of the third sonship. He also made to himself a Son wiser than himself, and he became the creator and governor of the aërial world. This region is called the *Hebdomad*. Meanwhile, in the heap and seed-mass, constituting the terrestrial stage, the realm of natural causation comes into being, "according to the preordained utterance of the Ineffable; and this has no ruler over it, since the scheme which the not-being One planned when he was forming all things is sufficient for its guidance."[3]

After the completion of the mundane and supramundane regions there still remained to be developed the third sonship, which was revealed in those souls that are naturally spiritual,

---

[1] This idea of a "Limitary Spirit" is thought to be taken from the Horus of Valentinus. It may also be partly borrowed from the notices of the Holy Spirit and the firmament in Genesis, ch. i. 3.

[2] *I.e.*, Ruler. The idea is perhaps that of an Angel.

[3] *I.e.*, there is no personal superintendent to interfere in its working, but natural causation proceeds by fixed laws in accordance with the original creative impulse.

and are left on earth to order, to guide, and to bring to
perfection the souls whose nature it is to remain in the terrestrial stage.   Historically, the period from Adam to Moses
represents the reign of the Great Archon, who is unname-
able by man, and therefore only revealed under the general
title of God Almighty.   With Moses the Archon of the
Hebdomad entered upon the scene, who revealed himself to
Moses by the name of Jehovah, and also spoke through the
prophets.   But when at last the entire creation was anxiously
looking for the revelation of the sons of God, and the Gospel
was ready to appear, the thoughts of the sonship penetrated
beyond the Hebdomad to the Son of the Great Archon, who
instructed his Father as to their immense significance.   Then
for the first time the Great Archon, smitten with sudden
enlightenment, realised that he was not the God of the whole
universe; he acknowledged a superior Deity, confessed his
own ignorance, and experienced that fear of the Lord which
is the beginning of wisdom.   This same wisdom was next
transferred to the Hebdomad; and from thence it came down
and lighted upon Jesus, son of Mary, not at His baptism as
most Gnostics held, but at the Annunciation, *i.e.*, the moment
of conception.

From the time of the Nativity onward the world continues
much as it is now, and will do so until all the sonship that
has been left behind follows Jesus and is purified and
becomes subtile, so that it can mount of itself upward like
the first sonship.   " When every sonship shall have arrived
above the Limitary Spirit, then the creation shall find mercy,
which now groans and is tormented and awaits the revelation
of the sons of God, that all the men of the sonship may
ascend up from hence."

When this has come to pass, God will bring upon the whole
world the Great Ignorance, that everything may remain in
the stage of its appointed development, and may neither
know nor desire anything beyond it.   This idea recalls that
of the River of Lethe, which is an integral part of the
Platonic system.   Its function, however, is different; for
whereas Lethe throws oblivion over the past to prepare each

life for a fresh start on the path of transmigration, the Great
Ignorance rivets the soul's hold on the particular form of
life which is assigned to it. This ignorance will extend to
the Hebdomad and to the Ogdoad. " And in this wise shall
be the restoration, all things according to nature having been
founded in the seed of the universe in the beginning, and
being restored in their due seasons." The birth of Jesus is
considered by Basilides to be the first process of sifting things
hitherto confused, through the division between his own
bodily and psychical parts: for the former alone suffered,
and so were restored to formlessness; the latter rose above
the world, re-entered the Hebdomad, and finally bore aloft
the third sonship by purifying it, and raised it above the
Limitary Spirit to the realms of the first or blessed sonship.

Ethical Side of his Doctrine.

We gather this from Clement's criticisms. They are
directed sometimes against Basilides, sometimes against
the Basilideans, but it is doubtful whether any distinction
of doctrine is intended to be made between them. In the
ethics of Basilides, faith played a highly important part,
being praised in lofty and enthusiastic terms. But since in
his view faith was the work of nature, not of responsible
choice, it cannot be identified with the faith of Christians.
Indeed, he pushed this view of election so far as to sever a
portion of mankind from the rest as alone entitled to receive
faith, or the higher enlightenment. This same conception of
congenital inability to accept beliefs which transcend the
fixed stage of the soul's development, led Basilides to confine
the remission of sins to those sins which were committed
involuntarily and through ignorance. This part of his theory
is involved in much obscurity; for whereas Origen declares
that he depreciated martyrdom and spoke lightly of the sin
of sacrificing to idols, Clement accuses him of treating all
suffering as a punishment for past sin, that of the martyr
included; a principle which Basilides, when pressed, extended, though with great apparent hesitation, even to the

human Christ. He also entertained the conception of sin in a prior state (even a non-human one) as working out its appointed penalty of suffering here, the elect souls suffering honourably through martyrdom, and those of a less noble sort being purged by their appropriate chastisement.

Discipline and Worship.

In these departments we hear of few changes introduced by Basilides. Clement mentions his practice of celebrating the eve of Christ's Baptism by a watch-night service. According to Agrippa, he followed the Pythagorean fashion of prescribing a five years' silence to his disciples. Agrippa is also an authority for the statement that he enforced his views by quotations from two prophets, Barcabbas and Bar-coph, and other fictitious authorities, bestowing barbarous appellations on them to strike the vulgar with amazement. These alleged prophecies, which we need not accuse Basilides of fabricating, were doubtless current among Gnostics and Manicheans, and were drawn from the apocryphal Zoroastrian literature. Isidore, the son and disciple of Basilides, declared the theological allegories of Pherecydes to have been taken from the prophecy of Ham. Now there was a tradition that Mizraim, the reputed progenitor of the Egyptians, Babylonians and Persians, was identical with Zoroaster, and that he was taught the arts of magic by his father Ham. Hippolytus, however, says nothing of these apocryphal prophecies; but speaks of the sect of Basilides, boasting that they took to themselves the glory of Matthias, by which he probably means that they borrowed doctrines from a work entitled the *Traditions of Matthias.*

General Characteristics.

To sum up the general characteristics of his theory, we may say that he was influenced in varying degrees by Orientalism, Greek philosophy,[1] and Christian doctrine. It

---

[1] The influence of Aristotle is traceable in the softening of antitheses, and in the assignment of regular causation to the realm of φύσις.

is uncertain whether he was, as is usually assumed, anterior to Valentinus, or, as is more likely, contemporary with him, and subjected to his influence, though rather by way of repulsion than of attraction. He reveals a decided tendency to soften those oppositions which Gnosticism delights in, as matter and spirit, Jewish and Christian, creation and redemption. He was careful to preserve in theory the original oneness of the Deity; yet he ascribed the chaotic nothingness out of which the universe was to spring to Him who was its Maker and source. Notwithstanding this, however, Creator and creation were not confused by him, but melt away together in a vista of obscure thought. In his ethical system, though faith was allowed its right of pre-eminence, yet it was conceived as an energy of the understanding, confined to those who had the requisite inborn capacity, while the dealings of God with man were shut up within the limits of a mechanical justice.

He seems to have been a solitary thinker with no disciple of any eminence except his son **Isidore,** who is alluded to in this connection by Hippolytus and Clement. Isidore wrote a treatise called "*Expositions of the Prophet Parchor,*" in which he put forward the plea that the higher thoughts of Pagan philosophers and mythologers were derived from a Jewish source. Clement also mentions a treatise by him *On Adherent Soul,*[1] which took up a position somewhat antagonistic to that of his father with regard to the connection of the passions with the soul. Basilides had regarded them as "appendages," and so had excused their aberrations; but Isidore contends for the unity of the soul, and the necessity of overcoming, through the reasoning faculty, the inferior creation within us. Though the fame of Basilides was so great, and his name is familiar as an eponym of heresy, yet his original teaching lacked the elements of vitality. It was a system of lofty speculation, obscure and difficult to grasp. Moreover, in some points it lent itself to serious misinterpretation. His imposition of a five years' silence seemed

---

[1] περὶ προσφυοῦς ψυχῆς. The passions seem to have been considered as sprouting out of the soul, as the young zoophyte sprouts from its parent.

to countenance the existence of a secret and presumably immoral esoteric teaching; his doctrine of election admitted of an Antinomian construction. On the whole, while with Mansel admitting a Platonic, and also a considerable Stoic leaven in his system,[1] we are compelled to recognise a no less considerable admixture of genuine Christian elements, which entitle him to be classed among those Gnostics who are less widely removed from the Christian faith. The school of spurious Basilideans who at a later epoch professed to follow his views in reality misrepresented them in every essential particular, and he must in no respect be held responsible for the excesses either of doctrine or practice by which they became justly infamous.

The Pseudo-Basilideans.

For this school our ultimate authorities are Irenæus and the lost Compendium of Hippolytus, both interwoven into the account of Epiphanius, and perhaps employed by the Pseudo-Tertullian. Its theology was founded on the notion of a supreme Deity, from whom were descended various personified attributes in lineal succession, who constituted the First or Highest Heaven. In all they reckoned no less than 365 heavens and 365 sets of angels, by the lowest of whom our world and man were made. Their Archon was the God of the Jews, who provoked such discord among angels and men that the Supreme Father sent down Nous (Mind), his Firstborn, who is also Christ, to redeem the world. Christ appeared on earth, but only in outward phantasm, and did not really take flesh. It was Simon the Cyrenian who was crucified; for Jesus exchanged forms with him as he bore His cross on the way to Calvary. The supreme power and source of all being is called Abraxas or Abrasax, a Greek word, the letters of which make up the numerical total of 365. But this imaginary being must not be confounded with the unnamed supreme Deity.

---

[1] He also shows distinct traces of the influence of Aristotle, especially in the pure intellectualism of his ideal.

In their moral theory these Pseudo-Basilideans denied the value of martyrdom, on the ground that it was casting pearls before swine and throwing children's meat to the dogs. They considered themselves to be no longer Jews, and in the ordinary sense no longer Christians, though in a higher sense more than Christians, *i.e.*, in their spiritual enlightenment and in their freedom to indulge in moral laxity. Clement complains of their degeneracy from the high standard of conduct maintained by Basilides himself, and there seems no reason to doubt that a licentious and impure life was among their most prominent characteristics.

CHAPTER VII.

FIRST DIVISION CONTINUED :—VALENTINUS AND THE VALENTINIANS.

IF Basilides was content to indoctrinate a small circle of philosophic adherents, the brilliant theosophist **Valentinus** attempted nothing less than to thrust his interpretation of Christianity upon the entire Christian world. In influence second only to Marcion, if second even to him, his extraordinary popularity aroused the defensive strength of orthodoxy to its most determined efforts, and called into existence an armoury of aggressive warfare, keen, trenchant and effective, but of which the forging lacked the true Christian temper. In estimating the character of the Gnostic teachers, we must make some allowance for the natural exasperation of their orthodox opponents. But, nevertheless, there seems sufficient reason to believe that they added to brilliancy of doctrine and the resources of a profound erudition an element of thaumaturgic imposture, and often the seductions of a not too scrupulous gallantry. There can be no doubt that in the eyes of a vast multitude they represented the main stream of Christianity. The attractive glitter of their theories eclipsed the sober doctrines of the Church, and we cannot wonder if it provoked a harsh and often unjust method of refutation. In Valentinus all the fascinations of the Gnostic reached their highest point. It was opposition to his influence that roused the calm spirit of Irenæus into unwonted indignation, and drove him to arm himself with the uncongenial weapon of an awkward pleasantry. But to this opposition we owe these concentrated efforts to expound the whole Christian system on which the great edifice of dogmatic theology was ultimately reared. If the battle had not been

fought out between Valentinism and Christianity, first by
Irenæus and then by Tertullian, with a prolixity wearisome
perhaps, but admirable in its searching thoroughness, we may
be sure that the task of Athanasius in the succeeding age
would have been far more difficult, nay, humanly speaking,
impossible.

Having regard therefore to the extreme importance of this
prince of heresy in the dialectical evolution of the Church's
doctrine and philosophy, we shall make no apology for treating his views at greater length than their intrinsic worth-
lessness demands. In him we see the most comprehensive
attempt to fuse Christianity into the vast fabric of religious
speculation erected by the various schools of Pagan thought,
and while recognising its supreme value, to deprive it
nevertheless of its essential foundation, and virtually to
destroy it altogether. Some critics have represented the
system of Valentinus as a Philosophy of Religion, analogous
to that Science of Religions with which Professor Max
Müller has made the English world familiar. But this
view, though partially true, is not an adequate account of it.
Valentinus was not a philosopher: if anything, he may be
called a theosophist. He did not maintain the genuine
critical attitude, external to all religions, while sympathising
with all. Neither the temper of the age nor the character of
the man was adapted to such a position. He rather aspired to
include revelation within his spiritual purview as an integral
element, but he based his acceptance of it not on the principle of faith acting in accordance with the higher reason, but
on a natural affinity of spiritual perception, which enabled
him at once to accept, and by interpreting to transcend it.

The following sketch is founded mainly on the views of
Neander, though with additions from other sources rendered
necessary by the progress of scholarship.

His Life.

The country and origin of Valentinus are doubtful. Irenæus, who treats his opinions fully, is silent on both these

points.   Epiphanius mentions a tradition that he belonged to
the *Phrebonite* Nome, a word nowhere else found, but which
may be a corruption of *Phthenotite* or *Ptenetite*, a *Nome* or
District in the Delta mentioned by Pliny.   He was certainly
educated at Alexandria.   Jerome speaks of him as a learned
man, Origen as "no ordinary person."   Tertullian says he
was a student of Plato, and this is highly probable.   It is
also likely that he was acquainted with the Philonic philosophy.   Clement says his disciples boasted that he had been
taught by Theudades, a disciple of S. Paul.

As to his date, we are told by Tertullian that he lived
until the pontificate of Eleutherus, A.D. 177.   Irenæus[1] says
"he flourished under Pius, and remained until Anicetus."
Eusebius[2] in the Chronicon for the year 141 says, "Under
Hyginus, Bishop of Rome, Valentinus the founder of a
special heresy was acknowledged at Rome."   In another
place[3] he speaks of his heresy being recognised under Pius.
It is most likely that he passed as a Catholic for some years,
and did not reveal his heretical tendencies, in Rome at any
rate, before the pontificate of Pius.   Driven from the Roman
Church, he fled to Cyprus, where he probably elaborated his
remarkable system, and where he must have died.[4]   It is
best to accept the statement of Irenæus in preference to
that of Tertullian, and to suppose that he did not survive
the pontificate of Anicetus.   It is possible that earlier in
his life he began the dissemination of his views in Egypt.
Certain it is that by the time of Justin his doctrines were
well known in the East: for in the dialogue with Trypho,
professed to be held at Ephesus (before A.D. 150), he is
already mentioned as giving his name to a sect.   Moreover, in
Justin's work on heretics published before his first Apology
(A.D. 145) Valentinus was attacked.   We may therefore fairly
conclude that his heresy began as far back as the closing
years of Hadrian (died A.D. 138), so that supposing Valentinus to have died about A.D. 158 at the age of 73, his birth
might have taken place as early as 85 (in which case he

---

[1] I. xi.   [2] Chron. *Anton. Pii. III.*   [3] *Anton. Pii. VI.*, *i.e.*, A.D. 144.
[4] Neander thinks that he spent the last years of his life at Rome.

may have seen Ignatius); though it is better to put it a little later.

His writings comprised Letters and Homilies. Pseudo-Origen, in the Dialogue against the Marcionites, mentions a treatise of his on the origin of evil. Tertullian does not accuse him of tampering with the canon, but only of wrongly interpreting it. His disciples wrote a new Gospel. A fragment is found in Epiphanius,[1] which some have attributed to Valentinus, but it belongs to one of his disciples.

His System—Theology.

In giving a sketch of his system, we must premise that it is far from easy to distinguish between his doctrines and those of his followers; but as their general tendency is the same, this is of no great importance.

In the first place, he assigns a tri-partite character to the Universe of Being. It consists of three spheres—the Pleroma or Divine Sphere, the realm outside the Pleroma, and our mundane world. The primal essence and root-principle of the whole is an illimitable and incomprehensible Being whom he calls *Bythos* (*i.e.*, depth), a word employed in preference to *God*, because, without any theological implication, it suggests at once the attributes of incognisability and fecundity of life.

From Bythos, as the fountain-source, a succession of spiritual powers were thrown off by a process of pullulation or emanation ($\pi\rho o\beta o\lambda\acute{\eta}$), analogous apparently to that by which the zoophyte (hydra) multiplies its individuality. The distinctive term for these spiritual powers is *Æon* ($a\acute{\iota}\acute{\omega}v$), a word which, among Gnostic thinkers, has three grades of meaning—(1) its original sense of eternity; (2) the primary divine Powers or personified attributes; (3) the whole emanation-world as contrasted with the whole world outside the Pleroma.

In this supernal process of self-development the powers that successively appeared stood as complementary one to another, in pairs or *Syzygies* ($\sigma v\zeta v\gamma\acute{\iota}a\iota$), one male and one

[1] § 5.

female. Of this mystic sexual distinction a symbol or copy may be traced more or less clearly in every sphere of existence. And not only so, but the entire series of Æons as a whole, which is called the *Pleroma*, or fulness of God-head, is itself conceived of as female in relation to Bythos, and called Ennoia, *Reflection*, and sometimes Sigè and Charis, *Silence* and *Beauty*. This primeval pair generates a second pair, Nous or *Mind*, and Aletheia or *Truth*, and these four form the first *Tetrad*. The second Tetrad follows, consisting of Logos (*Reason*) and Zoë (*Life*), who in their turn produce Anthropos (*Man*) and Ecclesia (*Church*), by which we are to understand not earthly humanity and the earthly church, but the archetypal humanity and the pre-existent church of the celestial sphere. These eight æons complete the *Ogdoad*, a name which appears frequently in the Valentinian contro-versy. After this there is a double line of generations, partly from Logos and partly from Anthropos and Ecclesia. From Logos as a root comes the *Decad*, also in syzygies or pairs, Agerătos (*the Ageless*), and Henōsis (*Unification*); Autophyes (*the Self-produced*) and Hedŏne (*Pleasure*); Akinētos (*the Unmoved*) and Syncrāsis (*Intermixture*); Monogenes (*Only-Begotten*) and Macaria (*Blessed*); Bythius (*the Abysmal*) and Mixis (*Conjugal union*). From Anthropos and Ecclesia is derived the *Dodecad*, consisting of six pairs, viz., Para-cletus (*the Paraclete*) and Pistis (*Faith*); Patrĭkos (*the Pater-nal*) and Elpis (*Hope*); Metrĭkos (*the Measurer*) and Agăpe (*Love*); Ainos (*Praise*) and Synĕsis (*Appreciation*); Eccle-siasticus (*Preacher*) and Macariŏtes (*Happiness?*); Thelētos (*Willing*) and Sophia (*Wisdom*). These complete the *Triakad* or group of thirty divine powers which make up the Pleroma. Of these Nous alone was sufficiently pure of essence to be able to apprehend Bythos. Sophia, the last of the æons, had an uncontrollable desire to do so, but, being conscious of her inability, was fain to pine away and melt into infinitude, when in her wanderings she met with Horus (*Limit*), a solitary Virtue, who succeeded in assuaging her madness. She was prematurely delivered of a shapeless birth called Enthymesis or *Thought*, who, immediately on entering into existence, was excluded from the Pleroma and sought a refuge in the terrestrial world.

In order to prevent any recurrence of such misadventures, Bythos caused to be put forth two fresh æons, Christus and Spiritus Sanctus (*Christ* and the *Holy Spirit*), who should have the power of revealing to the æons the ineffable nature of Bythos. Strictly speaking, even these favoured æons can neither know nor explain it, but they can discern it in its self-manifestation as displayed in the development of the æons, and this is what *we* mean by knowledge of the Divine. Bythos, by his self-limitation, is the cause of existence ; were this limitation removed, existence would be annihilated. This is why Horus, the Genius of Limitation and the condition of all existence, must be placed outside the Pleroma, for he fixes and guards the spiritual existences within the Pleroma as well as the inferior ones of this lower world. In every act of producing phenomenal existence two separate functions are attributed to Horus ; one by which he purifies the original spiritual individuality from those foreign elements which must necessarily enter into it, and into which, unless purified, it threatens to lapse ; and one by which he establishes the individuality, when thus purified, in that particular form of equilibrium which is to be its proper nature. Valentinus found signs and types of this mysterious process in the natural world, and also in the words of Scripture. For instance, when John the Baptist announced that Christ's fan was in his hand, and that He would burn up the chaff with fire unquenchable, this was interpreted to imply the double activity by which Horus would destroy the vitiated elements (matter) of the world and purify the redeemed. Again, in Christ's recommendation to take up the cross and follow Him, he saw a description of that Divine Potency, symbolised by the heavenly Stauros, and on earth by the crucifixion of Jesus, whereby each individual, being purified from all that is foreign to his nature, and thus attaining to self-conscious realisation of his higher life, first becomes a true disciple of Christ, capable of identification with Him.

The contact of the Pleroma with the world is originally

indirect. Though there is on earth a certain manifestation of Divine Wisdom, it is not the Æon Sophia, but her immature birth, Enthymesis, which comes into the material world, and there only gradually attains to maturity. By the appearance of Christ and His redemption, Enthymesis (or Thought) was matured. And it is only when the development of the world is summed up and, so to speak, read backwards by the light of Christ's Redemption, that it presents the spectacle of Divine wisdom at work, and satisfies the cravings of thought. In this way the heavenly Sophia is spoken of as rejoicing to recover her lost offspring; for now for the first time the manifestation corresponds to the idea, and the idea presents itself to immediate intuition through its manifestation in the finite.

Thus we can understand the Valentinian distinction between a Higher Wisdom and a Lower. The latter, which he calls *Achamoth,* is identical with the Mundane Soul, from whose mingling with matter springs all living existence in its three gradations. These gradations are as follows:—

(1.) The spiritual natures, endowed with divine germs of life, akin to Sophia, and also to the Pleroma.

(2.) The psychical natures, separated from the former by an appreciable admixture of matter—these would be represented by ordinary moral people.

(3.) The ungodlike natures, immersed in matter, whose tendency is to disruption and dissolution.

We now come to an important and difficult part of his theory. He reasons thus. Since every process of development ultimately leads back to Bythos, who (it may be remembered), though the source of all being, cannot come into contact with matter, a type or analogue of the Bythos must be imagined, who should stand in a similar relation to the material world in which Bythos stands to the Pleroma, only that he must act involuntarily as the unconscious instrument of Bythos in perfecting actual existence.

This Being is the Demiurge or World-God, a hybrid conception common to almost all Gnostics, partly derived from a false construction of Plato's hypothesis given in the

Timæus,[1] and partly borrowed from a warped and shallow estimate of the character of Jehovah as revealed in the Old Testament. The Demiurge's character is variously repre sented according to the different sects. To Valentinus he appeared as a just and holy Power, inferior in intelligence to members of the Pleroma, and therefore deficient in the loftiest spiritual goodness, but nevertheless having within him some traces of it. These he is able to impart to the spiritual natures among men, giving them their essential character of unity ; while to the psychical natures he assigns the quality of multiplicity subordinated to a higher unity, which may be raised from the unconscious to the conscious stage. The ungodlike natures are under the guidance of Satan, and they are characterised by negation of being. Only the spiritual natures contain within them the principle of immortality ; the psychical either gain immortality or fail of it, according as they yield their will to the godlike or the ungodlike ; while the ungodlike tend inevitably to death, which yet is not wholly evil, since it is the appointed con-dition of their being vanquished by the higher wisdom, and so finally saved.

Redemption.

This thought leads us naturally to Valentinus' theory of Redemption, in order to understand which it is necessary to bear in mind certain points which are implied in what has gone before.

(1.) That a constant process of vital development pervades every region of existence.

(2.) That the first disturbance of the primeval harmony (by the Æon Sophia) originated within the Pleroma.

From these positions it follows :—

(1.) That Redemption must begin within the Pleroma by the re-establishment of its broken harmony.

---

[1] Plato, while attributing the creation of the world to God, does not clearly define His relation to that which is essentially imperfect, except in so far as to deny that He either created or arranged it. See Jowett's Plato, vol. ii. pp. 478 *sqq.*

(2.) That this re-establishment will inevitably image itself forth in all other grades of existence, and among them, of course, in our mundane system.

(3.) That the same agent who reveals the hidden God in all the different spheres must reunite with Him all the alienated modes of existence, working continually until the consummation of all things.

This agent, it will be remembered, is the Æon Christus, under whose name, as well as those of Monogĕnes, Logos, and Soter (Saviour), the idea of a Redeemer is embodied. The latter is the counterpart of Christus outside the Pleroma, in whom the Christus of the Pleroma reflects himself, and through him works in individual beings until they are perfected. Thus the Æon Christ is the efficient cause of Redemption; the Soter is the receiver and perfecter of his operation. Since the Æon Christ is anterior to the world, it follows that Redemption in its earliest stage is coincident with creation. The Soter, who stands in the same relation to Achamoth, the Mundane Soul, as Christ does to the Holy Spirit, inspires in her the Creative Idea, which she communicates to the Demiurge, who believes himself to be acting independently, though in reality he is but an instrument of Bythos.

In all this we see plainly the influence of Plato's theories. To Valentinus, as to Plato, the world becomes a picture, more or less distant, of the divine glory; but it is only the spiritual natures akin to the Pleroma, as in Plato's view it is only the philosophic mind, that can discern in external things the reflection of the unseen glory; and it is these natures alone who acknowledge the Demiurge to be a true prophet.

Anthropology.

In close connection with this hypothesis was the position assigned to man in the universe. Through the invisible revelation of God, unwittingly made through the Demiurge in man's spirit, man was destined to be the link of connection between the prototype and the copy, and so to make good the imperfect testimony of the world to its Divine Origin. It is for this reason that MAN is represented as one of the æons in the Pleroma; and Irenæus quotes a Valentinian aphorism, " When God willed to make a revelation of Himself, this was called Man."

The Demiurge, in creating the actual race of man, unconsciously infused some of the seed of the Archetypal Man into his nature, so that man really transcended the Cosmos into which he had been created, and of which the Demiurge had supposed him to be merely the highest product. But, on observing his extra-cosmical affinities, the Demiurge was struck with awe, and forthwith combined with the cosmical powers to hold man in subjection by suppressing his consciousness of his higher affinities. In this, though he knew it not, he was acting under the direction of the Supreme Deity, since in no other way could the process of redemption be extended to the whole sphere of living being, and matter and death be destroyed.

Consequently, we must look to the spiritual natures alone for a true manifestation of humanity. They are the salt of the earth. The animal soul ($\psi\nu\chi\eta$) is but the vehicle, by which the spiritual part enters into the temporal world, and develops itself to maturity. It will be left behind so soon as the freed spirit rises to join its angelic consort in the Pleroma.

Doctrine of the Messiah.

The Demiurge, it will be remembered, had all along acted, though unconsciously, under a higher divine influence. This he showed by experiencing a strong attraction for the more spiritual natures among his chosen people the Jews, whom he selected for his special favours, making them prophets, priests and rulers. These men were able to point onwards to the higher order of things to be introduced by the Soter. This led Valentinus to form a theory of inspiration, which, according to him, consisted of two parts, an influence exercised by the Demiurge upon ordinary minds, and one exercised by the Soter upon the spiritual natures. To the former category belong the predictions of future events in prophecy apart from the perception of their inner meaning: to the latter belong the higher Messianic aspirations and the antici- pations of the Christian dispensation. We discern in this a genuine attempt to reconcile the conflicting interests of the religious and scientific standpoints in the exposition of Holy Scripture. It is uncertain whether, in addition to this, Valentinus acknowledged any apprehension of higher truth among Pagan thinkers, but, on the whole, it is probable that he did, regarding it as part of the world-wide preparation for the coming of the Soter into the world in the form of a Jewish Messiah.

The Soter, who had directed the development of the spiri- tual life-germs that fell from the Pleroma to form a new world, found it necessary at last to interfere immediately in the mundane course, in order to extend the Act of Redemp- tion, which he had already accomplished in his consort Achamoth (the Mundane Soul) to all the spiritual and psychical life that had emanated from her. To do this effectually, he had to unite with a human soul. The Demiurge had pro- mised his people a Messiah who should liberate them from the Hylic power (the principle of Matter), rule over all the world, and reward his faithful subjects with earthly bliss. He sent down from heaven this being, who is known as the Psychical Christ. This Christ, who appeared as Jesus of Nazareth, had an animal soul, a spiritual principle derived from Achamoth, and a body, which according to the Italian or Western Valentinians was suffering, but according to the Eastern school was wholly ethereal and impassible. Both schools agreed in declaring that He was not born of the Virgin Mary's substance, but conducted through her womb as through a pipe (σωλήν). At His baptism the pre-existent Soter descended upon Him, but together with the spiritual principle deserted Him at His passion, the animal soul (ψυχή) and the quasi-ethereal body alone remaining. These exhibited on earth an exact representation of what had happened before on the heavenly Cross (σταυρός). Such is the Docetism of Valentinus. The descent of the Soter first gave Messiah consciousness of the true nature of His kingdom, a sense as much beyond the comprehension of the Demiurge as it had been previously beyond His own. This illuminating process of Christ's baptism must be repeated in each soul, in order that truly sanctifying effects may follow from communion with the Soter. While Valentinus admits to a certain extent the efficacy of the Cross for the destruction of evil, it is hard to reconcile this admission with his erroneous conception of Christ's body. In the words, " Father, into Thy hands I commend My spirit," Neander thinks that the psychical Christ is made to commend to God the spiritual germ, that it might not be detained in the kingdom of the Demiurge, but mount in freedom to the upper sphere. The psychical Messiah finally rose to the Demiurge, who gave him sovereignty and right to govern in his name, while the pneumatic Messiah ascended to the heavenly Soter, whither all redeemed spiritual natures will follow Him.

Ethical Results.

The results of redemption upon mankind, though all are affected by it, are not the same for all. The psychical man, indeed, obtains forgiveness of his sins, is released from thraldom under the principle of matter, and receives power to withstand it. The spiritual man is, through communion with the Soter, incorporated into the Pleroma, exalted altogether above the Demiurge's kingdom, and attains to a fully developed divine consciousness.

The two classes differ also in the manner in which they appropriate and apprehend Christianity. The one are led to faith by outward phenomena, such as miracles, preaching, precept, and historical testimony. The other are seized immediately by the intrinsic might of the truth, and, as they apprehend it by pure intuition, their faith is raised above the assaults of doubt. The one apprehend only a lower or psychical Christianity : they recognise its historic evidence, and receive the Gospel on the authority of Christ. The other rise to the apprehension of the higher pneumatical Christianity, which they grasp in its vital connection with the entire theogonical and cosmogonical process. It is these by whom humanity is purified and regenerated; and in them lies all the hope of the future, which, when all is accomplished, will unite the Soter with the Mundane Soul and receive them into the Pleroma, and the Demiurge, at length fully enlightened, will enter into his eternal rest.

Such is a brief and sketchy outline of this extraordinary theory, which had vitality enough to engage the champions of the Church for several generations, and even then died hard; and yet is now so completely passed into the limbo of extinct phantasies that few even of professed students of philosophy care to master it. Yet there can be no manner of doubt that the effort necessary to grasp, and still more to refute, these seductive hypotheses was in itself an education for the Christian controversialists; and the disentanglement of orthodox gnosis from the half Jewish, half heathen personages which play so rampant a part on the Gnostic stage, represents no mean victory of sober thinking over "reason gone mad," won by Christian athletes for the cause of humanity.

Other Writers of the School.

Among the most distinguished writers of the Valentinian school may be mentioned **Marcus,** a native of Palestine (circ. A.D. 160), who set forth his system in a poem, in which the Divine Æons were introduced discoursing in liturgical forms, and using gorgeous symbols of worship. He discovered mysteries in the number and position of the letters of the alphabet. He held the entire creation to be a continuous utterance of the ineffable. He has an idea that the hidden source of the Divine has various voices, which descend to an echo and finally to a cessation of all sound; and again that this echo increases to a clear tone or a distinct word for the revelation of the Divine to man.

The Saviour is spoken of by **Heracleon** also as the Word, i.e., the Revealer of the Divine. All prophecy which foretold His coming, without being distinctly conscious of the higher spiritual Messiahship, was only a series of isolated, inarticulate *tones* that preceded the revealing *word*.   John the Baptist, standing midway between the Old Testament and the New, is the *voice*, which is already almost a *word*, for a *word* expresses a thought with consciousness.   The *tone* becomes a *voice* when the Prophets of the Demiurge attain to the knowledge of the higher Messiahship, and the *voice* a *word* when John becomes a disciple of Christ.[1]   Heracleon was distinguished for his scientific cast of mind.   His commentary on S. John's Gospel is partly preserved by Origen.   He also wrote on S. Luke.   The profundity of S. John's ideas was specially attractive to Gnostics.   Heracleon probably imagined that he drew his theology from S. John, but his perceptions were so warped by his system that he everywhere read his own views into the words of the Apostle.   Like Basilides, he depreciated martyrdom on the ground that it was but a single act of confession, whereas the consistent self-abnegation of an entire life forms a truer correspondence to the teaching and example of our Lord.

Another celebrated member of the Valentinian School was **Ptolemæus**, who presented his views in a highly attractive form, and against whom Irenæus directs his most telling arguments.   He was especially active in disseminating the principles of the sect.   His letter to a lady named Flora is still extant in the treatise of Epiphanius ; in this he draws a distinction between the ordinary Christian doctrine and an apostolic tradition corresponding with the words of Christ, of which he professed to be the special repository.   He endeavours to prove that not only are those in error who attribute the creation of the universe to an evil being, but those also who like Christians regard it as the work of the Supreme God, whom Christ came to reveal, and whom alone He pronounced to be good.   His theory of inspiration, like that of his master, presupposes the co-operation of several agents in the production of the Old Testament.   He divided the religious polity

---

[1] Our readers will recall the remarkable passage of Ignatius which Lightfoot renders "the Divine Word which proceedeth from Silence ; " also the distinction he makes between a *voice* and a *Word* of God, pp. 89 *n.* and 90.

of Moses into three parts, coming respectively from the Demiurge, the independent reason of Moses, and the additions subsequently made by the elders. Of these the first was the most important, and was thus sub-divided:—

(1.) A moral portion, unmixed with any evil elements, the same which Christ said He came not to destroy but to fulfil. This required completion, not abrogation.

(2.) A retributive portion with which evil was mixed, though he excuses it on the ground of its educational and disciplinary necessity. It is, however, wholly alien from the goodness of the Eternal Father, and was probably extorted by the Hylic principle from the Demiurge. This portion is entirely abrogated by Christ. The *State*, which represents retributive justice, belongs to the kingdom of the Demiurge, and cannot be made a manifestation of God. Our readers will remember the much discussed remark of a bishop of our Church that civil laws and civil constitutions cannot be derived immediately from the Sermon on the Mount.

(3.) The ceremonial law. This he regarded as wholly typical. Its outward observance was abolished by Christ, but it was by Him glorified and transfigured. In the spiritual service which Christ came to announce, the names of the old ceremonial (priest, sacrifice and the like) are preserved, but the things are altered and spiritualised. For example, sacrifice is not of victims, but of praise and thanksgiving; fasting is not from meat and drink, but from lust; the Sabbath is not a rest from work, but from evil-doing. In this respect Ptolemæus penetrated to the spiritual significance of Christianity.

CHAPTER VIII.

SECOND DIVISION: THE ANTI-JUDAIC GNOSTIC SYSTEMS: OPHITES—CARPOCRATES—BARDAISAN— JULIUS CASSIANUS.

AMID the seething ferment of opinions in this tumultuous epoch many sects arose which, though not closely connected with each other, agree in their antagonistic attitude to the Judaic revelation of the Old Testament. The most important of these are the **Ophites** or **Naassæans,**[1] who held the doctrine of the Sophia or Mundane Soul as the source of spiritual life, which they conceived to have the power of attracting to itself whatever had emanated from it. In them the Christian element recedes much further into the background than in the Valentinians, from whom they borrowed a considerable portion of their principles. They held the doctrine of the Demiurge much as the Valentinians, but gave him the mystic name of Ialdabaoth.[2] They regarded him not as a limited and unconscious agent of the Supreme Being, but as his unremitting and eternal antagonist. The higher light which he receives from Sophia he misuses for the purpose of erecting himself into an independent sovereign, thus provoking Sophia to withdraw, if possible, her ill-starred gift. Nevertheless, the Ophites admitted that the Demiurge was unconsciously subject to the power of the Supreme, whose purpose he works out by constraint, but without thereby becoming entitled to the claim of goodness. Indeed, he is represented as a radically evil being.

His empire is the starry world, which, in conjunction with him, strives to deceive and coerce the human spirit. The six

---

[1] From נָחָשׁ, a serpent.   [2] Origen, Cels. vi.

planetary angels create man, a mere lump of matter, into
whom Ialdabaoth breathes a soul, thus unconsciously infusing
some trace of the higher Sophia, by which man centres within
himself the reason and soul of the entire creation. Ialdabaoth,
jealous of this prerogative, strives in every way to quench
man's consciousness of himself. The better to effect this, he
gives him a series of commandments, but the Mundane Soul
employs the serpent-spirit[1] to defeat Ialdabaoth by tempting Adam to disobey. According to some schools of Ophites,
the serpent was only a disguise of Sophia herself; and these
really worshipped the serpent as a sacred symbol.

All of them were agreed in holding that it was Sophia
who opened man's eyes. The fall of man was a transition
from the state of unconscious limitation to that of conscious
freedom. Man renounced Ialdabaoth, who in anger drove
him from his abode in the upper air, and enclosed him in a
dark body and tied him down to earth. He now found himself between two opposing forces; on the one hand the
thraldom of the seven planetary spirits, and on the other,
on the part of the material principle, the incitements to sin
and to incur Ialdabaoth's wrath. But Sophia, man's constant
friend, supplied him with new force to withstand these new
dangers, and through the seed of Seth she preserved the
higher spiritual ideas for mankind.

In their Christology they imitated the Valentinians. The
psychical Christ, the man Jesus, is related to the æon-world
as in that system. The heavenly Christ united with Jesus at
His baptism, and left Him at His passion. This is indicated
by the fact that He performed no miracle before His baptism
or after His resurrection. Ialdabaoth, the Judaic God,
being jealous of the heavenly Christ, determined to get rid of
Him by bringing Him to death. This he was able to effect.
After the resurrection Jesus remained eighteen months on
earth, teaching a few select disciples His inner doctrines.
He was then raised by the celestial Christ to heaven, where
He sits at Ialdabaoth's right hand, drawing back to Himself
the emancipated spiritual natures, and thus enriching His

---

[1] Called in their system Ὀφιόμορφος.

kingdom and impoverishing Ialdabaoth's. Intermingled with this teaching are many pantheistic ideas wholly foreign to Christianity, on which it is not necessary to dwell. The moral result of this intellectual *farrago* is an utter subversion of the moral principle.

Origen, indeed, in his work against Celsus, denies the Ophites the title of Christians, declaring that they would only admit to their assemblies such as cursed Christ. Some have drawn from this the inference that the Ophite doctrine represents a pre-Christian form of Gnosis, introduced about the time of our Lord's birth by one Euphrates: but the formulæ of exorcism, cited by Origen, contain plain allusions to Christian ideas. It is possible that the hostility of the Ophites was directed not to Christ as such, but to the psychical Christ as they regarded him, confessed by the Church, whom they contrasted unfavourably with their own pneumatical Christ. And this hostility may have gone so far as to take the form of a requirement to curse the limited Messiah of psychical natures.

Carpocratians.

The Alexandrian **Carpocrates,** who taught in the first half of the second century, has many points of affinity with the Ophites, but in him the Hellenic element is far more prominent than the Oriental. He is deservedly regarded by the Fathers as a traducer of Christ, and a baseless pretender to the name of Christian. Nevertheless his heresy was sufficiently widespread to demand refutation at the hands of Hippolytus and Irenæus. The latter states that he was the first of so-called Christians to assume the name of Gnostic, though others attribute this to the Naassenes.

It is not necessary to do more than indicate the outlines of his system. He assumed as the origin of all things a single First principle, incognisable and incommunicable. From Him in various grades of emanation Powers had come forth, among the lowest of whom he ranked the Creator of the world.

Christ he regarded as a mere man, who by superior insight into truth had shaken himself free from Jewish prejudice,

P

and risen superior to the dominion of the Ruler of this world. The practical conclusion he drew from this theory contributed to render his name infamous among Christians. It was the absolute indifference of external conduct; nothing on earth was essentially good or bad. The Gnostic might practise what men regard as immorality without scruple, if it conduced to the tranquillity of his spirit. Indeed, a man could hardly be said to *know* in any real sense the comparative value of actions, unless he had had experience of all and selected those which best secured his unimpeded course to perfection. The reader will remark the similarity of this view to that of some modern Hedonists, who regard the just discrimination of higher and lower pleasures as only possible to him who has had experience of both.

The Carpocratians had a curious custom of securing mutual recognition by certain signs or marks, one of which was a brand on the lobe of the right ear. This custom is probably referred to by Minucius Felix.[1]

Carpocrates was succeeded by his illegitimate son **Epiphanes,** who also taught at Alexandria, and whose career of precocious talent closed at the boyish age of seventeen. He was the founder of what was known as the "Monadic Gnosis," and it was through him that the members of the sect received the name of Carpocratians. His best known work was a treatise "On Justice," in which he insisted on an equality of right to everything as a Divine ordinance, extending this principle not only to property in the conventional sense, but even to the relations of the sexes. We owe this account to the testimony of Clement, who had evidently read the book.

More doubtful is the ascription to him of the doctrine of "The Tetrad," mentioned by Irenæus as proceeding from a renowned master of the school.[2] He, however, does not give the name, and it is much more probable that Marcus is the author referred to.

---

[1] Chap. ix. 31. Cf. "Having his mark in their foreheads" (Rev. xx. 4).

[2] ἄλλος ἐπιφανὴς διδάσκαλος αὐτῶν. Ir. iv. 25 (clarus magister eorum) reproduced in the Greek by Hippolytus, Ref. H. vi. 38. Epiphanius carelessly takes the word ἐπιφανὴς to be a proper name.

Sethites, Cainites, and Nicolaitans.

More or less closely connected with the Ophites were those obscure sects who held that the Æon Sophia found means to preserve through every period of the Demiurge's world a race bearing within it the spiritual seed which was akin to her own nature.

Thus the **Sethites** regarded Cain as representing the hylic principle, Abel the psychic, and Seth, the elect nature, the spiritual. The **Cainites,** on the contrary, assigned the highest place to Cain. In their wild hatred of the Old Testament and the Demiurge, they took for representatives the worst characters of the Old Testament, as being rebels against the tyranny of the Demiurge, and, as such, children of Sophia. The Apostles appeared to them narrow-minded; Judas alone was truly enlightened, and he betrayed Christ from a good motive, as the only way to dethrone the Demiurge. Under the name of Judas they concocted a gospel embodying their gnosis. In moral respects, their licentiousness was unbridled.

Somewhat similar tendencies are to be found in the obscure sect of the **Nicolaitans,** mentioned by Irenæus as the same who are condemned by S. John in the Apocalypse.[1] But it is questionable whether in the passage referred to the Apostle has before him an already existing sect, and does not rather mean to characterise by a telling epithet opinions which he regards as unwholesomely seductive.[2] Irenæus, like the still more uncritical Tertullian, is prepared to find all existing heresies disposed of by anticipation in the New Testament. But as Clement also mentions the sect as one actually existing, and tracing its origin to Nicolas or Nicolaus the proselyte of Antioch spoken of in the Acts, there can be no question as to its historical reality, though it is in the highest degree improbable that Nicolas, who died in the faith and left faithful children, had anything to do with it. The chief tenet of the Nicolaitans was the advisability of subduing the animal

---

[1] Rev. ii. 15.

[2] νικόλαος has been thought by some to be a rendering of בִּלְעָם, Balaam, according to its supposed derivation from בָּלַע עַם, *populum substravit.*

nature by yielding to it. Clement mentions a story that Nicolas, being charged by the Apostles with jealousy of his wife, refuted the imputation by bringing her forward in the assembly, and offering her to any who might be willing to marry her. This is, of course, wholly apocryphal. The Nicolaitans, wishing to shield themselves under some famous name, and observing the title of Nicolaitan applied to antagonists of the detested Apostle, they determined to assume it, and jumped to the uncritical conclusion that it was derived from Nicolas. They appear to have been strongly anti-Judaic in their prejudices, and to have acknowledged S. Paul as the only apostle.

Bardaisan or Bardesanes.

This somewhat isolated thinker was a Syrian theosophist, and perhaps is without sufficient reason classed among the Gnostics. He was born at Edessa A.D. 155, of noble parents, and is said to have left the heathen doctrine of the priest of Hierapolis to receive holy baptism. Possibly Christianity was already partially recognised at the court of Abgarus the king. In 216 Caracalla intervened in the politics of Edessa, where he seems to have espoused the cause of the heathen conservative party. Bardesanes, put on trial, proved his faith to be sincere, and almost attained the honours of a Confessor. He seems to have preached Christianity as he understood it to some of the wild tribes, and to have held a religious conference with some Indian philosophers in the reign of the latest Antonine (*i.e.*, Elagabalus). His death is placed in A.D. 223, at the commencement of the reign of Alexander Severus.

His Theology.—Hardly any of his writings survive, for the *Book of the Laws of Countries*, which embodies his views, is from the hand of a disciple. Epiphanius asserts that he was the distinguished author of many orthodox books, but was afterwards corrupted by the Valentinians. Eusebius, however, reverses the process, dwelling on his controversial writings against Marcionism, and enlists him on the side of the Church. Ephraim Syrus speaks of a treatise in which he denies the Resurrection, and of his hundred and fifty heretical hymns, though Theodoret attributes the first Syrian hymns to Harmonius, Bardaisan's son. Ephraim himself wrote a counterblast in the shape of fifty hymns against heresies, of which only a small number are directed against Bardaisan's views.

That he acccepted the ordinary Christian faith is very probable; but he ran riot in an outer region of speculation, of which he had drunk deeply in his heathen days, viz., the theory of the divine influences of stars, whom he spoke of as living beings, in apparent defiance of the Divine Unity. He may have held the eternity of matter, but this is doubtful, and his doctrine of evil is also doubtfully dualistic. He is said to have called the Holy Spirit the "Secret Mother," probably with reference to Christ, after the manner of the Gospel according to the Hebrews.[1] He denied the resurrection of the flesh; attributed to our Lord a heavenly, not an ordinary body; mixed up the problem of human destiny with that of the seven stars, which he taught held sway over man's birth until the Star of Bethlehem appeared. As it is, baptism (not the washing, but the concomitant illumination of spirit) frees men from astral bondage, and makes the art of the astrologer of none effect.

His Affinities.—Although Hippolytus, Irenæus, Epiphanius, Moses of Chorene, and Barhebræus all speak of him as a Valentinian, there is really little in his authentic doctrine which savours of Valentinus. Hippolytus, in his Sixth Book against Heresies, distinguishes between the Christology of the Eastern and Italian Valentinians. It is possible that Bardaisan passed under this Eastern influence before becoming a Christian, and his account of Christ's body may be a trace of it. He seems to have held a position intermediate between Gnosticism and the Church—a sort of semi-heretic.

His Writings.—These were in Syriac, but early translated into Greek, and so known to several of the Fathers. They include Dialogues against the Marcionists, an Apology issued

---

[1] Origen in John iv. 63.

under the persecution of Antoninus (Elagabalus), and the Dialogue of Fate, which perhaps, however, is identical with the *Book of the Laws of Countries*, discovered and published by Cureton in his *Spicilegium*, but partly preserved by Eusebius in a Greek dress.[1] In form it is a dialogue between two young men concerning the mysteries of Providence. Their doubts are taken up and resolved by Bardaisan, whose opportune arrival gives rise to a somewhat lengthy exposition. The work is probably posterior to Bardaisan, but fairly represents his views. It treats of free-will, the two commandments ("eschew evil and do good"), the power of destiny and of nature, the moral customs of different countries, and the final victory of the great and holy Will that none can hinder. It is probable that the Greek translation was employed by the author of the ninth book of the Clementine Recognitions, though others give him the priority.

Results.—This school of thought spread little, if at all, beyond Syria, until in the latter years of Constantine two anonymous Greek dialogues were written to controvert the followers of Marcion, Valentine, and Bardaisan. The heretical adversary is introduced as insisting on three divergences from the Catholic faith, viz., a denial of the creation of Satan by God, of the birth of Christ from a woman, and of the resurrection of the body. In this later form of his theory, while admitting evil to be self-sprung, he does not believe it to be eternal or indestructible. The local speculations about the stars are now dropped, and a more distinct Greek colouring is adopted throughout. We observe also an increased readiness to appeal to Scripture, and a slight trace of Manichean influence.

Julius Cassianus.

A few words must be given to **Julius Cassianus** (about A.D. 200), to whom reference has already been made. He is one of those Gnostics who regard matter as essentially evil, and condemn the marriage union, referring all sexual intercourse to the temptation of the Serpent. He quotes in

[1] Præp. Evan. vi. 9, 10.

support of his doctrine an apocryphal saying of our Lord, quoted also in the Pseudo-Clement's Epistle,[1] which Clement of Alexandria notices is contained in the Gospel according to the Egyptians. His Encratite views are closely connected with his Docetic theory already noticed; the birth of children being *per se* an evil, Christ evidently could not have been born, and His humanity was therefore illusory. He also taught that man had not been originally created with a fleshly body, but that the coats of skins mentioned in Genesis as having been made by God for Adam and Eve were in reality our fleshly integument, then first formed. The coincidences between him and Tatian are too numerous to be accidental. It is uncertain which borrowed from the other.

APPENDIX A.

A few words may here be said with regard to the curious Gnostic work preserved in a Coptic MS. in the British Museum, written in the Thebaic dialect, and edited and translated into Latin by Schwartze, and generally known as *Pistis Sophia*. It probably belongs to a later period than that with which we are concerned, though many scholars believe that an earlier recension of it existed as far back as the middle of the third century. The Greek original has perished, but many of the Greek terms are embedded in the Coptic version which remains. It comprises four books or sections. The first two treat of Pistis-Sophia; the third and fourth are entitled μέρος τεύχων σωτῆρος. The fourth is defective, and represents an older form of the teaching. The three books represent Jesus as giving instruction to His disciples for eleven years after the Resurrection. He then ascends into heaven, completes the work of redemption, and returns to give the finishing touches to His scheme of higher knowledge. The fourth book represents Jesus as standing after His Resurrection on the ocean shore, surrounded by men and women clothed in white robes, who retire with Him to the middle sphere. The æons, archons, and cosmical powers stand aside, while He instructs the elect in many secret mysteries. Mary Magdalene takes a prominent part in addressing questions to Christ. Now Epiphanius mentions a book in use among the Ophites, called

---

[1] See pp. 42, 165.

ἐρωτήσεις Μαρίας, or *Questions of Mary*, and another called the
Gospel of Philip. The Pistis-Sophia can hardly be identified
with either of these, but we observe that in it Philip is mentioned,
together with Matthew and Thomas, as one of the three chosen
by Christ to write down His revelations. We therefore class this
work among the productions of the Ophite school, though it does
not agree exactly with any of the Ophite tenets that have come
down to us. It is Pantheistic rather than Dualistic. Its source
is not Syrian, but Alexandrian, and it was originally written in
Greek, not Syriac. It has also some affinities with Catholic doctrine. It greatly modifies the distinction between psychics and
pneumatics, so dear to the Ophites. It shows a tone of moral
earnestness which recalls Basilides alone among Gnostic writers ;
and it represents the path of salvation as twofold, partly by the
mysteries of redemption and partly by moral holiness, while it
utterly condemns the immoralities permitted by the genuine
Ophites.

APPENDIX B.

A work which Epiphanius declares to have been used by the
Sethites, and which in its original form belongs to the second century, is *The Testament of Abraham*, recently edited by Professor
James in the Cambridge "Texts and Studies." It was subjected
to several recensions, and translated into various dialects. It can
hardly be called a Christian treatise, though used by Christians,
and influencing to no small extent their popular beliefs. It contained a romantic account of the last hours of Abraham, followed
by a thrilling apocalyptic section supposed to be his vision of the
future world. The most remarkable feature of this is its pronounced pessimism, the proportion of the saved to the lost being
variously given as 1 in 7000 or 1 in 60,000 ! So despairing an
estimate of Christ's redemption was not likely to find a welcome
in the early Church, where the conception of the Christian's inheritance stood so high. Many small communities of enthusiasts
sprang up everywhere on the fringe of Christianity and Judaism,
who were to some extent influenced by their teaching, and adopted
much of their nomenclature, but knew little or nothing of the true
spirit of either. Such unquestionably was the origin of this
work, which, being now well edited and generally accessible, may
be read with advantage by the curious in matters theological.

WE have now to consider a far more interesting personage. Of all the Gnostics, **Marcion** is unquestionably the greatest and the best. In some respects he is not a Gnostic at all. The very essence of Gnosticism is to make religion a speculative theosophy instead of a practice of righteousness. Into this error Marcion did not fall. His system, though mistaken, was really religious. His theoretical position, however, like that of the Gnostics, was dualistic. But this was the least original part of his work. If tradition may be believed, it was borrowed by him at Rome from the genuine Gnostic Cerdo (A.D. 140). The doctrines which issued from their combined efforts were such as we have met with already in slightly different forms : that the Creator of the world was not the Supreme God, but a far lower and strictly limited being; that Moses and the prophets were not divinely inspired; that Jesus Christ was sent down direct from the Supreme God, and had no real connection with the world of matter; that the body, which draws its elements from evil matter, cannot after death rejoin the soul, which alone enters the pleroma of light; that those parts of Scripture which teach otherwise are corrupted and pseudonymous.

Such, in very brief outline, are the speculative tenets of Marcion's school; but they do not reflect his true genius: this was practical, not speculative. His true distinction is the prominence he gives to Christ and Christ's work. To him Christianity is no longer one of many tendencies, albeit the greatest; it forms the inspiration of his whole mind; all the Jewish and Pagan elements are recast under the influence of a remarkable and highly original Christology.

In order to appreciate his teaching, it will be necessary to touch on the few incidents we possess of his life. He was born, early in the second century, at Sinope in Pontus, the same city that had given the great Cynic Diogenes to the world. Epiphanius asserts, and there is no reason to doubt the assertion, that his father was bishop of the church there. It is not absolutely certain that he was brought up in the Christian faith, but it may be assumed as in the highest degree probable. There is even some ground for thinking that he may have held the office of suffragan to his father, inasmuch as his own followers subsequently recognised him as bishop. The depreciatory epithet of *nauclerus* (shipmaster or passenger) flung at him by Tertullian, need not mean more than that he had travelled much by sea. It is obvious that he was of a restless, inquiring mind. The speculations of Basilides and Valentinus were attracting widespread notice. Possibly Marcion may have fallen under their spell before he conceived the project of visiting Rome, and broaching his opinions in the metropolis. He seems to have arrived there just at the close of the episcopate of Hyginus (about A.D. 140).

The Roman Church was at first disposed to receive him graciously. His munificent contributions to its common chest, his father's character, his own strictness of life and conspicuous abilities, for a time secured him favour. But this did not last. His ambition began to display itself, and the austere type of piety which he cultivated was distasteful to the Roman clergy. For this and other reasons they looked coldly on him, and finally refused him communion. He now proceeded to feel his way towards the position of a heretical teacher. The Syrian Gnostic Cerdo was at Rome, and to him Marcion attached himself as disciple or comrade, with the results which have been already indicated. It is, however, possible that Marcion had already thought out his leading ideas before his contact with Cerdo. At any rate they were now embodied in a coherent system, and Marcion lost no time in propagating them throughout the Empire.

His influence was enormous, his activity incessant, and the importance of his sect or church may be gauged by the number of eminent men who wrote against it. The attack was begun by Justin, continued by Dionysius, Theophilus, Irenæus, Hippolytus and Tertullian. Two centuries later Epiphanius found Marcionite congregations in Italy, Syria, Palestine, Lower Egypt, and even in the Thebaid, Arabia, and Persia. He paid a second visit to Rome during the episcopate of Anicetus (A.D. 154–166) and, according to a doubtful story of Tertullian's [1] begged for readmission into the Church. This was promised on condition of a full recantation of his errors, and an undertaking to bring back those whom he had led astray. He gave the pledge; but his death, which happened shortly after, prevented him from redeeming it. It was during this Roman visit that he met the aged Polycarp, whom he had known in happier days. Seeing the bishop's face averted, he accosted him with the words, "Dost thou not remember me, Polycarp?" to which the stern old man replied, "Aye! I remember thee for the firstborn of Satan." His death may be placed about the year 166. His career therefore cannot have been a long one measured by years, though it covered the episcopates of no less than five Roman bishops.

His Doctrines.—Our chief source of information as to his doctrines is the exhaustive treatise of Tertullian. Irenæus, besides supplying many facts of interest in his great work against heresies, probably wrote a separate dissertation, in which he followed the method of convicting him by his own inconsistencies. Tertullian, whom in other respects we know to have been largely indebted to Irenæus, imitates him in this point also with considerable success. His first book against Marcion was written A.D. 208, shortly before the *Syntagma* of Hippolytus appeared, which also dealt copiously with Marcion and his views.

The three cardinal points of his system are as follows:—

1. That the Supreme God, who is absolutely good, cannot

---

[1] Irenæus tells nearly the same story of Cerdo: and it is possible that Tertullian is inaccurately reproducing Irenæus.

possibly enter into any union with matter. The world therefore cannot be created by God, but is the work of an inferior being, who is ever in conflict with matter but cannot overcome it.

2. That the Supreme God has once and once only revealed Himself in Christ. Christ and Christ's religion is therefore for man the only possible manifestation of the absolute good.

3. That true goodness consists in love and in love only. Justice or the retributive principle is in its nature opposed to love, and therefore cannot be affirmed of the Supreme God.

Important consequences follow from each of these principles. From the first is derived the violently anti-Jewish attitude which distinguished Marcion above all other heretics. The God of the Jews according to him does not work after the pattern of ideal perfection, but is the independent Creator of an imperfect world answering to his own imperfection. He can infuse no truly spiritual essence into the soul of man, for he has it not himself, while man's body is of course wholly evil. The Demiurge gives men commandments, but no power to keep them. To the Jews he gave indeed a revelation of himself, and a religion of worship and morality corresponding to his own character, with a limited heaven to the obedient and perdition to all the rest. Conscious of his inability to make his subjects truly good, he promised them a Messiah who should raise them to his own level, gather them from the dispersion, and grant them earthly felicity in a world-embracing kingdom. The true God, however, could not consent to this over-severe system; His heart swelled with pity for the perishing. He does not issue a law confessedly impossible to be fulfilled; but reveals Himself, and enters into communion with all who will accept His revelation. His self-manifestation of the Supreme is the appearance of Christ, who brings a new God into the world, unknown before. This is the dualism of Marcion, so mercilessly satirised by Tertullian.

From his second principle it follows that Christ's appearance in the world was a sudden phenomenon, like an earthquake, wholly unconnected with the past either by way

of prediction or preparation. The transcendental relation of
Christ to the Supreme God is not clearly defined by Marcion.
While distinguishing them in some sense, he nevertheless
regards Christ as an immediate manifestation of Deity.
Thus his theory of Christ's person is necessarily *Docetic;* for,
had he sprung from a human mother, he must have been con-
nected with matter and therefore a subject of the Demiurge.
Hence the Gospel of Marcion commences with these words,
" In the fifteenth year of Tiberius Cæsar *Christ came down
from heaven.*" We have his views on this subject fully
given in Tertullian's treatise, " On the Flesh of Christ " (*de
Carne Christi*).

Christology of Marcion.—It is an essential feature of
Marcion's Christology that Jesus was not the Messiah promised by the Demiurge through the Prophets. He strongly
contrasts the Christ of the Old Testament with the Christ of
the Gospel, and declares that Jesus only accommodated Himself to Jewish prejudice in allowing Himself to be styled the
Jewish Messiah. His immediate power over nature, and His
godlike acts of mercy and pardon to His enemies, proclaim
His true Divinity and dissociate Him from the Demiurge.
It is this that accounts for His readier reception among the
heathen than among His own countrymen, for they were
less prejudiced by preconceived interpretations of the Old
Testament. The Demiurge, unable to comprehend such an
invasion of superior Godhead, sided against Christ, and
stirred up the Jews and Romans to crucify Him. Though
in Marcion's view Christ did not really suffer, yet the
Demiurge imagined that He did, and wished to consign
Him to the hell of those who had disobeyed him; but Jesus
again disappointed him by raising the souls of the Gentiles
who were undergoing punishment to His own heaven. Then
at length the Demiurge was made to understand the drift of
what had happened, and to acknowledge his own blindness.

It seems as if Marcion taught that the Messianic predictions of the Old Testament would be accomplished for such
as believed in the Demiurge. He would bring to judgment
those who had not been freed from his power by faith in the

higher Christ, and they, together with the Old Testament saints, would enjoy the reward of an earthly millennium. The eternal and heavenly kingdom into which Christians enter is the antithesis of this millennial paradise. The God of love does not punish, but He gives over to the Demiurge and the sphere of justice those who refuse Him, while those who even on earth enter into fellowship with the Father, through faith of the Son, are made partakers of a life superior to matter and to the Demiurge. For such there is no more judgment. The providential care of the Supreme God is reserved for the elect alone; while for those outside the Demiurge has his own providence, both general and special.

From his third principle of the antithesis between justice and love follows the absolute incompatibility of the Law and the Gospel. The latter alone had power to sanctify. Marcion's own life, and the moral standard of the community which he founded, were marked by a lofty rigour. His asceticism was based on the disparagement not only of meats and drinks, but of marriage, which, as perpetuating the material element, he regarded as no less blameworthy than fornication. Life itself he valued little. The seriousness of his discipline provoked the hatred of the Pagans. The success of his church organisation inflamed the anger of the orthodox. Persecuted by both alike, he and his adherents were daily inured to suffering. "Fellow-objects of hatred and fellow-sufferers!" thus he addresses his co-religionists. He urges them never to lose an opportunity of testifying their belief by dying for it. Like the Montanists, though from a different motive, these sectaries were always ready for martyrdom.

To Marcion belongs the merit of a genuine enthusiasm, an inspiring personality, and a truly organising genius. It was this last feature that enabled him to perpetuate for centuries a system of doctrine so absolutely irreconcilable with the true doctrine of the Church. But harsh and unphilosophical as it was, it paid homage to Christ, and it professed to be built on Him. In the words of Christ and the apostolic comments on them was to be found the only source of truth. Much of his influence was due to his bold claim to possess the authentic words of Christ and the true key to their interpretation. He dealt with the New Testament with the utmost freedom. Like Luther, he discovered a gospel within the Gospel, but he carried the process infinitely further. He found in S. Paul the only genuine representation of Christ, and consequently rejected all the New Testament that was not Pauline. He re-wrote the Gospel on this supposed Pauline plan, which was substantially S. Luke's, only that he rejected all such portions as did not square with his Docetic views. "Marcion's Gospel" is frequently alluded to by the Fathers, and quoted so freely by Tertullian, that we can almost reconstruct it from his writings. The other Gospels he rejected, not on critical grounds, but because he thought them corruptions of the original. He seems to have considered this corruption due to the Galilean Apostles! Even his mutilated and abridged S. Luke is so uncritically put together that many inconsistencies remain in it. Besides this book, he admitted also the Epistles of Paul, excluding those to Timothy and Titus; but even these he claimed the right to correct, and to expunge from them every shred of Judaism. The Epistle to the Hebrews he rejected, not from its defective authority, for that would have no weight with him, but from its sacrificial ideas.

Another celebrated work of his was the *Antitheses*, or sets of passages showing contradiction between the Old and New Testaments, frequently alluded to by Tertullian. They appear to have been arranged with much acumen, and were doubtless effective enough from his point of view, according to which the two Testaments proceed from different deities, and therefore it was vain to bridge over external discrepancies by the hypothesis of a spiritual unity, which obviously was out of the question.

His Disciples, Apelles, Hermogenes.

In the community that he founded differences of opinion soon appeared. His system had so little speculative completeness that inquiring minds were not satisfied. His most ardent follower, who afterwards, according to Tertullian, turned "deserter," was **Apelles,** an Asiatic by extraction, who was born about 120. He is said by Tertullian to have been taught by Marcion at Rome, from whence he was obliged, owing to an act of incontinence, to emigrate to Alexandria. He was induced to regard the utterances of a woman named Philumene, a possessed virgin or clairvoyante, as the inspired oracles of the Holy Ghost; and his intercourse with her gave rise, as might be expected, to scandalous stories, which, however, appear to be entirely without foundation. He lived to a green old age, as we learn from the account given by *Rhodon*, an opponent of his doctrine, whom Eusebius places in the reign of Commodus (A.D. 180–193). A writing by Philumene entitled "Manifestations" was considered by Apelles as authoritative, and selections from it read in his conventicle. He himself wrote a series of *Argumentative Proofs* (συλλογισμοί) criticising the Mosaic theology, which in their turn were controverted by Rhodon. As he grew older, he became more tolerant, confessing that he had failed to prove his views, and desiring, above all controversial victories, to inculcate a genuine love of Christ and moral purity as the only essential requisites for salvation.

His later contemporary **Hermogenes,** against whom Tertullian wrote one of his most brilliant pamphlets, is said to have been by profession a painter and to have resided at Carthage (circ. 170–210). In his case the bias of Greek philosophy predominated over that of Orientalism. His most important deviation from orthodox teaching was the thoroughgoing application he made of the tenet of the eternity of matter. He was much occupied in contesting the spread of Montanism, the ascetic pietism of which was highly repugnant to his Hellenic fastidiousness. He also combated the emanation theories of the Gnostics, on the ground that if the human soul, through however many successive departures, originated ultimately from God, the fact of man's sinfulness could not be satisfactorily explained. He was careful, however, to guard himself against the popular Platonic doctrine that evil is necessary as a foil to good, thus betraying a certain indebtedness to the Christian principle. Tertullian calls him a Stoic; but no doubt his philosophy was a syncretic compound of many diverse systems. He endeavoured to account for the existing state of the universe by supposing that God's creative power is conditioned by an inorganic matter which is equally eternal with Himself. This matter was in a chaotic ferment, over which the Deity had from all eternity exercised a creative attraction, analogous to the influence of the magnet, or of beauty,[1] by which the mere presence of Godhead tends to give form to the formless and life to the lifeless. Thus creation was eternal and yet progressive; while the opposition of matter to the creative attraction was also eternal, and in this consists the origin of all imperfection, including moral evil. It was from the controversy with him as well as with the earlier Gnostics that Irenæus and Tertullian successfully established the doctrine of a creation out of nothing, which is by no means clearly expressed, though it is undoubtedly implied, in Scripture.

[1] Compare the Aristotelian conception of the relation of the Supreme Good to the phenomenal Universe, "κινεῖ ὡς ἐρώμενον :" "He influences it as the beloved object influences the lover."

Q

CHAPTER X.

THE EARLY UNITARIAN TEACHERS.

WE have given the above title to our chapter in order to bring before our readers in as simple a form as possible the controversy we now propose to treat. The word Unitarian is of comparatively recent origin, and is opposed to Trinitarianism; and the Trinitarian doctrine was not precisely formulated until some time after the close of our period. The term used by these teachers to describe themselves was **Monarchian**, or believers in the essential oneness of Deity.[1] Yet this term was really inadequate and misleading; inadequate, since it included very different forms of doctrine, and misleading, since it was equally applicable, in a modified sense, to the orthodox creed.[2] Hence, although the term Unitarian as applied to these early writers is an anachronism, yet, essentially, it better expresses their dogmatic position than the name they gave themselves.

Our plan will not require us to criticise on orthodox grounds the difficulties of the Unitarian view, but only to bring out its distinctive characteristics, and to show how divergent were the two main channels in which it flowed. These may be named after their two most celebrated exponents, the **Paulianist** and **Sabellian,** the former having more affinity with the Deistic tendencies of later Judaism, the latter being connected with the purely metaphysical theology

[1] From μόνος, single, and ἀρχή, source (of Godhead); implying that those who held it admitted but one original source of Deity, denying consubstantiality or personality to other Divine essences.

[2] The Church held the Father to be the πηγὴ θεότητος; the deity of the Son and Spirit, though consubstantial, being derivative. See, on the question of Orthodox Monarchianism, the note on p. 439 of vol. ii. of Neander's Church History (Bohn's edition).

of the Greek schools. Both claimed to be Christian, but both were at once rejected by the common Christian consciousness as subversive of the faith. Their history, as imperfect, unsuccessful tentatives of development, extends over a considerable period. But the student is invited to consider them all together, and at the present stage of our subject. He will thus be in a position to give his subsequent attention to the main stream of Church literature, undiverted by allusions to doctrinal difficulties or disputes.

The two embodiments of the Unitarian idea arose in different ways. The first originated in a zeal for the Divine Unity as the exclusive basis of Biblical revelation. It held that the Church's system did not sufficiently mark the difference between Christ and the only true God. It therefore emphasised His humanity, and finally denied in any real sense His Divine Nature. The second arose from a zeal for the true Godhead of Christ, which seemed to be impaired by the Church's doctrine of a Logos distinct from and subordinate to the Father. This theory tended to recognise in Christ only the one undivided God, and to regard the titles Father, Son and Spirit as mere modal designations of the same absolute Being.

It is evident that we have here two divergent and even contradictory forms of teaching, the one verging on Deism, the other tending to Pantheism. And in fact we find that on more than one occasion they were more violently opposed to each other than they were to the Church.

The earliest traces of the first form appear in an obscure sect called **Alogi**, from their denial of the Logos doctrine of S. John. They existed in Asia Minor during the prevalence of the Montanist New Prophecy, to which they offered a fierce resistance, but seem to have had little influence beyond that sphere. It was in Rome that the first systematic Monarchian theory was broached. Its founder was one **Theodotus,** a leather-dresser from Byzantium, who attracted notice about the end of the second century. He did not question the supernatural birth of Christ, but he denied the indwelling Deity, and regarded Him as influenced by the

Holy Spirit in the same way as, though in a higher degree than, other saints.   He is said to have been excommunicated by Victor, but he had already formed a school, consisting mostly of dry mechanical logicians, who treated theology like a mathematical problem.[1]   One man, however, came over to him of a different stamp, the saintly confessor Natalis; but we are told that before his death he returned to the Orthodox faith.

Of somewhat greater importance is the name of **Artemon,** who followed a more decidedly rationalistic course.   Against his heresy the work known as the " Little Labyrinth," ascribed to both Caius and Hippolytus, was directed.[2]   He also admitted Christ's supernatural birth, but held that His union with the Father was moral only.   In the twenty-eighth chapter of his fifth book Eusebius gives an account of these theories, and quotes an anonymous author, probably Caius, for their refutation.   The main interest of his discussion turns on the question whether this heresy found favour with the bishops of the Roman Church.   Artemon's most telling argument was that his views were substantially those of all the Roman bishops until Victor, whose successor Zephyrinus first formulated the Catholic theory, thereby, according to Artemon, corrupting the simplicity of the faith.   The writer quoted by Eusebius indignantly repudiates this allegation. He quotes a long list of Fathers, from Justin downwards, who had affirmed in unmistakable terms the true deity of Christ, and alludes to some very early hymns, composed in the sub-apostolic age, in which this doctrine was evidently set forth.   Unfortunately this passing allusion, though confirmed by the celebrated testimony of Pliny, that the Christians sang hymns to Christ as God, is insufficient to enable 'us to determine exactly the dogmatic import of these verses.   The researches of Neander, Lightfoot and others have, however,

---

[1] Asclepiades, Hermophilus, and Apollonides ; and perhaps his own son, the younger Theodotus, though this writer seems to have had affinities with the Gnostics, and with the little known sect of the Melchizedekians, who imagined a mystic connection between Christ and the Captain of the angelic army.   [2] See Book iii. ch. 10.

abundantly disproved the hypothesis of Baur in support of Artemon's view, and have vindicated the Early Roman Church from any taint of Ebionism, whether open, or veiled under the guise of Monarchianism.

At the same time we must admit the probability that Callistus, who succeeded Zephyrinus in the Papacy, did really for a time either accept Artemon's views or profess to accept them. His unscrupulous character, combined with his complete ignorance of theology, made him ready to coquet with any party that appeared likely to help him in his ambitious plans. But Hippolytus opened upon him the battery of his powerful arguments and biting satire. Callistus was greater at abuse than at discussion. By way of reply, he tried to fasten on his opponent the opprobrious epithet of Ditheist. The Roman Church followed Hippolytus. It held none the less firmly because as yet only implicitly, the Trinitarian form of belief; and the uniformity of its teaching from the apostolic age onwards, forms the great practical test of Orthodoxy both for Irenæus and for Tertullian.

Another example of this form of Monarchianism is **Beryllus,** Bishop of Bostra in Arabia, whose doctrines are briefly and obscurely described by Eusebius. His theology seems to have affected only the Person of Christ, and to have made no pronouncement on the Nature of God. He taught that Christ only arrived at distinct personal consciousness by His human birth. That ante-mundane participation in the Father's glory, of which S. John's Gospel speaks, Beryllus interprets not of self-conscious personality, but of an ideal existence in the Thought of God anterior to any outward manifestation. When these opinions became known, the situation was considered so grave that a synod was convened to sift the whole question. In order the more effectually to confute Beryllus, Origen was summoned from Cæsarea Stratonis. We learn from Eusebius that this Father, by his learning, skill and moderation, succeeded in convincing Beryllus of his error (A.D. 244). The latter addressed a letter to Origen, in which he admitted his fault, and promised to abstain from such teaching for the future. This is one of those rare instances in which theological discussion, carried on without theological bitterness, has led to union instead of discord. It is to Origen and his followers alone that we can look for examples of this sweet reasonableness, so much more precious than ability, so much more persuasive than anathema.

Paul of Samosata.

At a later date, and in a different part of the world, the teaching of Artemon was revived by the well-known **Paul** of **Samosata**, Bishop of Antioch. He belongs to the later half of the third century; but, as we shall not recur to this subject, we propose to give, for the sake of completeness, a short account of his views.

To the historian he is a highly interesting personage. Endowed with a striking presence, commanding personal ability, and an inordinate love of pre-eminence, he threw himself with vigour into the secular and religious life of Antioch, and soon became not merely its chief ecclesiastical officer, but its most prominent and powerful citizen. Zenobia, Queen of Palmyra, who was known to favour the Jewish faith, gave him her patronage and protection. He used her influence to acquire the lucrative civil appointment of *Ducenarius*, or collector of revenue, thus affording the first instance of combined spiritual and temporal authority. He filled his double position with offensive arrogance. He claimed a general jurisdiction over all the Christian population, citing them before his civil tribunal, and assessing their judicial penalties. His ambition was equalled by his avarice, and both by his vanity. Large sums of money flowed into his coffers, which he expended in a display of magnificence as unsuitable to a Christian Father in God as absurd in the representative of an officially proscribed religion. The society of Antioch was frivolous, refined, and dissolute. The bishop's morals did not escape suspicion. His assemblies were thronged with ladies of fashion, among whom the courtier prelate moved with graceful assurance, inhaling the sweet incense of flattery from voluptuous lips. He resembled much more the ambitious and corrupt ecclesiastics of the Byzantine court than any prelate of whom the Church had as yet had experience. Relying on the countenance of the queen, he strove to force his doctrines on the churches of the neighbourhood. These silently resented a despotism they dared not resist.

His doctrines were those of Artemon pushed to their logical issue. He admitted no distinction of Persons in the Godhead. The Logos he explained to be merely the self-consciousness of God, analogous to the spirit of man, and in no sense a separate personality. Man might in this sense be truly said to be made in God's image, but not, even in the case of Jesus Christ, to partake of God's Nature. Paul did not, however, reduce the Divinity of Messiah to a purely psychological resemblance to God. He admitted a positive action of the Word on Jesus, but not so as to imply any union of essence. Jesus was indeed born of a virgin,[1] but in other respects was a man like ourselves, who had succeeded in realising human perfection, and in attaining by merit the fulness of grace. The Divine Word might be said to animate Him, but was not incarnate in Him. Thus the difference between Jesus and other men was relative, not absolute. He gained the title of Son of God by His holiness, though it might also be affirmed of Him in a certain sense from the time of His birth. Paul denied any possibility of union, except that of will, between the human and divine. In this metaphorical sense Christ was one with the Father; and Paul maintained that such union was superior to that of nature, for this would leave no scope for the exercise of moral freedom. The Holy Spirit, he said, dwelt in Christ in the same manner as a god dwells in his temple.

The reader will observe that Paul's theological standpoint is, like that of the later Jews, in reality Deism. He fixes an infinite and impassable gulf between the Creator and the Creation. Moreover, he substitutes an apotheosis for an

---

[1] It has been doubted whether Paul held this, but as Baur and Neander, from different points of view, both admit that he did, it seems best to accept it.

incarnation, after the manner of heathenism, and looks upon
our Lord as virtually the ideal man, a sort of conception
which the Stoic imagination had created.

His views were instinctively and at once repudiated. The
clergy under him almost to a man appealed against his teaching. The Eastern bishops, headed by Firmilian of Cappa-
docia, met in synod to sit in judgment on their metropolitan
(A.D. 264). He was asked to state his views. This, however,
he had no intention of doing. He protested vaguely that he
taught in conformity with the Apostles, and was willing to
accept the definitions prescribed by orthodoxy. His versatility
and command of evasive language prevailed over the suspicions
of judges unskilled in metaphysics or rhetoric, and he was
permitted to continue in his office, greatly to the disgust of
those who knew him best. On a second occasion, two years
afterwards, a conference was held, in which counsel and exhortation were employed, but with no effect beyond a renewal
of vain and delusive promises. At last his misgovernment
as well as false teaching became intolerable. A thorough investigation was demanded. A council met, which in learning
and piety, though not in numbers, may rank with the most
illustrious synods of the Church (A.D. 270). In this assembly
Paul at length met his match. A presbyter named Malchion,
who was or had been a rhetorician, and therefore understood
the artifices of Paul's controversial method, was able by his
pressing logic to pin him to certain flagrantly heretical ad-
missions.[1] On which, brought at length to bay, he boldly
announced his system, which was a virtual confession of guilt.

He was called upon to retract; and on refusing was excommunicated, deposed, and a successor appointed. It
was one thing, however, to pronounce his deposition, another
thing to compel him to vacate the chair. Relying on his
popularity and the good offices of Zenobia, he set the decree
at defiance, and remained ostensibly bishop for two years

---

[1] A curious incident in this council was the objection raised by Paul to
the term ὁμοούσιος, co-essential, as defining the relation of the Son to the
Father, and the allowance of his objection by the council. The term was
abandoned, and this abandonment proved the cause of much trouble to
Athanasius when striving to reintroduce the term.

longer. But on the overthrow of Zenobia by Aurelian, the bishops called in the Emperor's authority, thereby giving the first instance of an example often followed since with disastrous consequences, of appealing to the intervention of the temporal power. Aurelian acted with great consideration. He referred the business to the Roman bishop and his Italian colleagues; and, in accordance with their decision, enforced the ejectment of Paul. The deposed prelate founded a sect known as Paulianists, who lingered on in steadily diminishing numbers for more than a century and a half. In the 19th canon of the Nicene Council their baptism and orders are disallowed, on the ground that, notwithstanding their possession of apostolical succession, their denial of the Trinity made both baptism and ordination in that Name a purely nominal function devoid of meaning.[1]

Praxeas and Noetus.

We now pass to the second class of Monarchians, who proceeded less from religious than from metaphysical premises, and were even further removed from the true Christian doctrine. They all came from the East, and the first of them is **Praxeas,** who migrated from Asia Minor to Rome just when the Montanist party had succeeded in gaining the ear of the Pope. This Pope was probably Eleutherus (A.D. 185). Praxeas set forth strongly the weak points of Montanism, and induced the Pope to withdraw his support from it.[2] Hippolytus, however, whose information on this topic is full and accurate, mentions many names of Monarchian leaders, but never once that of Praxeas. This has led to the supposition that Praxeas was a nickname either given to him or assumed by him, and mistaken by Tertullian for his real name. There is a story that he had been a confessor. At any rate his influence with the Roman Church was very great. His doctrine was Unitarian in the strictest sense, and is called by

---

[1] On the question of heretical opinion as invalidating baptism, see the chapter on Cyprian.

[2] Neander says to excommunicate it. If so, the Pope in question must have been Victor.

Tertullian *Patripassian.*[1] He denied any essential triplicity in the Godhead. The Most High became incarnate in Christ by an act of sovereign will. In Jesus the Divine part is God the Father, the flesh is the Son. This view reduces the humanity to a mere semblance, the corporal envelope of the Divine Spirit, which is at the same time the Word and the Father. Victor and Zephyrinus may possibly have accepted his language without understanding his views. He left Rome for Carthage apparently with good credentials of orthodoxy. But he found there a controversialist of a very different stamp from those of Rome. It was in vain to palm upon Tertullian plausible speculations of ontology. He struck directly at the practical issue, and by his penetrating logic soon convicted Praxeas of unsoundness. The date of his treatise *Against Praxeas* is variously given as A.D. 206, 210, and 222.

Another name of mark is that of **Noetus** of Smyrna, who appeared at Rome soon after Praxeas had left it (A.D. 202), and somewhat developed his doctrine. According to him, the One God determined to go forth from the absolute mode of existence and to assume the relative. Christ is therefore at once Son and Father, according to these two phases or modes. Thus he explained the Theophanies of the Old Testament, the Father appearing as Son to the patriarchs. The Son does not proceed from the Father: He is as it were an imperfect presentation of the Father adapted to mortal apprehension. Thus Christ was the Son during His terrestrial career; yet discerning spirits could even then behold the Godhead of the Father in Him. This doctrine appears to safeguard the freedom of the Divine agency. But it comes perilously near to Pantheism, and to a theory of successive incarnations. Epiphanius asserts that he taught the transmigration of souls. He seems to have regarded Jesus as the type-product of humanity, His personality being one of the masks which the Author of Being assumes for a time in the long drama of self-manifestation.

---

[1] *I.e.*, that when Christ died upon the cross, it was God the Father who suffered in Him. This title, which is more creditable to Tertullian's ingenuity than to his scrupulousness, was not really merited by Praxeas.

The varying relations of Noetus to Zephyrinus and Callistus are described in the pages of Hippolytus. There seems no reason to doubt that these prelates committed themselves to a form of Unitarian doctrine. The Roman clergy were never strong in theology. Callistus made no difficulty about condemning the very men on whose shoulders he had mounted, so little was his mind impressed with any speculative bias. The Church resumed its orthodox level, and Noetus disappeared.

Sabellius.

By far the most eminent of the Patripassians or Monarchians was **Sabellius** of Libya.. If Paul foreshadowed Arius in importance, Sabellius was the precursor of Pelagius. In one respect Sabellius was in advance of the entire Church, viz., in his precise application of the three names, Father, Son and Spirit, to express co-ordinate relations. We find the formula first in S. Matthew's Gospel, and but little later in the assertion by Simon Magus that he had appeared as the Father to Samaritans, as the Son to Jews, and as the Holy Ghost to Gentiles. In each of these a co-ordination of relations appears, but is left indefinite. In the definite theology of the early Church the subordination of the Son to the Father in dignity is more dwelt on than His co-ordination in respect of essence; while the inclusion of the Holy Spirit in such co-ordination is only worked out in the most rudimentary manner. Justin, for example, seems to waver between ascribing true Godhead to the Spirit, and depicting Him as an angelic nature created by God. Now to Sabellius belongs the logical merit of bringing to the front this conception of a co-ordinate triplicity. We say logical rather than theological, because Sabellius really gave to his doctrine of the Trinity no more than a logical value. Over and above the threefold manifestation of Godhead and far behind it lay in his eyes the absolute incommunicable essence, the Monad; and the Trinity merely denoted the different relations of the self-evolving monad to the creation. His language, however, was not always consistent. At times he identified the Father with the Monad, and so could say, "The Father remains the same, but evolves Himself in the Son and Spirit." This is the cardinal distinction between Sabellius and the other Monarchians, that he received the whole Trinity, and, with the rest, the doctrine of the Holy Spirit, into his Unitarian theory.

It should always be remembered that to Sabellius the Trinity does not mean the same thing as to an orthodox churchman. A characteristic of his system lies in his using the established language of Christendom in a new sense. This gives an appearance of obscurity to his ideas which does not really belong to them.

With regard to the Person of Christ, he held that the Divine power of the Logos appropriated to itself a human body, and begat by this appropriation the Person of Christ. In himself the Logos was only Logos; it was by his humanisation that He first became the Son of God. This view led Sabellius to regard Christ's personality as only a transitory manifestation. In the final end, God will resume into Himself the power of the Logos, which has been thrown forth as a self-subsistent personal existence, and this personal existence will thereby be annihilated. The ultimate resumption of all difference into absolute unity is the goal of his system. It merges by insensible gradations into Pantheism, though of a logical and metaphysical, not of a cosmological or physical type.

Summary of Heretical Teaching.

We have now traced the outlines of the three great types of heresy which distracted the Ante-Nicene Church, together with some of their combinations. We have shown that they proceeded from three main sources—(1) Judaism, pure or mixed; (2) Oriental or corrupted Platonism, including a mass of doctrines from the remotest regions imperfectly fused together; and (3) the dialectical apparatus of Greek philosophy, playing upon conceptions at bottom Judaic or Pantheistic.

The first of these produced the Ebionite form of Christianity, the second the Gnostic, the third the Unitarian. These three forms have died out so far as their outward presentation is concerned, but their spirit is by no means dead. In the seething ferment of opinions at the present day, it is not difficult to perceive the analogues of each of them. Ebionism is reviving under the guise of Biblical theology, which seeks to restrict the genuine Christian dogma to that form of it which historical criticism educes from the New Testament. The brilliant and suggestive works of Matthew Arnold are the best known exponents of this line of thought, whereby the Person of Christ is reduced to nearly human dimensions, and the miraculous element in it classed as *aberglaube*. Unitarianism, as the name implies, still holds its ground; and in the works of Martineau and others, rises to a lofty height of spirituality, far transcending the metaphysical restrictions on which the system is logically based. But it is Gnosticism, the hydra-headed, the Protean, that looms highest on the horizon, and once more darkens it by its huge but shapeless bulk. We are not alluding to the current supernaturalism of a magical or theurgic character, which in divers forms is nevertheless making way both in Roman Catholic and Protestant countries. We speak here only of its intellectual aspect, which in the twofold sense of a theosophy and a science is manifestly reappearing among mankind. As a theosophy, Gnosticism rests upon the faculty of spiritual intuition among those favoured souls who, by discipline or natural insight, are enabled to transcend the physical sphere and penetrate the mechanism of the unseen universe. The recent influx of Oriental ideas and systems into the higher culture of Europe has undoubtedly opened a path of development of which at present we see only the beginning. As a vast syncretistic edifice of religious thought, Gnosticism is even more distinctly reappearing, though in place of the cosmogonical structures of the old Gnostics we meet with a comparative survey of the religious ideas of humanity founded on the method of science, from the point of view of the critical philosophy introduced by Kant. The science of religions has not yet proceeded far enough in its synthesis to evolve the conception of a universal religion. But unless the human mind is to rest content with the dogmatic *non possumus* of Agnosticism, which is a highly improbable result, we may expect to see in the not distant future a vast religious structure essentially corresponding to the great systems of Basilides and Valentinus, transcending them indeed in the soundness of its metaphysical basis, and in the purity of its method, but equally with them including the Christian revelation as one of many elements to be absorbed in its comprehensive scheme.

Meanwhile the dogmatic system of Christianity itself will have before it the task of proving its adaptability not only to the scientific consciousness of the western world, but also to the widely different modes of religious thought that have prevailed immemorially in the East. The Hellenic mode of presenting Christian dogma which has exclusively prevailed during the long interval since Justin Martyr first undertook it, may possibly be awaiting a new phase of development more nearly approaching universality. We have remarked in our introductory essay that, so far as the world has already received Christianity, no other mode of connecting it with man's primary intuitions of the metaphysical order has been available ; and that the Greek intellect alone has hitherto supplied an expression for these which could fairly be called universal. But it remains to be seen how far the necessity for stating Christian dogma in a way intelligible to the metaphysical systems of China, India and Japan, may involve a reconsideration of its ontological aspects. In any case it must become increasingly clear that the Person of Jesus Christ in the future, as in the distant past, will be the centre round which the whole problem will revolve. And as we read the record of these ancient systems and ponder on their fate, we, who accept Jesus Christ as the one perfect manifestation of Deity in the human sphere, and recognise His unique and transcendent power over mankind, cannot doubt that the Spirit of God will again move over the face of the waters and educe from their turbid mixture the ray of eternal light.

BOOK III.

THE APOLOGISTS.

(A.D. 130–250.)

CHAPTER I.

THE APOLOGETIC LITERATURE.

I. General Remarks on the Subject.

THE environment in which the Christian faith had to work out its destiny was a highly complex one. Under an external uniformity, due to the strong hand of Rome, there heaved a multitudinous sea of passions, prejudices and faiths.

These, though divided by profound mutual antipathies, could combine, when occasion required, to withstand the new religion. It is impossible, within the limits of a short essay, to do more than single out those particular forces which came most directly into collision with the Church, and to indicate the manner in which the Church confronted them.

There are four such forces which stand out conspicuous above the rest. With each of them, separately or united, the Church had to reckon; over each she triumphed, but her triumph was not gained without a considerable reaction of the conquered principle upon herself.

The first antagonistic principle was Judaism, from which Christianity sprang; the second was Philosophy, or the effort of the human spirit to win its own way to truth; the third was Paganism, by which we are to understand the manifold religions of the nations; the fourth was the attitude of the secular power, which was based on the apotheosis of Cæsar and the omnipotence of the State. We propose to consider these in order.

1. The Hostility of the Jews.

From the earliest spread of Christianity the Jews had been among its most implacable foes. Their hostility was twofold. On the one hand, there was the bitter rivalry of

R

the Synagogue, that is, of Judaism proper; on the other, the impracticable obstinacy of the Judæo-Christians, or those who had embraced Christianity without renouncing the Law. Both assumed at the outset positions from which they never withdrew. Already in the New Testament this is clearly manifest. The Acts of the Apostles and the Epistle to the Galatians give the key to all the subsequent relations of the Church and the Circumcision. The Jewish position was this: "Whatever else may be accepted, the Mosaic Law must remain untouched. Circumcision and the Sabbath are not abrogated by Christianity."

The unconverted Jew rejected Christ, the converted Jew accepted Him, but both held equally to the Law. The one insisted on its permanence, the other on its universality. The dislike of the Jews to Christians of their own blood is witnessed by the assertion of the Roman Synagogue to S. Paul, "As concerning this sect, we know that everywhere it is spoken against." [1] But this dislike had not yet passed into the organised propaganda of hostility which it soon became. For "We neither received letters from Judæa concerning thee, neither any of the brethren that came showed or spake any harm concerning thee." [2] A generation later such language would have been impossible. Justin (A.D. 145) complains that in every city where there was a Jewish Synagogue emissaries were despatched from the leading Jewish communities to prejudice the Christian cause; and not only so, but in every outbreak of popular fury it was the Jews who goaded the people to madness, the Jews who heaped up the faggots and applied the first torch to the stake.[3] Their own terrible sufferings, instead of teaching them pity, served only to inflame their hate, and none gloated with fiercer joy than they over the dying agonies of the martyr.

It is true there were Jews of a very different stamp, men of whom Philo is the type, who had drunk at the well of Greek thought, and, while remaining loyal to their faith, had

---

[1] Acts xxviii. 22.   [2] Ibid. v. 21.

[3] We learn this from the account of Polycarp's death, already referred to in the chapter on Polycarp.

cast aside much of its bigotry. An interesting picture of such a Jew is preserved in Justin's celebrated dialogue. Though not of Alexandrian but probably of Ephesian birth, the grave and thoughtful Trypho shows none of that fierce spirit of condemnation which animates some of his fellow-disputants, but listens courteously to the Christian apologist as he handles the Old Testament evidences for the Divinity of Christ. But, benevolent as he is, he cannot comprehend the offer of salvation being made to such as reject the ceremonial law. This prejudice is too inveterate to be outgrown. The question has not advanced a step since the Council of Jerusalem. If anything, it has gone backward. Trypho does not exactly deny the possibility of salvation to a Gentile believer who rejects the Law, for this position would be manifestly untenable. But, with regard to the Christian of Jewish birth, his conviction as to the ever-binding force of the Law is absolute.

The same controversy appears in the Latin Church in Tertullian's short treatise, "Against the Jews."[1] In this the arguments of Justin are repeated, though with less fulness. In these and all other writings addressed to Jews, the final court of appeal is always the Old Testament, and, to the Christian party at any rate, pre-eminently the prophetic books. The following are the main points made by the apologists against their Jewish opponents, and on them they rest their case:—

1. The fact that the Law of Sinai is a temporary dispensation, being preceded by the Law of Eden, the Noachic precepts, and the covenant of promise with Abraham, and being followed by the prophetic announcement of a new law written in the hearts of the faithful.

2. The prediction of Christ's coming in humility before His final and glorious Advent, and the important chronological indications thereof in the Book of Daniel.

3. The indications throughout the Old Testament of a plurality of Persons in the Godhead, and the fulfilment of these allusions by Jesus Christ and by Him only.

[1] Adversus Judæos.

4. The abrogation of the claims made by Israel to be the exclusive people of God, and the incorporation of the Gentile world into the spiritual Israel or Church of Christ.

Many other matters are discussed, and many other proofs alleged; but the above form the leading topics of Christian apologetic as directed against Jewish and Judaising writers.[1]

The net result of this controversy is the establishment of certain fixed canons of Old Testament interpretation, the germs of which are already present in S. Paul's epistles, and are pursued to a very full development by the skill of successive apologists. Individual writers no doubt allow their fancy or their prejudice to carry them away, as when Justin sees the Cross in almost every situation in the Bible, or when Origen sacrifices grammar and history for his favourite allegory; but the main principles of patristic exegesis are struck out by the long conflict with Judaism, and after seventeen centuries remain in vogue at the present day as a striking witness to the ingenuity and thoroughness with which the Old Testament was studied.

2. The Opposition of the Philosophers.

The august tradition of Greek philosophy, from its first outburst in Ionia in the seventh century B.C. to its last expiring effort in Alexandrian Neo-Platonism, offered many elements that might well have combined with Christianity, had there not been others, still more influential, which repelled it. It will be worth while to dwell briefly on these two sets of characteristics.

No one will do injustice to Greek philosophy as a system of reasoned truth, metaphysical in its presuppositions, dialectical in its method, simply aiming, at any rate in its best

---

[1] The Fathers were at a disadvantage when arguing with Jews, owing to their ignorance of Hebrew. It was open to the Jew to reply, when pressed with a convincing text, "The passage you quote is not in the Hebrew." The Fathers, stung by Jewish taunts, accused the Jews of mutilating the Old Testament to suppress evidences of Christ's Messiahship. With so much suspicion on both sides, it would be hopeless to expect unprejudiced discussion.

period, at understanding that which is. But there is another aspect of philosophy, not quite so universally appreciated, but, from our present point of view, even more important. We mean its religious protest against the falsehood and immorality of polytheism, and its distinct assertion of the Unity and goodness of God. A parallel, and that no fanciful one, might be drawn between the philosophers of Greece and the prophets of Israel. In each case the higher teaching was directed against prevailing religious ideas, often at no small risk to the teacher. In each case the main element of that teaching was the Unity of God, though the Greek conceived of Him as Intelligence or Force, the Hebrew as a Personal Creator.[1] In each case the superior insight of the thinker gave him influence in public affairs, and governments were guided by his advice, though at times scarcely understanding it. In each case that which began as a spontaneous inspiration degenerated into a technical discipline, though in the case of prophecy this was never able to supersede the genuine utterance, whereas in the case of philosophy the mere method often survived the thought. And in each case the moral example held up to the world was of the nature of a stern rebuke, and the world in return expected the preacher of righteousness to renounce it.

Modern writers (and among them the late Dr. Hatch) have justly drawn attention to the pure and spiritual ideas at which the later Stoic and Platonist thinkers had arrived, and have spoken of them truly as "Seekers after God." Nor did this point escape the notice of the apologists. It seemed to them so striking that they could only explain it by the theory of direct indebtedness to the prophets of the Old Testament or the apostles of the New. If Plato spoke as an Attic Moses, Seneca spoke as a Roman S. Paul: both were retailers of borrowed wisdom. Our insight into the

---

[1] I cannot bring myself to accept Matthew Arnold's theory that the only really essential substratum in Israel's conception of God is the Unseen Power, not ourselves, that makes for righteousness. The element of what, for want of a more exact name, we must call Personality seems to me a primordial part of the conception.

progress of the human spirit is larger than theirs; hence we can afford to smile at the simplicity of the hypothesis that satisfied their critical sense. But however we may explain it, the fact remains and is of the highest possible significance, that philosophy had become more and more religious, and that the Gospel seed was sown in prepared ground.

How came it then that Greek philosophy, instead of welcoming Christianity as an ally, treated it with mistrust, first as alien to itself, then as hostile?

The answer is to be found mainly in the exclusiveness of the claim put forward by Christ for His religion. Nothing of the sort had ever before been suggested. Philosophies might be logically incompatible; but as a matter of fact they existed side by side. Platonist and Aristotelian might wrangle, Stoic and Epicurean indulge in mutual abuse; but at bottom each understood the other, and their common interests outweighed their differences. But the GOD whose unity was preached by Christians was a jealous God: His existence was neither to be guessed at by conjecture nor proved by argument. He had revealed Himself once for all to man, and man's part was to accept the revelation.

The pride of reason was thus touched in its tenderest point, and it could not forgive the slight. The splendid achievements of human intellect, laboriously wrought out in the seats of the highest culture through centuries of unaided toil,[1] were, so it seemed, to be unceremoniously superseded by the miracle-mongering supernaturalism of a race of barbarians who had contributed nothing to the civilisation of mankind.

Nor did the first Christian preachers on their part seek to conciliate philosophy. With harshness indeed, but with a prescience that fully justified it, they insisted on the incompetence of human wisdom to solve or even to illustrate the problems with which revelation dealt. The instinct of the

---

[1] The Greeks, too, regarded their intellectual life as an inspiration from heaven, given specially to their race They made the words of the old bard their own—

αὐτοδίδακτος δ' εἰμί, θεὸς δέ μοι ἐν φρεσὶν οἴμας
παντοίας ἐνέφυσεν.—Hom. Od. xxii. 347.

Apostle did not err when he declared that his message was to the Greeks foolishness, and warned his readers against the seductions of philosophic antitheses.[1]

The attitude of such men as Celsus and Porphyry abundantly confirms the Apostle's view. These men could not see the superiority of Christian theology to their own. On the contrary, they were firmly convinced of its inferiority. They admitted, indeed, the moral excellence of the Gospel, but they denied that its ethical theory was so coherently framed or so elegantly expressed as their own.

The idea of sitting at the feet of a comparatively uncultivated teacher in the guise of humble learners was utterly repugnant to their pride ; and yet it seemed to both parties as if revelation permitted no other attitude. So the gulf became wider, and the hope of mutual understanding more remote. Yet all the time each party was receiving influence from the other: heathenism in its ideas, Christianity in its methods. This becomes obvious when we consider the Neo-Platonic system. In this vast fabric of eclecticism many Christian ideas are introduced, more or less altered to suit their surroundings ; and certain features are borrowed from the Christian moral standard. Even Julian attempted to import into his reformed Paganism more than one Christian element which, though his prejudice might still despise, his judgment could not but adopt.

The best philosophers, indeed, were not indisposed to consider the claims of Christianity. When Christian thinkers approached them in a philosophic spirit, they generally gave them an attentive hearing. It was otherwise with such men as Crescens the Cynic, whose pretentious ignorance Justin exposed. These men, from mortified vanity, became bitter enemies of Christianity, and were too often able under colour of the public weal to carry out their schemes of revenge.

In Alexandria, at any rate, the pleasing spectacle is presented of Christianity and philosophy discussing with equal learning and without passion their rival claims. And it was precisely at Alexandria that the Gospel was first successfully presented as a system of religious philosophy. The great

[1] 1 Cor. i. 23 ; 1 Tim. vi. 20.

Catechists, Clement and Origen, attended philosophers' lectures themselves, and numbered philosophers among their own converts. This process was not free from risk, and in fact it proved detrimental to the simplicity of their faith. Nevertheless the effort was a noble one ; and even those who condemned and mistrusted it were unconsciously influenced by its results.

To sum up our remarks on this head, philosophy, in spite of its lofty and often spiritual influence, must be ranked on the whole as an antagonist of the Gospel. This assertion, however, requires two qualifications. First, it must be limited by the earnest effort after a mutual understanding made by the Catechists of Alexandria, showing that they did not regard philosophy as an alien ; and secondly, it must be limited by the powerful reaction of Greek metaphysic upon Christian theology, which endures to this day, and has made Christianity virtually a Greek religion.

3. The Hostility of the Heathen Religions.

The religions of the Empire were as diverse as they were numerous. Some were purely rational, some were proselytising and aggressive; some were imaginative, others sensuous, others harsh and cruel; some tended to a dreamy asceticism, others to fanatical excitement, others to impure orgies. The tendency of one was to priestcraft, of another to magic, of a third to ceremonialism, of a fourth to mystery. But all found a home in the Imperial City; all, except a few sanguinary superstitions which still lingered in remoter provinces, were not only tolerated but gained fresh adherents. The rivalry of sectarianism which prevails to-day within the Christian sphere was in those days spread over a multitude of contradictory faiths.

It is perhaps hard for us to do justice to the genuineness of Pagan belief. We do not allude so much to those dark mysterious doctrines which we find in Egypt or eastern Asia, for we know from the Old Testament how intense and even fanatical was the devotion which these inspired. But it is in the case of Greece especially that we fail to realise how sincere the people's religious convictions were. We are so accustomed to draw our notions of the Greek mind from the great classical writers, that we insensibly regard their attitude towards the popular religion as representing that of the people. And yet no conclusion could possibly be more erroneous. If we desire to criticise with sympathy the manifestations of religious belief in Greek history, we must put out of our mind once for all the great aristocrats of thought, and apply our attention to writers who stand on a more genuinely popular level.

That the polytheistic creed was tenaciously held, and defended when necessary by the weapons of bigotry, is absolutely certain. To go no further than Athens, the imprisonment of Anaxagoras and the death of Socrates are sufficient proofs of this. But these happened in the fifth century B.C. In leaping over a period of six hundred years, a period marked by continuous intellectual progress, and so presumably of scepticism, we hardly expect to find the same general prevalence of sincere belief. During all this long interval poets and philosophers had continued to explain away and ridicule the popular mythology. They had addressed an ever-widening circle of hearers. It seemed impossible but that their views should spread. They could point to the fact that few men of any position professed religious belief;[1] they could prove with crushing effect the impotence of the so-called deities to resist the Roman arms. And the conclusion would seem irresistible that the religion which acknowledged these deities must be felt to be false.

[1] It is instructive to compare the present indifference of men, both in Protestant and Catholic countries, to dogmatic religion. It is obvious that religion in its spiritual sense had no part in the life of the public men of Rome under the later Republic. Cicero's letters show no trace of susceptibility to spiritual influence. Cæsar made in the Senate a public avowal of his unbelief. Juvenal declares that religious sanctions of conduct were all but universally discredited in his time. Yet the remarkable religious revival which meets us at the close of the first century A.D. must have been sufficiently visible to discerning eyes as far back as Augustus, who tried by every means to encourage it, though personally he could have had no sympathy whatever with it.

Yet it is evident that this conclusion, natural as it appears, was not drawn. The mass of men never have been, and we may safely affirm never will be, without belief in the supernatural. Gibbon is nearer the mark when, speaking of these times, he says—"The various religions of the Empire appeared to the people to be all equally true." Certain it is that unless there had been a genuine conviction of the truth of Paganism, men like Tertullian and Augustine would not have set themselves so energetically to confute it.

The reason is to be found in the universal craving of the human spirit for some religious belief. In default of a nobler faith, the oft-refuted fables of mythology were still cherished as the only traces left of something beyond the hard realities of the visible world, as the only link that bound the spirit to a higher and happier past.

Nations like the Gauls, who had no such mythology, or like the Asiatics, to whom power is the symbol of Deity, doubtless accepted the apotheosis of Cæsar as something more than an artifice of state policy. The Emperor, if not conceived of as actually Divine, was certainly regarded as the representative of heaven. And in the general decay of spiritual and moral life this may have seemed the only barrier against pure materialism, and have been held with a grasp, unreasoning, and yet despairingly strong.

From these and other causes there arose about the end of the first century of our era a very decided religious reaction. The leaders of thought, as we have already remarked, display for the first time a distinctly religious tone. Among the masses also religious sentiment became extremely and even morbidly active. The physical interpretation of mythology, which satisfied men of science, had no attraction for the vulgar. For them a different path of satisfaction was thrown open, the chief extant representative of which is Apuleius. Taking his stand on one aspect of Plato's philosophy, especially that revealed in the Timæus, he reconciled mythology with the religious sense by identifying the old gods with those intermediate spirits who act as agents of the supreme Deity in the material world. These spiritual beings, to whom was given the name of Demons (δαίμονες), were held to partake in some degree of a carnal nature, and to their dominion were assigned nearly all the departments of human life. They might still be worshipped under the old familiar names of the gods, and thus man's spirit might still expatiate in the sense of its union with the unseen world. So profoundly suitable was this doctrine to the wants of the age, that it was accepted by a large portion of mankind. Not only to the Pagan idolater, but to the Christian apologist, it seemed to embody an important truth. But whereas to the one it opened out a new field of soul-satisfying worship, to the other it appeared as the terrible penalty of a judicial blindness by which the powers of evil were mistaken for those of good. Almost all the apologists assume the reality of these intermediate beings; they never doubt the probability of their influencing the minds of men; and no small portion of their arguments is spent in proving by incontestable evidence their malignant nature, and the intolerable bondage to which they had reduced mankind.

We are apt to marvel at the wearisome reiteration with which one controversialist after another traces the phenomena of sacrifice, augury, ritual, magic and astrology, to a demonic source; at the prolix minuteness with which they describe the attributes of these beings, and the triumphant energy with which they challenge them to the critical ordeal of exorcism. But unless we clearly apprehend the connection in their minds between the demonology of the Platonic schools and the doctrine of evil angels which had come to them through Jewish channels, we shall fail to appreciate the task which they set themselves to accomplish.

Simultaneously with this popular reformation of heathenism there rose into prominence a very different form of religious influence, which appealed to the purer and more devout minds. The Mysteries or secret religious rites had long existed in various parts of the world, in connection with the older and more awe-inspiring cults. Paganism had by them striven to purify the souls of its votaries, and raise them to higher and more spiritual beliefs. It is not our purpose to

give any description of these deeply interesting efforts of the
ancient world to satisfy the aspirations of the individual soul.
But there is evidence enough to show that for many centuries they preserved broken reminiscences of the primal
revelation, faint glimmerings of the "Light which lighteth
every man that cometh into the world." And so striking
was their analogy to the inner doctrines of the Church that
some of their distinctive terms came to be applied to parallel
features of the Christian faith.

The very word μυστήριον is used for the Christian sacraments. The terms φωτισμός (i.e., illumination) and τελετή
(i.e., initiation) are often employed to designate baptism. The
expressions μεμνημένοι (initiated) and ἀμύητοι (uninitiated)
are common to the mysteries and to Christianity. While
therefore we emphasise the double conflict that engaged the
Church, on the one hand with the grosser Paganism, on the
other with its higher esoteric forms, we must also remark
that the attitude of the Christian apologist was different in
the two cases. Towards the one it was simple, uncompromising hostility. Towards the other, it was sympathetic so
far as concerned the object aimed at, but antagonistic so far
as concerned the means employed, which it showed to be but
a vain shadow of the real method of salvation.

From these two sources of renewed religious vitality it is
impossible to doubt that a genuine though perverted religious
enthusiasm arose. It would be unjust to the popular Paganism to see in it nothing but blind unreasoning hatred of
Christianity. No doubt the moral laxity which everywhere
accompanied heathen rites proved a fatal stumbling-block to
the acceptance of a purer faith. And this widespread depravity
was encouraged by the cynical indulgence allowed by the
Roman authority to the coarse and brutal passions of the
multitude.

The introduction of gladiatorial shows had fearfully
whetted that thirst for blood which is inherent in unre-
generate human nature. And the temptation to gratify this
appetite by a display of zeal for the insulted gods proved too
strong for a degenerate and corrupted world. Nevertheless,

it should be remembered that the government as well as the priesthood had encouraged the disposition to regard the Christians as atheists. Moreover, the secrecy of their assemblies, the absence of image or altar, and their apparent adoration of an obscure Jewish Criminal, made the charge sufficiently plausible. To this must be added the jealous silence under which they veiled their doctrines, and their vague predictions of an impending destruction of the world by fire, which, when judged through an unfavourable medium, might seem to justify the opprobrious epithet of enemies of the human race. The reputation of an atheist was not more favourable then than it is now. And we need not fear to admit that the blind rage of the populace was founded to some extent on a genuine horror of atheism, as well as of those nefarious immoralities of which the calumniators of Christ's religion asserted it to be the cloak. That Christians were in fact condemned to death as atheists we know from abundant testimony. And the horrors which they were accused of perpetrating at their nocturnal rites, if really believed, would be sufficient to arouse a fury which no considerations of common sense or justice could avail to control.[1]

Accordingly, we find that in their popular treatises the apologists direct their arguments to the proof of two points in especial—first, that they are not atheists, but worshippers of the only true God; and secondly, that their religious rites and Christian practices are such as deserve from the community nothing but gratitude and praise. In proving these points, they naturally retort upon their adversaries, and, in clearing themselves, show with unsparing cogency that the charges both of atheism and of unnatural lust are in reality applicable to the heathen systems.

As time rolled on, we find that these charges, founded on

[1] How terribly inveterate this sort of prejudice is may be seen from the periodical outbreaks of popular rage at the present day in countries like Austria and Russia, where the belief prevails that Jews occasionally murder a Christian infant for religious purposes. This sort of prejudice defies the strongest disproof.

calumny and ignorance, were gradually dropped, and others of greater plausibility put forward. Celsus makes no allusion to them. He substitutes for them others which he considers equally damaging; for instance, that Christians are the cause of the calamities which the offended gods hurl upon the earth; that they are bad subjects and conspirators against the Empire; that they engender a spirit of faction, hatred and distrust; that they embroil the relations of social life.

All such accusations are dealt with at length by the apologists; but so inveterate were they that even in the time of Augustine, when Christianity had fully established its supremacy, it was still felt necessary to give them a formal and at length a final refutation.

4. The Hostility of the State.

The last, and in some respects the most formidable obstacle to the acceptance of Christianity within the Empire, was the attitude of the supreme power towards it. This attitude was not clearly understood by the early Christian apologists. It appeared to them vacillating and inconsistent, depending on the caprice of individual rulers; whereas a deeper study of the phenomena has shown that a continuous line of policy may be traced connecting measures apparently at variance.

The key to this policy is the conception of religion entertained by Roman law. Religion was regarded not as a body of spiritual truth, nor as a matter of conscientious belief, but solely as a department of the State.[1] To coerce the conscience to embrace any set of opinions was a thing unknown to Græco-Roman civilisation. Provided obedience was rendered to the requirements of the State, the peculiarities of national religions were respected, and allowance made for conscientious difficulties. This is clearly shown by the treatment accorded

[1] The French Republic imitates the Roman Empire in this respect. Yet the two positions are not really analogous. For whereas the French State, as a State, is indifferent to religion, and merely provides for the needs of its subjects' consciences, the Roman State regarded the right worship of the gods as an essential condition of its own well-being.

to the Jews.   No nation in the world was more disliked by
the Romans, and no religion in the world was so incomprehensible and so distasteful to them.   Few of the conquered
peoples had given them more trouble, probably none bore
them so little good-will.   If anything could excuse a policy
of coercion of conscience, that excuse might have been urged
in their case.   And yet, what do we find?   The conscientious
scruples of the Jews were on the whole respected by the
Emperors.   Their occasional violation was the result of insane
caprice or of uncontrollable anger, sometimes of unintentional
blundering.   The Jews themselves made no allowance for the
inexperience of their rulers in matters spiritual.   They gave
no facilities for the carrying on of the work of secular government.   Their turbulence was not, as in the case of other
nations, the result of ordinary motives, such as the secular-
minded Romans could appreciate while they punished, but
was complicated with mysterious expectations of a divine
kingdom and an ever-increasing multiplicity of unintelligible
scruples, which the Romans, utterly unable to understand,
felt compelled to ascribe to the worst of all motives, hatred
of the human race.   In spite of these elements of provoca-
tion, the Jews demanded, and the government granted them,
the free exercise of their religion, with due provision for the
safeguarding of their abhorrence of every form of idolatry.
Judaism was one of the *Religiones Licitae* or State-protected
religions, which the Emperor and all his officials were bound
by law to respect.

In the modern sense of the word, therefore, the Roman
government was truly tolerant.   It exacted no more from
the adherents of the subject religions than it exacted from
the adherents of its own.   It interfered in no respect with
freedom of conscience, except so far as that freedom interfered with obedience to its own institutions.   Even atheism,
so far as it was merely speculative, received no condemnation
from the law.   Only those opinions or rites were forbidden
which were considered injurious to public order or public
morals.   Not once, but many times in Roman history had
the State interfered to suppress religious rites which had a

disturbing or immoral tendency. The permission accorded to the Jews to exercise their religion without hindrance, while limited by these two conditions, was in harmony with the whole spirit of Roman legislation.

How then are we to account for the apparent inconsistency of its attitude towards the Christian faith? In the first place, by its ignorance of the true character of Christianity; in the second, by its instinctive discernment, so soon as the true character of Christianity began to be understood, that it was irreconcilable with the established government. In the early days of Christianity, its origin in Judæa, and the fact that its preachers were nearly all Jews, led to its being regarded as a mere sect of Judaism. Thus it would be allowed to avail itself of the impunity accorded to Judaism, as a permitted faith. And for a time it undoubtedly enjoyed this privilege. The first troubles through which the Church passed were not, strictly speaking, persecutions by the central government. Even the atrocious cruelties of Nero, when, taking advantage of the unpopularity of the Christians in Rome, he made them the scapegoats of an anger directed against himself, were not acts of legal violence, but merely the extension of Imperial authority to an outburst of blind hatred, which demanded a victim, and for which no other victims equally acceptable to the multitude were at hand. It was only gradually, and in a great measure owing to the hostility of the Jews, that the Roman authorities came to apprehend the distinctness of Christianity from Judaism, and that it was in truth a wholly independent religion. When once this was understood, Christianity lost the position it had hitherto unwittingly occupied, of a religion allowed by the State. It sank at once to the status of a cult unrecognised by law. Only two courses were now possible to the government. It might ignore Christianity, or it might suppress it. The great statesmen who directed the Empire were as indisposed as modern rulers would be to spread the devastating horrors of religious persecution. The famous rescript of Trajan shows a clear grasp of the situation as it appeared to the wisest ruler of that time, and one of the wisest of any time. He forbade inquisition to be made for Christians, but at the same time he ordered that, when their offence was proved, they should be punished according to law.

It has been shown by Lightfoot and others that a Roman Emperor was prevented by his position of guardian of the laws from extending indulgence to such as refused to sacrifice. By a terrible irony of fate, the most conscientious and patriotic Emperors were precisely those who felt least able to pass over what they were bound to regard as a direct act of treason to the State. Nothing in the whole course of human history is more mournful than the fact that the wise and enlightened Trajan, the gentle and deeply religious Aurelius, have to be counted among the persecutors. It is true that the Church, with noble generosity, chose to forget Trajan's attitude to the Bithynian Christians, and to award to his lofty character the sacred tribute of her prayers. And it is also true that many apologists speak with real enthusiasm of Marcus Aurelius, and his occasional protection of their brethren. But the *gravamen* so pointedly urged by Tertullian, *non licet esse vos* ("you have no legal right to exist"), still remained. It was still the great and standing offence of Christianity, that in spite of its intrinsic holiness, in spite of its daily increasing numbers, in spite of its good services to the community, it could produce no certificate of birth; that it persisted in existing, in growing, in claiming a place among a society which had refused to make room for it.

And in this lay the whole strength of the power to persecute. The laws afforded Christianity no protection. The utmost that a favourable ruler could do was to discourage information against the Christians by imposing penalties upon their accusers. And this was actually done by more than one Emperor.[1] But wherever the Christians were conspicuous from their number, or for any reason specially obnoxious to the multitude, it was not difficult to oblige the magistrate to set the law in motion against them.

[1] *E.g.*, the rescript of Hadrian, preserved in Justin's first Apology, chap. 68, which forbids attention to mere rumours, and insists upon proof of unlawful action being given.

Looking at the different persecutions, we observe that in the majority of cases it was not the representative of the Emperor, but the mass of the people that instigated them. Often a prefect or proconsul was reluctantly compelled to pass sentence on one whom he had tried hard to save. And, on the whole, it is clear that, had the law allowed a discretionary power, the magistrates would in many cases have refused to condemn. But the Empire was erected on the popular will, and the prince could not venture to override its manifestation. In later times, when the adherents of Christianity were as numerous as their opponents, and their support was clearly worth possessing, the personal bias of the Emperor would count for much more. He could extend his protection to the Church with an effect that Marcus Aurelius could not have rivalled; or he could nerve the weakened arm of Paganism to strike its last blow, with an interest in the contest far more direct and personal than the early Emperors could have conceived.

The great preliminary task of the Christian writers was, therefore, to explain their true aims and character to the Emperor, to remove the misconception as to their disloyalty to the government, and so to secure a place among the tolerated sects. Let us consider for a moment the justice of their request from the Imperial point of view. There were two prejudices so engrained in the minds of the Cæsars that they seem to have admitted no argument upon them. The first was the prejudice against clubs (*sodalitates*), associations, or guilds of every sort, which they could not help believing must be utilised for purposes of political disaffection. The result was that, except under the most careful restrictions, all such associations were forbidden. The correspondence of Trajan and Pliny reveals this to be a cardinal feature of the great Emperor's policy. The closely-guarded love-feasts of Christian believers, and their gatherings before daybreak for common worship, were inexplicable except on the ground of some secret purpose; and as they refused to explain the details and meaning of that worship, it seemed reasonable to conclude that that purpose must be fraught with danger to the State.

The other prejudice concerned the refusal to burn incense before Cæsar's image, which was universally interpreted to imply disloyalty to Cæsar's power. It was true the Jews were not required to perform this act. But the Jews' religion was a strictly national one, and for such the Romans had always respect. Again, the Jews' religion was ancient, and the Romans reverenced antiquity more than any other people. Moreover, the Jews showed no desire to convert all mankind ; still less did they speak of a kingdom soon to come, which should embrace all the nations of the earth, and involve the existing fabric in one awful destruction. Hence the attitude of the Christians, though not theoretically different from that of the Jews, was practically different, which laid it the more open to attack, because the ingrained political suspicion and jealousy, which had grown with Rome's growth and deepened with her extending power, were roused by the rumours current about the rise of Christianity, and unconsciously confirmed by the language of Christians themselves.

Yet, if we turn to the Christian standpoint, we shall see abundant cause to endorse the complaint that they could not obtain a fair hearing. If such an emperor as Trajan, Hadrian, or either of the Antonines had been at the pains to study thoroughly the statements of advocates so highly qualified as Melito, Justin, or Tertullian, or if they had instituted a commission to inquire into the political influence of Christianity and draw up a formal report, it can hardly be doubted that some concession would have been made, sufficient at any rate to redeem the Empire from the terrible stigma of injustice towards its loyal subjects. At the bar of history, the great and in many ways beneficent administration of the Empire must plead guilty to the grave error of not considering it worth while to obtain full information before it acted in a matter of life and death to subjects whom it was bound to protect. It may be that even so the conclusion drawn would have been adverse. It may be that the incompatibility of a monotheism which intended to convert the world with a despotism based on the divinity of Rome and of Cæsar would have been clearly realised by the Ruler, and the suppression

of the new creed deliberately resolved on. But in that case
the bitter complaint of the apologists could not have stood
in its present form. The taunt that they were condemned
unheard would have lost its force, and the Empire would
have stood higher in the estimation of mankind for not
having shrunk from the most painful of all the duties that
fall upon a human being, that of frankly facing and resolving
honestly to grapple with an unwelcome truth.

Besides the above four opposing forces, of which we have
attempted to give a slight sketch, there were many other
obstacles to the spread of Christ's religion. There was the
prevailing degradation of moral and social life, the licentiousness of both sexes, the constant admixture of idolatry
with every transaction of business or of pleasure, the public
amusements, the horrors of slavery, and all the thousand
inconsistencies which a society based on heathenism brought
every day before the conscience of a Christian. But these
things belong to a history of the Church rather than to a
history of its literature. We therefore pass them over, merely
remarking that the writings of the earlier Fathers are full
of references to the difficulties which surrounded the profession of Christ, difficulties of which it is impossible for us to
form an adequate idea unless we are acquainted at first hand
with the works not only of the Christian writers, but of the
heathen historians and satirists, who show us plainly that the
Christian picture is not overdrawn. It is our desire to state
as temperately as possible the actual problems that were
present to the minds of the pioneers of Christian civilisation,
so as to indicate how, under the guidance of the Divine Spirit,
these problems were met, and how the leaders of Catholic
thought laid down the lines on which the immense superstructures of dogmatic faith were afterwards so successfully
raised.

CHAPTER II.

THE DIFFERENT CLASSES OF APOLOGISTS.

HAVING offered in the last chapter some general remarks on the surroundings of the Christian apologists, we now proceed to classify their writings. This is by no means easy. Several modes of division have been proposed.

The first classification divides them into (1) such as were addressed directly to the civil power under the stress of persecution, refuting calumnious accusation, and pleading for the removal of prohibitive legal enactments; (2) such as were addressed to the educated public in general, appealing indeed to their justice to give the Christian cause a hearing, but mainly concerned in proving that Christianity is the only true religion. These two classes of writing have very distinct aims: the first is strictly apologetic, the second mainly didactic. But nevertheless it is impossible to separate them. As a matter of fact, most Apologies belong at once to both classes. Those of Justin and Tertullian contain long expositions of the faith; yet they are both directly practical and forensic in their object: that of Minucius is a mere literary treatise addressed to a private friend, yet it would probably plead more effectively with a proconsul or an Emperor than almost any of those directly addressed to them.

Another classification is made to depend on the class of opponents which the writer had in view—according as these were (1) Jews or (2) Pagans. This has the advantage of corresponding to a genuine difference in treatment, since in their controversy with Judaism the Fathers make free use of the Old Testament, whereas in their controversy with Paganism they seek for other proofs. The reader will find in Smith's " Dictionary of Christian Biography " an admirable account of apologetic literature considered from this point of view.

But both these classifications have primary reference to the history and doctrine of the Church rather than to its literature. It will be necessary for our present purpose to go more deeply into the question, and to classify these important writings not according to their external object, but according to their internal spirit and method. We shall bring into the clearest possible relief the central principle which pervades each school of apologetic thought, and show its influence on the mind of Christendom.

The two main tendencies of apologetics are determined by the two fundamental conceptions of the relation between God and man already referred to in the Introduction, and correspond roughly to the two great divisions of Christendom into East and West.

The tendency of Greek Christianity is to lay down as a first principle the essential kinship between the Divine and human, so that whatever is most truly and perfectly human is really Divine, and the revelation of the Divine in human history is not the sudden apparition of an alien element, but the progressive manifestation of an abiding presence, brought to its culminating perfection in the Incarnation of Christ.

It follows from this that both Judaism and Paganism were stages in the progressive manifestation of God in man through Christ; and that both were Divinely appointed, the one to lead the Jews, the other to lead the Gentiles, to find themselves in Him.

The source of this fruitful thought must be sought in the Gospel of S. John, where it is stated with incomparable emphasis, though only as a germ, in which, however, all the legitimate developments of the Alexandrian theology are implicitly involved.

The first Church writer who attempts to found an apologetic system on this basis is Justin Martyr. He is not, indeed, able to maintain it with consistency; but to him belongs the credit of fixing it as a principle from which results of vast importance were in due time to follow.

He was succeeded by Athenagoras, whom an obscure tradition connects with the catechetical school of Alexandria. Pantaenus followed in the same direction, and impressed the doctrine, which is partly theological and partly philosophical, upon his eminent disciple Clement.

It is Clement who most distinctly and unflinchingly applies this principle to the whole domain of Christian thought.   His writings throughout kindle with a triumphant consciousness of the essential relationship between man and God.   This relationship he regards as no mere accidental act of grace conferred on one who had no original title to it.   Still less is it a necessary outcome of the Divine Nature expressing itself in man by a law of its own being.   It springs from the definition of God as Love, and from the conception of that Love as everlastingly manifested in the Son, in whom the Divine Fatherhood is eternally but freely realised;[1] and by whom, as the agent of creation, the rational creature is made to partake of the Divine Nature, though capable, owing to his freedom, of falling from his inheritance.   The Word of God, then, has always been present in human nature, wherever the true Light has not been quenched by sin.   And the gleams of truth and righteousness which have shone like stars amid the night of Gentile ignorance and guilt have been the Divine witnesses to the Son of God, which find at once their source and explanation in the Incarnation of Jesus Christ. Similarly the Jew received in the Law a higher but still partial illumination of God the Word, which he indeed misunderstood, but which Christ expressly connected with His own operation among the chosen people, and which was intended, side by side with Greek philosophy, as a preparatory discipline to open man's mind to Christ.

The same thought inspires Origen, the great disciple of a great teacher.   He certainly corrupts it by the admixture of hypotheses as to the origin and destiny of souls, which are

---

[1] The word *freely* is here used to guard against the theory that any eternal necessity surrounds the Divine Fatherhood.   Clement does not attempt to analyse the manner of the generation of the Word.   But as against the Gnostics he is careful to maintain the Divine freedom.

absent from Scripture and out of harmony with the mind of the Church. But the central truth that man is made for God, and by his likeness to God becomes, through Christ, capable of knowing God, shines out in his writings with peculiar lustre, and forms the firm foundation of his apologetic argument. The highest theological expression of this principle is not attained until Athanasius,[1] who, at once a master of dialectic and a great Church ruler, assigns to the Incarnation once for all its true place in human history, and also guards it from the tinge of mystic vagueness, with which Clement and Origen allow it to be encircled.

The main result of this principle is seen in the attitude assumed by this school of apologists towards Judaism, and still more towards Pagan philosophy. The preparation for the coming of Christ has been not negative only, but positive. The manifestation of God in human form came not as an absolutely new fact in the rational universe,[2] but as the long-expected fulfilment of the desire of man's heart, the reinstatement of his nature in its true position, and the guarantee of a spiritual progress which should again unite man to God.

A second class of apologists, which also numbers many illustrious names, took its stand upon the same fundamental truth, but refused to allow any progressive movement in human history towards the decisive fact of the Incarnation. It preferred to dwell on the advent of Christ as a sudden break in the Divine dealings with mankind, who had fallen wholly back from original righteousness, and who could only be said to have paved the way for Redemption by manifesting their utter incapacity for righteousness and truth. The writers of this class admit the primordial kinship

---

[1] Athanasius first connects the statement of the Trinity as an original fact of the Divine Essence with the Incarnation and the union of the two Natures in Jesus Christ, and by these majestic doctrines he vindicates the essential divineness of man's nature.

[2] Two mysterious thoughts were ever present to the minds of the great Greek Fathers, of which they earnestly strove to gather the significance —(1) The Image of God, in which man was created; (2) The Theophanies or appearances of a Divine Person in human form recorded in the Old Testament.

between the human soul and its Maker, but recognise it only when divested of all the trappings and disguises with which false creeds and philosophies have tried to smother it. Some of them extend their condemnation not only to Paganism, but also to the Mosaic law, regarding it as Divinely ordained only so far as it was imposed upon a disobedient people as a punishment for their sins. This attitude, which is first taken by Barnabas, is traceable in the writings of Tatian, Irenæus, and the writer to Diognetus,[1] and to a less extent in Tertullian. But it is in their attitude towards heathen thought that the second class of apologists differ fundamentally from the first. By far the most brilliant of them is Tertullian, and he is also the most typical. He will not allow any excellence whatever in Pagan philosophy. It is speculatively false and practically immoral, more plausible, no doubt, and less gross than Pagan religion, but none the less demon-taught and soul-destroying. If the appeal of God the Word to the human soul is to have any response at all, that appeal must be made not to the soul encrusted with the cancer-growth of civilisation, but to the soul naked and untaught, caught, as it were, unawares in its moments of infant unconsciousness, for then only will it bear spontaneous witness to its divine birth. This brilliant and striking thought is brought out with startling vividness in Tertullian's "Essay on the Testimony of the Soul that is naturally Christian." The whole progress of man's mind since the fall, with the single exception of the Jewish faith, has been one long apostacy, deviating ever more and more hopelessly from the path of truth.

This line of reasoning is more congenial to the Latin Church than to the Greek, and it is by Tertullian, the first Latin theologian, that it is most distinctly grasped. The weak point in its metaphysical basis is the position assigned to Judaism, which there was a general tendency to misrepresent. In the heretic Marcion, who offers several points of contact with this school, this tendency was carried to

---

[1] In this unknown writer the disparagement of Judaism attains its maximum. According to him it differs in no respect from heathenism, except that its superstitions happen to be directed towards the true God.

an extreme by his denying the Old Testament legislation to be the work of the good God. But both Tertullian and Irenæus bestow great pains on fitting in the Mosaic dispensation with their general system; and though they fall below S. Paul's solution, they are far removed from those of Tatian and the writer to Diognetus.

The third class of apologists, of whom Arnobius is the representative, proceed upon a totally different fundamental assumption. They regard man exclusively from the physical point of view, and deny to him any claim to kinship with God. Biassed by Gnostic prejudice, they even refuse to allow him to be the direct work of God, referring his creation to some intermediate power. The redemptive mission of God the Son becomes an isolated supernatural fact, caused indeed by the Divine Love, but incomprehensible to us, and demanding only our humble, adoring acknowledgment. It appears as if it might have been effected in some other way than by the Incarnation, so far as our reasonable apprehension of it is concerned. The system of thought here inaugurated is not only different from but incompatible with that of the Greek Fathers; it seeks to magnify God by degrading man, and, like Calvinism, of which it may be considered the precursor, it shows distinct affinities for non-Christian modes of thought. A Mohammedan may speak of God as the All-merciful, but in his theology this does not mean that the Divine heart beats with loving tenderness for the soul that proceeds from Him, but merely that, while He has the power and the right to destroy a guilty creature, He abstains from doing so, and offers him instead the gift of eternal life.

Arnobius himself has no claim to be ranked as a philosopher or a theologian. Lactantius, who followed on somewhat similar lines, though a thoughtful reasoner, does not construct a complete dogmatic system. But their influence is not altogether absent from the mind of their great successor S. Augustine, whose tremendous vindication of the sovereign power of God has proved a two-edged weapon, and imposed upon the conscience of Christendom a " fearfulness and trembling" which has interfered disastrously with the "glorious liberty of the sons of God."

Evidences of Christianity.

The Question of Christian Evidences is that on which the acceptance of Christianity by those to whom it is for the first time presented necessarily turns. That these should refrain from persecuting, should be benevolently neutral, does not content the apologist; he is aggressive, and urges the adoption of his faith. The Jewish or Greek doubter appeals for proofs. In supplying these, the Christian may lay the chief stress either on the inward and spiritual form of evidence, or on the physical and external. The former addresses itself to the conscience, starting from the principle that like is known by like; the latter addresses itself to the understanding, and convinces by shutting the opponent's mouth. Now, these two lines of proof correspond to the two ways of regarding man's nature before mentioned. The moral or spiritual proof is only of force on the supposition that man's conscience is the Divine voice within him, that his spiritual retina is sensitive to the light, and that if he will he can discern "things as they are." The essence of it lies in its confidence in man's freedom; he answers because he hears distinctly.

The external proof, which is most relied on and most effective, is nevertheless of a lower order of cogency, for it reasons with its opponent as a superior, not as an equal. It impresses not only the intelligence, but also the emotional nature, awakening hopes and fears, and the vague awe of the supernatural. Its effect is therefore more striking, and its application more widespread. At bottom it rests upon the manifestation of superhuman knowledge or power coming from without; and so does not differ generically from the evidence of non-Christian religions. It is its close connection with the moral proof which gives it its value, its inestimable value; for Christianity cannot dispense with external evidence, so long as it .accepts S. Paul's declaration that "if Christ be not risen our faith is vain." The Apostle's creed lays down the true lines on which an evidential system must be built. It gives us facts, one of them at least miraculous, to be explained; and the explanation of these facts is found to carry with it that regeneration of humanity for which the world had been longing and to which its progress had been tending.

A full and consistent presentation of Christianity must rest on both these proofs, but not in an equal degree. In combining them, either the physical must be subordinated to the moral, or the moral to the physical. In either case one gives its value to the other. This consistent attitude is, however, rarely maintained by any one Father. Justin, for instance, in his Apology rests the main proof of Christ's doctrine on the presence of the Divine Word in germ in the human heart, but in his dialogue with Trypho he lays greater stress on the theophanies and prophecies of the Old Testament and the miracles of the New. Tertullian, in his most original treatise, founds the truth of Christianity on the witness of the uncorrupted human soul, yet no one brings to bear with greater vividness the employment of portent and terror, of Divine Might acting out of the course of nature, in order to convince an unwilling world. Clement is the most consistent of the apologists; but he gains simplicity by subordinating that side of Christianity for which external proofs are required, namely, the redemptive work of Christ as finished by His death. Origen, the most spiritually-minded of the Fathers, does more justice than Clement to the power of the proof from miracle, though he restricts its province. His point of view is that, Jesus Christ having once been apprehended as the Divine Incarnate Word, it would be expected that He should stand in a different relation to external nature from ordinary mortals, and that therefore the alleged instances of His supernatural power are both in themselves credible, and, by their perpetuation in a weakened form to his own day, bear witness to their greater intensity during His presence on earth.

The student who will keep before him the two lines of

thought, as here distinguished, will not fail to obtain an additional help towards mastering the arguments of the great apologetic writers. He will study them according to their spiritual affinities rather than according to accidental similarities.

Next to the fundamental axiom of the kinship of the Divine and human, the link which binds the first school of apologists most closely together is the influence of Plato. Hippolytus alone in his extant works shows few traces of it. Justin, Athenagoras, Clement, and Origen, are all in a sense Platonists. Justin's Platonism comes out in his views on creation, on intermediate spirits or demons, and especially on the nature and attributes of the One God. Athenagoras shows traces of another side of Plato's mind, in his appreciation of a sceptical balance of judgment, which he refuses to condemn so long as it is not caused by moral obliquity, and is really searching after truth.

The Alexandrian Fathers are steeped in Plato, to an extent, indeed, that interferes with the proportion of their faith. The absolute self-sufficingness of the Eternal God, the distrust of matter, the idealistic presentation (at least by Origen) of Christ's humanity, the imperfect separation of the spiritual and intellectual spheres, and the presentation of Christ's redemption rather as a revelation ($\phi\omega\tau\iota\sigma\mu\grave{o}\varsigma$) whereby the eye of man's soul is turned round to the light and lovingly contemplates the Divine, than as an atonement whereby an alienated humanity is restored to its original destiny:—all these, and many other features of their system, which will be noticed in due course, are drawn rather from the fountain of Plato's genius than from the pure tradition of the Gospel.

The greatest masters of the second school are either uninfluenced by the Platonic philosophy, or have broken with it and freed themselves from its tendencies. Tatian had drunk deep of Greek thought, but he seems to have always been dissatisfied with it, and to have rejoiced in throwing it overboard. Irenæus stands midway between the Greek and Latin modes of thought, but he is far more of a divine than of a philosopher. Tertullian's mind, though capable of abstract thought, and moving with ease in the most subtle dialectic, has more affinity with the materialising views of the Stoics than with the metaphysic of idealism. Cyprian, who succeeded him, displays a mind still more restrictedly rhetorical and forensic. The cosmical views of Plato are traceable in the works of Arnobius and Lactantius, but the spirit of their systems is wholly anti-Platonic.

The canon of truth in all the apologists is the same, namely, the teaching of Christ and His apostles preserved in the written evangelical records and in the general tradition of the Church. None of the great writers, even while expatiating in the realms of transcendental theology or of man's free-will, ever willingly adopts any conclusion which he believes to be inconsistent with this Catholic tradition.

But while both the great schools of thought agree in accepting this as the supreme arbiter, they differ widely in their conception of its mode of application. To the first school the revelation of Christ is conceived as a self-manifesting process, in conformity with the workings of reason, freely moving among the phenomena of spiritual truth. The tradition of the Church is regarded as true because the expounders of it were more fully under the guidance of the enlightening Spirit, and their statements commend themselves more and more fully, in proportion as they are understood, to the purified conscience in which the same Spirit has awakened the power of discernment. Christ is the fulfilment not only of the Law—*i.e.*, of the spiritual progress of the chosen race—but of humanity as such, with all its imperfect aspirations, all its guesses at truth. He is acknowledged by the free exercise of a mind touched by His grace.

To the other school the apostolic teaching assumes a more directly authoritative aspect. Irenæus defines true doctrine to be the uncorrupted, unvarying testimony of those churches which were founded by apostles, and had continuously retained the deposit of truth once committed to them. And Tertullian goes so far as to declare that their teaching, even though incredible, is binding on faith: "Credo quia impossibile."

The domain of human freedom is here reduced to the power of accepting or rejecting that which the Catholic Church declares, on pain of eternal loss, to be Christian truth. It is evident, therefore, that between these two points of view there is at bottom an irreconcilable difference. The one reads Divine truth in the human spirit as taught by Christ and born again in Christ; the other looks on truth as a gift from heaven, of which man as such is the passive recipient. The latter view, which was definitely accepted by the Latin Church, is unquestionably the better fitted to secure the obedience of mankind. But it needs the periodical refreshment of the earlier and more philosophic standpoint if man's highest intellect is to be led as a willing captive by the triumphal car of Him who guides us into all truth.

CHAPTER III.

THE EARLIEST APOLOGISTS—ARISTIDES—QUADRATUS —AGRIPPA CASTOR—ARISTO PELLAEUS.

WE have grouped together in this chapter four writers who until recently were little more than names to us, but who, from their admitted antiquity and philosophical pretensions, hold a high place in the annals of the Church.

These are Quadratus and Aristides, Agrippa Castor and Aristo of Pella. The first two have much in common. Both were of Athens, both philosophers (the former perhaps also a bishop), and both authors of apologies believed to be addressed to Hadrian and described as highly important for the Christian cause. A few brief notices of their works were collected by the industry of Routh, the most circumstantial being, as usual, those of Eusebius. The impression. derived from these would be that these two writers were remarkable examples of intellectual power and philosophic acumen, as well as staunch defenders of the faith.

An opportunity of testing the value of this criticism has been afforded in the case of one of them, **Aristides** (whom, though generally placed after Quadratus, it will be convenient to consider first), through a remarkable series of discoveries in which nothing is more noteworthy than the promise it gives of similar discoveries in the future. For it turns out that, as we had all along had Tatian's Diatessaron in our hands without suspecting it, so we had been equally the unconscious possessors of the Apology of Aristides. The recovery of this work has excited so much interest, and is so good an example of the patient industry of scholars and the chances offered to those who know how to use them, that we propose to give a very brief account of the way in which it came about.[1]

[1] Taken from Rendel Harris' edition of Aristides (Cambridge Texts and Studies).

Some fourteen years ago the learned Armenian monks of the Mechitarist convent of S. Lazarus at Venice, who had done such excellent service in publishing the Armenian version of Tatian, issued to the world an Armenian translation of the opening chapters of the lost Apology of Aristides, accompanied by a Latin version. The fragment was so different from the preconceived ideas formed of it, that able critics, and among them M. Renan, unhesitatingly pronounced it spurious. Relying on the testimony of Eusebius as to its date, and of Jerome as to the talent of the author and his frequent citation of heathen philosophers, the French critic had no difficulty in showing that the work published was deficient in talent, and entirely without allusions to philosophy; that its mythological knowledge was unworthy of its reputed author, while its theological phraseology was three centuries too late.

In spite of this sweeping rejection by so high an authority, the fragment was found to be authentic after all; and theology has again to thank the Armenian monks for the first instalment of an invaluable gift. Mr. R. Harris, late of Cambridge, now of Philadelphia, while travelling in Syria in 1889, discovered in the convent of S. Catherine on Mount Sinai a Syriac manuscript, containing a practically complete translation of the whole of the missing Apology. This was in sufficient accord with the Armenian fragment to vindicate its substantial genuineness, while, by its omission of the fifth century theological terms, it showed that M. Renan's objections to the Armenian had not been altogether without weight. It proved further the erroneousness of Jerome's laudatory criticism, and prepared the way for doubts as to the accuracy of the date he assigned.

Mr. Harris thus characterises the Syrian document:—" The language and thought of the writer are simple and straightforward; in fact he is more of a child than a philosopher, a child well trained in creed and well practised in ethics, rather than either a dogmatist defending a new system or an iconoclast destroying an old one; but this simplicity of treatment, so far from being a weakness, adds often greatly to

the natural impressiveness of the subject, and gives the work
a place by the side of the best Christian writings of his age."

We now come to the strange part of the history. While Mr.
Harris was passing his Syriac MS. through the press he showed
the proofs to Mr. Armitage Robinson, the editor of the "Cambridge Texts and Studies contributing to the illustration of
Biblical literature." This eminent scholar, while shortly afterwards perusing in Vienna a Latin version of an old romance,
called "The History of Barlaam and Joasaph (or Josaphat),"
was struck with the resemblance of a portion of this to
the Apology of Aristides. The Greek text of the "History"
is printed in Migne's edition of the works of S. John of
Damascus, and Mr. Robinson soon found himself reading
the actual words of the apologist himself, transferred bodily
into the History as a defence of Christianity delivered by
Barlaam before the Indian monarch Abenner and his son
Joasaph.[1] As this work exists in several copies and numerous versions, a new field of criticism of the Apology was
opened up to the student, which will doubtless prove highly
fruitful. Sufficient to say, that the restored Greek text is,
on the whole, in fairly close accord with the Syriac, though
the latter, in accordance with the usual habit of Syriac
versions, contains amplifications and insertions, and circum-
locutions for the sake of avoiding difficulties. We may
therefore feel tolerably certain that we possess this ancient
and much valued Apology entire, and a few brief remarks
will now be made upon its main features.

The first thing that strikes one is that it must have enjoyed
a great reputation. This is proved by the fact that Jerome
and the author of the Roman Martyrology, influenced by popular opinion, perceive in it excellences it does not possess.[2]

---

[1] The work in question is a religious romance long attributed to S. John
of Damascus, but probably much earlier, and now recognised to be a
working up of the Indian legend of Sakya Mouni or Buddha, with other
ancient Eastern tales incorporated into it. It was immensely popular
during the Middle Ages, and translated into most of the European languages. The reader will find all details in the Dictionary of Biography.

[2] It is worth while to observe the growing amplitude of language employed. Eusebius, while mentioning the work as extant in his own day,

The selection of it by the author of Barlaam and Josaphat out of the multitude of apologies open to him is still stronger testimony to its fame. And if Mr. Harris' comparison of some of its views with those singled out for attack by the heathen Celsus be sufficient to prove that Celsus had it specially in his mind when he wrote against the Christian faith, we may be quite certain that it stood out prominently among its fellows as a recognised standard work. That it should have been so considered is not altogether unreasonable; for it has some merits of its own, rare among patristic writings. First, it is brief, simple, and to the point; secondly, it deals systematically with the opinions of the different races of men, dividing them into Barbarians, Greeks, Jews, and Christians, and taking each in order; thirdly, while contenting itself with a bare statement of doctrine, it brings into clear light the two dogmas most easily assailed by a heathen, that of the divinity of Christ, and that of Man being the final cause of creation. This last is mercilessly ridiculed by Celsus; and though it is found also in Justin (whom Jerome declares to have been an imitator of Aristides), yet most probably Celsus got it from the latter.

One highly interesting feature of this Apology is the evidence it affords of an already formulated Christian creed. Mr. Harris thus restores the fragments in their proper order:—

> " We believe in one God, Almighty
> Maker of Heaven and Earth :
> And in Jesus Christ, His Son
>
> . . . .
>
> Born of the Virgin Mary :
>
> . . .
>
> He was pierced by the Jews :
> He died and was buried :
> The third day He rose again :
> He ascended into Heaven :
>
> . . . .
>
> He is about to come to judge
> . . . . "

uses no term of praise.—H. E. iv. 3 fin. Jerome speaks of the author as " philosophus, vir eloquentissimus ;" the author of the Martyrology as "sanctus Aristides, fide et sapientia clarissimus."

That these clauses formed the whole Creed is not likely: but in one respect they point to a very ancient date. The clause "pierced by the Jews," which never occurs in any of the third century symbols, contains a point emphasised in the New Testament, and traceable in the apocryphal Gospel and Preaching of Peter and the Gnostic Acts of S. John, all early documents. And oddly enough, it appears here in conjunction with a far more friendly attitude to the Jewish people than was usual in later times. It is necessary therefore to carry back the Apology to as early a date as is compatible with the historical evidence. Eusebius speaks of it as delivered to Hadrian, who visited Athens in A.D. 125 and again in 129. But the recovered inscription makes it certain that the Emperor addressed was not Hadrian but Antoninus Pius, and that the prænomen of Aristides was Marcianus. Now this name is otherwise known as that of a Christian of great authority in Smyrna about A.D. 138–140. On a review of the probabilities, Mr. Harris concludes that the Apology should be assigned to the early part of Antoninus' reign, and that it was possibly presented to him, along with other Christian writings, during an unrecorded visit of his to his ancient seat of government in Smyrna.

The notices of **Quadratus,** the companion-apologist to Aristides, are somewhat more exact, but it seems doubtful whether they are founded on any more certain data. Eusebius says:[1]—

"Quadratus presented an Apology to Hadrian, which he wrote in defence of our faith, because certain ill-disposed persons tried to injure our people. The oration is still extant and in our possession: we can judge from it the writer's talent and the correctness of his apostolic doctrine. The writer sufficiently attests his early date by the following words: 'Our Saviour's works were always present, for they were true: those who were healed, those who had risen from the dead: who were also ever present. Nor only during the Saviour's lifetime, but after His departure did they live a long time, so that some of them have remained even to our own day.'"

[1] Eus. H. E. iv. 3.

The chief difficulty in accepting the remote date thus claimed for Quadratus lies in another passage of Eusebius,[1] which refers to a letter of Dionysius of Corinth in the time of Antoninus, which speaks of Quadratus as succeeding to the see of Athens after the martyrdom of Publius, when the Church was scattered by persecution. If Quadratus the apologist and Quadratus the bishop are the same person, it seems impossible to believe that Dionysius could have been mistaken as to the time, and Quadratus must therefore be brought down to the early years of Antoninus. On the other hand, the account of Eusebius is so precise, and the quotation itself so graphic and explicit, that it seems best to admit the existence of two Quadratuses, the first an apologist under Hadrian, the second a bishop under Antoninus.[2]

There would be no doubt whatever as to Quadratus' early date, if the details given in S. Jerome's biography could be trusted. But that great writer, so learned and acute-minded in controversy, contents himself for the most part in biography with working up into a more elegant literary shape the facts supplied by Eusebius. When he appears to be giving additional details, one often finds that these when analysed can be traced to some Eusebian notice, hint or allusion. Otherwise his account of Quadratus is precise enough. "Quadratus, a disciple of the Apostles, after Publius Bishop of Athens had been crowned by martyrdom, was elected in his place, and by his faith and industry reunited the church, which the terror of persecution had dispersed. When Hadrian wintered at Athens and visited Eleusis, having been initiated into almost all the heathen mysteries, this gave occasion to such as hated the Christians to harass them without receiving an imperial order. Quadratus submitted to him a most telling apologetic treatise, full of reason and faith and worthy of his apostolic teaching," &c.

In another passage taken from the Chronicon of Eusebius, Jerome says that Quadratus and Aristides sent their Apologies

---

[1] Eus. H. E. iv. 23.

[2] The chief difficulty of the hypothesis lies in this absence of any other testimony for a persecution at Athens under Hadrian : whereas that under Antoninus is attested also by Melito.

to Hadrian, and that Serenus Granius, the Legatus, himself wrote in the same sense: whereby Hadrian was so much moved that he sent a rescript to Minucius Fundanus, Proconsul of Asia, laying down that the Christians were not to be condemned without certified charges. This rescript is preserved in Justin's Apology and in the Chronicon and History of Eusebius. There seems no reason to doubt its genuineness: for it follows in the line of Trajan, forbidding clamorous and irresponsible accusations, but ordering Christians to be punished if proved to have done anything against the laws. Justin places too mild an interpretation upon it, in conformity with his charitable, hopeful nature.

The next writer we have to notice is **Agrippa Castor,** whom Eusebius mentions as a celebrated opponent of the heretic Basilides.[1] He wrote under Hadrian probably about A.D. 135, and is the earliest recorded controversialist against heresy. He exposed the grandiloquent terminology of Basilides, especially ridiculing his imaginary prophets Barcabbas and Barcoph (or Parchor) and his mystic name for the Supreme Deity Abrasax (or Abraxas). Of the method of his treatise we know nothing, but we may infer that it enjoyed a wide reputation.

Another writer of this period was **Aristo** of Pella, of whom, however, the scanty notices that remain are somewhat conflicting. Eusebius quotes him as an authority for Hadrian's having forbidden the Jews, after the suppression of Barcochba's revolt, to settle in or near Jerusalem. But he does not say to what work of Aristo he is alluding.[2] Maximus, in commenting on the work on Mystical Theology ascribed to Dionysius the Areopagite,[3] declares him to be the author of a Dialogue between Jason and Papiscus, which, he says, Clement of Alexandria ascribed to S. Luke. If this reference to Clement be correct, the work must have been produced at a very early date. Jerome twice mentions the Dialogue by name, but without naming the author; and Origen quotes Celsus as having read it, but he too is silent as to the author's name. Some critics have doubted whether we have

[1] Eus. H. E. iv. 7.   [2] Eus. H. E. iv. 6.   [3] Routh, Rel. Sac., vol. i. p. 96.

sufficient evidence to connect the work with Aristo at all; but this scepticism is unnecessary. The two fragments quoted by Jerome are (1) "*He that hangeth is a reproach of God*,"[1] alluding to the current Jewish objection to a crucified Messiah; and (2) "*In the Son God made heaven and earth*,"[2] which, he says, is an inaccurate representation of the Hebrew sentence, "*In the beginning God created the heavens and the earth*."

The dialogue was supposed to be held between Papiscus, an unconverted Jew, and Jason, a Christian, or perhaps a converted Jew. Celsus, who read it, dismisses it with the contemptuous remark "that it is worthy not so much of laughter as of pity and indignation."[3] Origen does not offer a very warm defence of the writer, but he deprecates Celsus' criticism as misleading and unjust, begging the reader to judge for himself by a perusal of the book, and excusing its superficiality by remarking that its purpose was rather to confirm the faith of believers than to convince an intelligent opponent.

It was translated into Latin by another Celsus, whose preface is still extant, and used to be appended to the works of Cyprian. The fragment is given in Routh, and is here translated for the benefit of the reader :—

"There comes into my mind that great, memorable and glorious discussion between the Hebrew Christian Jason and Papiscus the Alexandrian Jew, how the obstinate hardness of the Jewish heart was softened by admonition and gentle reproof, and Jason's doctrine, by the infusion of the Holy Ghost, won the victory in the heart of Papiscus. By it Papiscus was admitted to an understanding of the truth and fashioned to the fear of the Lord by the Lord's own mercy, so that he believed in Jesus Christ the Son of God, and entreated Jason that he might receive the sign of baptism. This is attested by the written narrative of their contest, which is expressed in the Greek language, showing how they strove with one another, Papiscus withstanding the truth, and Jason maintaining and vindicating the dispensation[4] and fulness of Christ."

[1] λοιδορία Θεοῦ ὁ κρεμάμενος. Jer. lib. ii. Comm. Gal. cap. iii. comm. 13. —*Routh.* [2] Jer. Quæst. Heb. in Genesin., tom ii. op., p. 507.—*Routh.*
[3] Origen *contra Cels.* iv. ch. 52.
[4] *Dispositionem.* Others translate "commission."

CHAPTER IV.

EARLY APOLOGETIC WRITERS CONTINUED:—ATHENA-
GORAS—EPISTLE TO DIOGNETUS—DIONYSIUS OF
CORINTH—MAXIMUS—THEOPHILUS.

WE have already noticed how two champions of the faith
arose in Athens to testify to the vitality of S. Paul's work
there. A third writer now comes before us from the same
capital, superior to them both in culture and intelligence,
though, strange to say, little spoken of in the annals of the
Church. We allude to **Athenagoras,** whose *Apology* and
Treatise on the Resurrection still remain to us, and are highly
favourable specimens of his controversial method.

Before criticising them, it may be well to pause a moment
and consider the difficulties which must have beset the
planting of the Church in Athens.

If the burning zeal of the great Apostle ever permitted
him to feel diffidence in addressing an assembly, he may well
have felt it when he addressed on Mars' Hill for the first
time an Athenian crowd. No doubt the Athens of his
time was in her decay, inferior in opulence and grandeur
to many younger cities. Yet even to a Jew, provided he
had received some educational impressions beyond the
fanatical shibboleths of Pharisaism, there was much in
that wonderful centre of intelligence to shake his most
inveterate prejudices and inspire him with unwilling
respect.

Shorn indeed of her political greatness, deprived even of
her philosophical supremacy, she still shone with a brilliant
after-glow of æsthetic and intellectual prestige. Her monuments flashed on the visitor memories recent enough to
dazzle his imagination. Her schools claimed and obtained

even from Emperors the homage due to her unique past. Recognising her as the true nurse of Hellenism and the chief missionary of human refinement, the best spirits of the age held her worthy of admiring love not unmixed with awe. As the seat of the most brilliant and popular university, young men of talent and position flocked to her from every quarter, studied for a time within her colonnades, and carried thence the recollection of a culture which was not always deep, not always erudite, but was always and genuinely Attic.

To subject to the criticism of this people a doctrine professing to come direct from God, a religion and not a philosophy, depending not on argument but on revelation, was a task of which the difficulties might seem insuperable. When we consider what the Athenian character was, this language will not seem exaggerated. Keen, subtle, capricious, satirical, sated with ideas, eager for novelty, yet with the eagerness of amused frivolity, not of the truth-seeker: critical by instinct, exquisitely sensitive to the ridiculous or the absurd, disputatious, ready to listen, yet impatient of all that was not wit, satisfied with everything in life except its shortness, and therefore hiding all references to this unwelcome fact under a veil of complacent euphemism—where could a more uncongenial soil be found for the seed of the Gospel? Had the Apostle been susceptible of moral doubt, he might well have experienced a momentary misgiving. Imagine a zealot of the Salvationists mounting the pulpit of S. Mary's Oxford on Show-Sunday, and we can form a faint idea of what the frequenters of Athenian lecture-halls thought of S. Paul. Yet even this comparison falls far short of the mark. To an Athenian the Jew was not so much an object of hatred (as to the Roman), nor even of contempt (as to the rest of mankind), as of absolute indifference. He was simply ignored. To the eclectic philosophy which now dominated the schools of Athens, Judaism alone among all human opinions was as if non-existent. That Athenians should be convinced by the philosophy of a Jew would be a proposition expressible in words but wholly destitute of meaning.

On the other hand, the Jew was not altogether uninfluenced by Greek thought. Wide apart as the two minds were, the Hebraic proved not insensible to the charm of the Hellenic; witness the Epistle to the Hebrews, witness Philo, witness the intrusion of Greek methods of interpretation even into the text-books of Rabbinism. And it was Athens, as the quintessence of Hellas, Athens as represented by Socrates, and still more by Plato, which had gained this subtle power. And just as Judæa alone among all the Jewish communities retained its exclusiveness wholly unimpaired by Hellenism, so Athens, more than any Pagan capital, was likely to ignore or repel a faith coming in the garb of Judaism. And yet within less than a century we find this faith so well established there as to yield to the Church the good fruits of martyrdom in the person of its bishop, and of able defences in the person of three of its teachers.

The early and the later fortunes of the Athenian Church are buried in oblivion; it comes but for a brief period before the scene of history. But the undying interest of that one dramatic moment when Paul proclaimed a bodily resurrection to the authors of the conception of a spiritual immortality, will always cause us to linger with strange sympathy over every relic of the Christianity of Athens.

Of the personal history of Athenagoras we know next to nothing. Philip of Side, a very inaccurate writer of the fifth century, says that he was the first head of the school at Alexandria, that he was converted to Christianity while wearing the philosopher's cloak and presiding over the academic school, and from a zealous impugner became an ardent defender of the Christian faith. These statements, with the exception of the first, may not improbably be true, but the date assigned by Philip is contradicted by the Apology itself, which is clearly addressed to M. Aurelius and his son Commodus, as joint rulers of the world, and by several allusions enables us to fix the time of writing to A.D. 176–177.

The style of the treatise proves the education of the writer, and the clearness and vigour of the arguments shows his intelligence. He calls the work an *Embassy*,[1] which may indicate that he was in possession of some formal introduction to the Emperor. At any rate, he writes with a practical object, in the anticipation of securing Cæsar's attention.

His main purpose is energetically to repel the three standing charges against the Christians, of atheism, incest, and cannibalism, and also to state, in a way intelligible to heathens, the main outlines of the Christian creed. His theology closely resembles that of Justin: God the Father is conceived of mainly as the self-subsisting Being and Cause of all existence, God the Son as the Eternal Reason operative in creation, God the Spirit as an emanation from the Eternal God, who spoke by the prophets. Like Justin, he mentions the angels as holding a place in Christian theology. His philosophical position is eclectic, with a decided leaning to Plato, but tinged with ideas from many sources. He has been suspected of belonging to the Montanists, from his account of the passive attitude of a prophet under the action of the Holy Spirit, and from his absolute prohibition of second marriages; but it would not be difficult to find similar views in orthodox writers such as Justin and Hermas. It is unlikely that a writer so cultured and temperate would have sympathised with the ill-balanced enthusiasm of Montanus.

As to the "Defence of the Doctrine of the Resurrection," this was a peculiarly difficult subject for a Greek philosopher, and probably no dogma proved so great a stumbling-block to thoughtful Gentiles. There lay at the root of all heathen speculation the axiom that matter is *per se* imperfection; and the union of form with matter in an individual and eternal relationship seemed not merely inconceivable but contradictory to the highest idea of God. Athenagoras has approached his theme in a reverent and not over-combative spirit, and confines his reasoning to those broad principles of God's Nature and man's final cause which will never lose their point.

Almost all historians put a high value upon his work.

---

[1] πρεσβεία. It seems, however, that in later Greek this word is used in a more extended sense.

"He writes," says Donaldson, "as a man who is determined that the real state of the case shall be exactly known." And the steadfastness with which he keeps this object before him is worthy of all praise. But he was not the first and will not be the last to experience the difficulty of making the truth appear when those to whom it is addressed are determined not to recognise it.

In connection with Athenagoras, though far removed from his spirit, we may notice a short satirical work on heathen philosophy by one **Hermias,** which is found in the older editions of the Fathers annexed to his writings. Nothing whatever is known of the author. His date is disputed, but the general tone savours of the time of Lucian and Plutarch. The work is entitled, *A Ridicule of Outside Philosophy,*[1] implying that Christianity is the true philosophy, a theory which was most earnestly put forward in the second and early part of the third century. It contains a large assort-ment of absurd and contradictory opinions on God, the soul, and the world, placed side by side, to show their mutual repugnance, but neither criticism properly so called, nor constructive doctrine. Its only value arises from its antiquity. We may probably assign it to the time of M. Aurelius.

We come now to one of the choicest gems of early Christian thought, the anonymous **Letter to Diognetus,** formerly ascribed to Justin. This little treatise was first published in 1592 by Henricus Stephanus, from a mediæval transcription of a very ancient and defective manuscript, which contained the following works :—(1) Two pieces, each by the "holy Justin," "*On the Divine Monarchy,*" and "*An Admonition to the Greeks;*" (2) an exposition, said also to be by Justin, "*Concerning the Trinity;*" (3) two discourses by a person designated as "the same," but not otherwise specified,

---

[1] Διασυρμὸς τῶν ἔξω φιλοσόφων. The Sophists of this period wrote short essays of a satirical character called σκώψεις. Sometimes they published ironical panegyrics of trifling or unworthy subjects, of which the *Laudes fumi et pulveris* is an example. The work of Hermias belongs to the former class.

"*To Greeks*" and "*To Diognetus;*" (4) the treatises of Athenagoras "*On Behalf of Christians*" and "*On the Resurrection.*"

The work on the Trinity is now generally believed not to be Justin's. But even if it were his, it would not follow that the copyist of the other two treatises, in prefixing "*By the same*" as a mark of authorship, meant thereby to ascribe them to Justin. As Professor Birks remarks, they may have been taken from a torn copy with a piece missing at the beginning, and this missing piece may have contained the first of the series of writings, together with the name of the writer. And this is what he thinks actually occurred. He therefore groups together the Address to Greeks and the Letter to Diognetus as Nos. 2 and 3 respectively of an apologetic series, of which No. 1 is lost. He supposes the author to have taken some public step which in the eyes of his equals compromised him as a Christian; that the first treatise gave an account of his motives in renouncing heathenism, the second depicted the falsehood of the Pagan creed, the third explained the nature of Christianity, and that, in spite of their different titles, they were virtually all addressed to Diognetus. If we ask whether any light can be thrown upon their authorship, he mentions that Cureton, in his *Spicilegium Syriacum,* publishes a version of what appears to be another set of notes to the same discourse *To Greeks,* which is there ascribed to **Ambrosius,** a chief man of Greece, who became a Christian, and justified his conduct to his fellow-magnates in the reply commented upon, which is found to be the same with the existing discourse. Pursuing this clue, he points out that there is some ground for believing that an Ambrosius of noble lineage at Athens, during the time of Marcus Aurelius, may have been the founder of the Ambrosian family of the *gens Aurelia,* of whom one member was the correspondent of Origen. And as the only Diognetus known to us in times after Christ is the painter-philosopher who acted as tutor to the boyhood of Marcus Aurelius, it is tempting to connect the two names together, and to imagine Ambrosius, the Athenian noble, to have pleaded with Diognetus, the courtier-philosopher, the cause of the faith he had adopted.

It may be objected by a critical reader that this assignment of authorship is inconclusive and uncertain. This is admitted; but we are nevertheless of opinion that it is desirable to give, whenever possible, a human interest to every writing of antiquity by connecting it with some writer's name. How much more satisfaction we derive from a treatise when we can form some idea of its author! How much more stimulated we are to grapple with its difficulties! Unfortunately, this cannot always be done; but even where the author is unknown, plausible conjectures as to who he was may greatly help towards a sympathetic study of his work. Who can deny that we lose immensely by conceiving of the deutero-Isaiah as merely the "Great Unknown"? Criticism may compel acquiescence, but the loss remains. What would we not give to know who wrote the Epistle to the Hebrews? And yet surely it is better to study it with some hypothesis of authorship, if we desire to penetrate to its inner spirit. In proportion to the grandeur of a writing, so is the pleasure of knowing its author. It is the high value of the Address to Greeks and Epistle to Diognetus that makes us favourably inclined to adopt Birks' theory of their authorship, hanging though it does upon a more than slender thread of tradition.

At any rate, it assists our study of the two works. For, in the first place, they breathe a tone of calm dignity and aristocratic reserve as different as possible from the plain, middle-class sociability of Justin's mind. In the second place, though coloured with philosophy to some extent, their philosophical view is that of the high-bred man of the world rather than of the quiet, unpretending student. In the third place, their stately language and pure Attic culture bespeak an intellect of far higher order than was given to the martyred saint of Flavia Neapolis. Everything in both works, and especially in the so-called Epistle, points to a writer whose rank and opportunities agree exactly with those ascribed to the Athenian Ambrosius.

It has not been usual to consider the two works together, nor do we believe that Professor Birks' hypothesis has met with any general support. And as the Letter to Diognetus is far the better known of the two, and for some time was accorded a place, which is still claimed for it by some, among the works of the sub-apostolic age, it will be convenient to confine our criticisms to it, only observing that, if it be read in connection with the Reply to the Greeks, the real resemblance between the two treatises will be at once apparent.

In our opinion, the hypothesis of its anteriority to Justin is inadmissible. The use of the word οἰκονομία with reference to the inner relation between the First and Second Persons of the Holy Trinity points to a later date. If one must fix a time for its composition, one would incline to place it in the time of Aurelius, between Justin and Athenagoras, and to regard it as emanating either from Athens or Rome, the former by preference, in accordance with the tradition already mentioned.

Unfortunately, the single MS. in which it was preserved (which perished in the conflagration at Strasburg in 1870) was in two places defective. The work as we have it consists of twelve short chapters. The first break is in chap. vii., where the critics are of opinion that the insertion of a few words is sufficient to bridge it over. The second is after chap. x., when the sequel takes the form of a peroration, and is so completely different from what goes before, both in matter and manner, that many critics believe it to belong to a different work. These two concluding chapters are so obviously the end of a sermon or address to catechumens, that if we accept them as genuine, we are compelled to regard the whole work as a homiletic discourse and incorrectly described as an epistle at all. The arguments on neither side are convincing. But, on the whole, we incline to think that the peculiar loftiness of style points to one and the same author, and that the difficulties of separating the two chapters are greater than those of retaining them.

In these the author describes himself as a disciple of Apostles and a teacher of Gentiles. These epithets, however, must be understood rhetorically and not historically; as indicating the spirit of his research, not the actual persons from whom he drew it. His spiritual affinity with the writer to the Hebrews is manifest, and his indebtedness to the theology of S. John is also traceable, and in that sense he may without presumption call himself their disciple.

In the Letter he sets himself to answer three questions propounded by Diognetus—(1.) "On what God relying and how worshipping, Christians all look above the universe itself and despise death, and neither reckon those gods who are so accounted by the Greeks nor observe any superstition of the Jews." The first part of this question is treated very briefly, probably because of its much fuller discussion in the treatise to Greeks, but the section devoted to Judaism is longer, and contains some very striking and brilliant remarks.

(2.) The second question is, "What is this kindly affection that Christians have for one another?" To this he replies in the section chaps. v.–ix., pointing out the supernatural character of the Christians' mutual love, the mysterious nature of their polity, and the regenerating power of their leading doctrines. The most important chapters for theology are the seventh, eighth and ninth, in which he describes the eternal love of God the Father, as shown in His sending His Royal Servant ($\pi\alpha\hat{\iota}\varsigma$), whom He also calls His own Son (ἴδιον υἱόν), and affirms to be truly God and man, the Creator and Ruler of the universe, to redeem mankind. He speaks of God in philosophical language as not only Almighty, Invisible, Good, and True, but also as Wrathless (ἀόργητος) and Unconstraining, "for force," he says, as Irenæus after him, "belongeth not to God." The theology of this section has by some been thought to savour of Sabellianism, but incorrectly, or of Marcionism, but with still less ground. The platform on which it stands is genuinely Catholic, but, as in the case of Justin, the theology is not fully developed either in its view of the Person of Christ or in its apprehension of the co-equal Godhead of the Holy Spirit.

(3.) The third question of Diognetus is thus stated by the writer, "What, in fine, is this new race or practice that has invaded society now and never before?" The answer to this seems to begin with chap. x. It is then interrupted by a *lacuna* of unknown length, and perhaps concluded with the oratorical rhapsody of the last two chapters. It probably included a discussion on the "fulness of time," giving reasons why the advent of Christ was delayed so long, and carefully establishing the continuity of His Revelation with that of the prophets of the Old Testament, which it completed, and by completing closed.

The writer never mentions the work of the Holy Spirit, though it is quite possible he may have done so in the portion that is lost, as it commences with a beautiful picture of the fruits of faith, emphasising the glorious privilege which Christians have of reproducing the Divine life in their own. The whole work is so exquisitely graceful and so concisely arranged that, even in its mutilated state, it conveys the impression (rare among patristic writings) of high literary power. The reader will be glad to have some extracts from it as justifying this praise. We have therefore selected two, one describing the life of Christians on earth, the other embodying an impassioned summary of doctrine in the last two chapters, the great difficulty of which taxes the translator's powers to the utmost, and, we fear, prevents him doing more than very imperfect justice to its beauty. It will be seen how saturated the writer is with the teaching both of S. Paul and S. John.

THE LIFE OF CHRISTIANS (Chaps. v. and vi.).

"The Christians are not distinguished from the rest of mankind either by nationality or language. They have no separate cities, they use no special dialect, they practise no peculiar mode of life. They inhabit the cities of Greece and the rest of the world just as each finds his place allotted to him. They follow the local customs in respect to meat and drink, costume, and other social habits, and yet they carry about with them the strange and avowedly mysterious signs of their true nationality. They dwell in their own country, but as strangers; they share in the privileges of its citizenship, but endure all the disabilities of aliens. Every foreign country is to them a native land, and every native land is to them a foreign country. They marry and bring up families like other folk, but they do not, like others, expose their infant children. They provide their meals in common, but theirs is no common meal.[1] They live in the flesh, but not after the flesh. They sojourn upon earth, but their citizenship is in heaven. They obey the established laws, and yet by their individual lives they surpass the laws. They love all men, and yet they are persecuted by all. They are not understood, and yet they are condemned. They are put to death, and yet are raised to life. They are poor, and yet make many rich. They are in want of everything, and yet in everything they abound. They are dishonoured, and yet by their dishonour are covered with glory. They are defamed, and yet are counted righteous. They are reviled, and bless. They are insulted, and entreat men honourably. They do good, and are punished as evil-doers, and when punished they rejoice as being raised to life. The Jews make war on them as Gentiles, and the Greeks persecute them, and yet those that hate them cannot state the cause of their dislike.

" In one word, Christians are to the world what the soul is to the body. The soul is dispersed through all the limbs of the body : so the Christians are dispersed through all the cities of the world. The soul dwells within the body, yet it is not part thereof: so Christians dwell in the world, and yet they are no part of it. The soul is invisible, yet is guarded within a visible body : so the Christians are visibly in the world, yet their worship is a thing invisible.[2] The flesh hates the soul and makes war upon it, though the soul injures it not, but only hinders it from indulging its lusts : so the world hates the Christians, though they injure it not, but only set themselves against its pleasures. The soul loves the flesh that hates it : so do Christians love those that hate them. The soul is enclosed within the body, while yet it is the soul that holds the body together : so the Christians are enclosed within the prison of the world, and yet it is they who hold the world together. The soul is immortal, and yet dwells in a mortal

---

[1] A play on the two senses of κοινὸς, common, viz., shared alike by all, and unclean or polluted, alluding to the abominable calumnies circulated about the Christian love-feasts.

[2] Alluding either to the secrecy of Christian worship, or perhaps to its spiritual and inward character.

tabernacle : so, too, Christians sojourn among things corruptible, waiting for the incorruption of Heaven. The soul is made better by being stinted in the matter of meat and drink : so Christians increase more and more by being daily punished. God has assigned them a certain place to fill, and it is not lawful for them to refuse to fill it."

A Summing up of the Doctrine (Chaps. xi. and xii.).

"I offer no strange exhortation, I submit no unreasonable request. But having become a disciple of the Apostles, I would fain become a teacher of the Gentiles, worthily ministering to the disciples of truth that which has been delivered to me. For who that has been rightly instructed and become a friend of the Word does not seek to learn clearly the things that have been openly shown to the disciples through the Word? To whom the Word appearing made them manifest, speaking with plainness, not understood by unbelievers, but declared by disciples, who being reckoned faithful learned from Him the mysteries of the Father. For this cause He sent forth the Word that He might appear to the world, Who, being dishonoured by His people and preached by Apostles, was believed in by Gentiles. This is He that was from the beginning, that appeared new but was found to be old, and ever newly is begotten in the hearts of saints. This is the Everlasting One, ever reckoned a Son to-day, by Whom the Church is enriched, by whom grace being simplified is fulfilled in the saints, who granteth insight, explaineth mysteries, announceth times, rejoiceth in the faithful, giveth gifts to seekers who break not the pledge of faith nor transgress the ordinances of the Fathers. Then the fear of the Law is chanted, the grace of the prophets is understood, the faith of the Gospels stablished, and the tradition of the Apostles preserved, and the grace of the Church exulteth. For which reason thou shalt know without sorrow what the Word exhorteth, by whom He wills and when He wills. For whatever purposes of the Word we at His bidding have been moved to utter with pain, of these we make you partakers out of love in all things revealed.

"By earnest reading and hearing of these ye shall know aright how great things God grants to those that love Him, who become a very paradise of joy, an all-fruitful flourishing tree, springing up within themselves, adorned with varied fruits. For in this place are planted the tree of knowledge and the tree of life : but it is not the fact of knowledge that destroys, but disobedience. For that which is written is not without meaning, how God from the beginning planted a tree of knowledge and a tree of life in the midst of Paradise, indicating that life was through knowledge. But our first parents by using it corruptly were tormented by the serpent's guile. For neither life without knowledge, nor knowledge without true life, is safe : wherefore the two were planted side by side. And this meaning the Apostle discerned, when blaming knowledge pursued apart from the bidding of truth unto life, he said, 'Knowledge puffeth up, but charity edifieth.' For he that thinketh he knoweth anything without the true knowledge that is certified by life, knoweth it not, but is deceived by the serpent, not having loved life. But he that knows with fear and seeks life, plants with hope, expecting fruit. Let thy heart be knowledge, let the true Word entertained by thee be (thy) life. Whose tree if thou bearest and whose fruit if thou choosest, thou shalt ever gather the things that with God are desired, which the serpent toucheth not neither doth error approach to, nor is Eve corrupted, but a Virgin is trusted :[1] and Salvation is made clear, and the Apostles become intelligible, and the Lord's passover goes forward, and the wax-lights are brought together, and supramundane things are set in order, and in teaching the Saints the WORD is made glad, through Whom the Father is glorified, to Whom be glory world without end. Amen."

In this condensed and pregnant passage we see the lines of a complete course of doctrine sketched out, though in terms designedly veiled and mysterious, culminating in that perfect communion with Christ the Enlightener, which is attained through His presence in the Eucharistic worship, the appointed orderly channel of heavenly grace and teaching of celestial mysteries.

Some have endeavoured to fasten upon the writer a tendency towards Gnostic error, but we should rather regard

---

[1] Or perhaps "is made faithful." The key to this difficult sentence lies in the conception of the Church of God as the spiritual Paradise, and also as the antitype of Eve, the virgin bride of the Second Adam. There is no doubt a further reference to the Virgin Mother of Christ.

his language as pointing to the high ideal of spiritual knowledge given by S. John, and at a later date wrought out into
a finished system by the great Alexandrian teachers. While
highly guarded and metaphorical, his language unquestionably implies that the true gnosis is inseparable from a pure
heart and a holy life; and as such the Catholic Christian
can find no fault with it. The view of the Holy Eucharist
here shadowed forth is exalted and ennobling, and though
perhaps our taste is a little offended by the introduction of
a material symbol, yet when we consider the use of wax-
tapers in the dark chambers to which Christians were driven
for worship as necessary for purposes of light, we shall hardly
find fault with their introduction into a passage otherwise
supremely spiritual and expressed in language chaster and
more exalted than we shall easily find in any other of the
Ante-Nicene writers. The reader who would enter fully into
the author's mind should compare the Epistle with the
Apologies of Justin and Athenagoras, and also with the
striking fragment already given from Melito.

Another interesting figure in the Church of Greece is
Dionysius, Bishop of Corinth (fl. A.D. 170), of whom the
following account is supplied by Eusebius.[1] He succeeded
Primus in the bishopric, and exercised spiritual supervision,
not only within his own diocese, but far beyond its limits,
and did excellent service to Christ's cause by writing Catholic
epistles. One of these, addressed to the Lacedæmonians, contained a catechetical scheme of doctrine, as well as powerful
arguments for peace and unity. Another, addressed to the
Athenians, exhorted to faith and heavenly conversation,
from which he reproached them with having fallen away,
since the martyrdom of their bishop Publius. A third,
inscribed to the inhabitants of Nicomedia, controverted the
doctrine of Marcion. A fourth, to the Gortynians, entered
into the question of a disputed episcopal succession, begging
them to accept the orthodox bishop and to avoid heretical
perversions. A fifth, addressed to Amastris and the Pontic
churches, whose bishops had requested him to intervene,

[1] Eus. H. E. iv. 23.

contained important exegetical matter, coupled with a request to receive Palmas. Recommendations were added concerning marriage and celibacy, and the desirability of re-admitting to communion on repentance every kind of sinner, including the schismatic and heretic. It will be seen how varied and influential was the activity of Dionysius, and how wide an authority he enjoyed.

But his recommendations did not always pass unchallenged. In his Epistle to the Gnossian Church, he exhorted **Pinytus,** the bishop, not to lay by his strict views on continence too heavy a yoke upon his flock, but to remember the infirmity of human nature. Pinytus replied with some spirit, that greatly as he reverenced Dionysius, he thought he might feed his people with stronger meat. As for his own flock, they had learned the wisdom of the full-grown, and did not mean to slide lazily into an infantile old age from imbibing doctrines that were but milk for babes. The liberal views of discipline held by Dionysius do not imply any personal laxity, but they spring from his organising statesmanlike temper, which discerned the impossibility of enforcing ascetic ideals in a church which was to include all classes and all types of manhood. The same thing meets us again in the controversy between Tertullian and the orthodox, between Cyprian and Stephen. Where comprehension is the object, rules must not be too rigid; at any rate, the way of penitence must be made open to all. Pinytus, however, must have urged his views with moderation, acuteness, and scriptural authority, for Eusebius commends him highly both for his sound theology and for his faithful pastoral solicitude.

. The last and most interesting letter of Dionysius that Eusebius mentions is that to the Roman Church, of which Soter was then bishop. It contains a remarkable testimony to the generous spirit of catholic sympathy in which the revenues of that Church were administered :—

" It has from the beginning " (he says) " been your custom in many ways to assist all Christians, and especially to send money to the various city churches, thus mitigating their home poverty, and more especially enabling them to send succour to their members who are labouring in the mines. And this custom, handed down from the first, you have adhered to with true Roman steadfastness. And your blessed [1] bishop Soter has even expanded its application by sending round the gifts of your munificence to the saints, and advising all those who come to Rome and seek his counsel with the patient care of a true father in God."

Dionysius complained bitterly of the way in which his letters were tampered with. "I write" (he says) "not to please myself, but because continually pressed by Christian friends to do so. And the Apostles of the Devil sow tares in my field; they pick out many true things and put in many false. It is no wonder men have striven to falsify the Scriptures of the Lord, if they spare not writings so inferior as mine." One of his letters was addressed to an individual named Chrysophora, and was full of wise counsel.

From these notices we may, as Salmon remarks, gather several facts of interest. First, we see the solidarity of Christendom. The bishop of a provincial church, apostolic in origin, but not otherwise pre-eminent, is in constant correspondence on matters of general business with the representatives of churches in many parts of the world. Then we observe the general prevalence of the Episcopal form of government. Though the bishop has not yet come to take the place of his church, yet he is at the head of it and represents it, though letters are still inscribed to the church and not to the bishop. Thirdly, we remark the value attached by Christians to their literature. Dionysius tells Soter that the Corinthian Church had read the letter of the Roman Church in their Lord's day service, and would continue to do so from time to time. He incidentally mentions also the use of Clement's Epistle in Divine worship. He alludes to the Gnostic interpolations and excisions of the Sacred Books in the interests of their heresies, and he

---

[1] μακάριος, an epithet generally applied to departed saints, here indicating an extraordinary degree of living sanctity.

implies that those attempts had been frustrated by the vigilance of Christian believers. The exegetical research which Eusebius attributes to him need not be confined to the Scriptures of the Old Testament, but was more probably directed towards some of those of the New. Salmon is of opinion that the few fragments we possess show traces of an acquaintance with the Gospel of S. Matthew, the Acts, the First Epistle to the Thessalonians, and the Apocalypse.

Contemporary with Dionysius were other able writers now lost, whose names are preserved by Eusebius. **Philippus** was bishop of Gortyna in Crete, and wrote against the heresy of Marcion. **Modestus,** whose see is not mentioned, was, according to the historian, even more successful in exposing his fundamental fallacy. Musanus or **Musianus,** who lived in the reign of Antoninus Pius, or, according to the chronicle, in that of Severus (if he is the same person), wrote in opposition to Encratism.

In the seventh chapter of the *Praeparatio Evangelica,* Eusebins gives a long quotation from a treatise *On Matter* ($\pi\epsilon\rho\grave{\iota}$ $\mathring{\upsilon}\lambda\eta\varsigma$) in the form of a dialogue, which he attributes to a certain **Maximus,** who flourished near the close of the second century. Some have considered him to be identical with a bishop of Jerusalem of the same name in the reign of Commodus. As Eusebius, however, was evidently ignorant of this identity, it is safer to assume that they were distinct, especially as the name was a very common one. The same fragment is incorporated in a work by Methodius on Free-will, borrowed, as is so often the case, without acknowledgment. It is also found embedded in a treatise or dialogue against the Marcionites ascribed to Origen, and also in the *Philocalia* of the same author. Routh has edited the text of the fragment with much care, and its excellence is such as to justify the constant use made of it by subsequent writers. At the same time, it affords an instance of the unsatisfactoriness of the metaphysical method in questions of theology. Many of the Fathers occupied themselves with purely metaphysical topics, notably Methodius, Tertullian, and Origen. Irenæus also handled the same subject as Maximus in a discourse now lost. The great importance attached to metaphysical discussion arose from the prominence given to it in many heretical systems, which sought to combine the ideas of revelation with those of heathen philosophy. To those who have studied the first beginnings of abstract thought among the Greeks, and carried on their research through the pre-Socratic systems to those of Plato and Aristotle, these later treatments of the same insoluble problems will appear deficient in interest. No new thoughts are introduced; the only novelty is the combination of the conception of God as Creator with the various antinomies of reason, but the result is still unsatisfactory to the speculative intelligence and always must be. The true position of the Christian is expressed once for all in the Epistle to the Hebrews : "By faith we believe that the worlds were formed by the Word of God, so that the things which are seen were not made of things which do appear."

At the same time, the treatise of Maximus is not without importance from the candid and evidently truth-seeking way in which he states the difficulties he endeavours to meet. He shows he is aware of the charge so often brought against apologists that they start objections only to demolish them by a preconceived theory. He strives to state his opponents' case with fairness, and does not shrink from meeting argument by argument. But the result of all such controversial literature remains, that it does not really remove the difficulties it propounds, but merely shows the incompetency of existing solutions. Such problems as the origin of matter and of evil are beyond the grasp of the human mind, and we must either be content to acquiesce in the statements of Scripture, or else with the modern agnostic confess our necessary ignorance of them.

We now pass for a moment to Antioch, the capital of Syria, the brilliant meeting-ground of Greek and Oriental culture. The celebrity of its church dates from the earliest days of Christianity. Founded by S. Paul, ruled by S. Peter as its first bishop, and counting the martyred Ignatius among his worthy successors, it maintained for centuries the high

traditions of its origin. It was specially distinguished for
scriptural knowledge and exegesis. The sixth bishop on its
roll was **Theophilus,** who held the see during the reign of
M. Aurelius, and died about A.D. 181. This learned and
genial man was the author of several important works, one
only of which has come down to us, the three books addressed
to Autolycus, a heathen friend, for the purpose of convincing him of the falsehood of idolatry and the truth of
Christianity.

It covers the usual ground of such treatises in a more
than usually systematic and readable way. Book I. treats
of the nature and attributes of God, how He may be known,
the difference between the worship of a real Being and
the cultus of mere symbols, the meaning of the term Christian, and the importance of a belief in the resurrection.
Book II. is devoted to an examination of the popular mythology, and of the more pretentious but equally unconvincing
theories of the philosophers, exposing their weakness and
inconsistency. On the other hand, the writer dwells on
the dignity and reasonableness of the Biblical account of
Creation, explaining in elegant language its main features,
accounting for its accommodations to human intelligence,
and justifying the Divine dealings with mankind. He gives
a short sketch of the early history of the human race as
recorded in Genesis, and shows how it is held together by
the thread of prophetic revelation, adding testimonies from
the Sibylline oracles, and the unconscious confirmation of its
doctrines by the best heathen poets. The third book continues the same subject, Autolycus having expressed his
inability to accept the reasonings offered in the second; it
then proceeds to expound more fully the Christian conception of God and His Law, especially its inculcation of repentance, of chastity, and of moral righteousness; it defends
the Christians from the charges so ignorantly and calum-
niously flung at them, and asserts in a long chronological
argument the superior antiquity of the revealed faith to all
philosophic systems, concluding with a short explanation
of the perversions of history by heathen writers.

The impression produced by reading the work is decidedly favourable to the writer. It is evident that Theophilus was a man of large heart and genuine sympathy, who strove with all the resources of learning but also with a humble trust in God, who alone can turn men's hearts, to bring Autolycus to a better judgment. To his half-mocking question, " Where is your God ? show Him to us ; " he replies : —

" Show me thy man, and I will show thee my God. Show me that the eyes of thy soul see, that the ears of thy soul hear. All have eyes to see the sun, but the blind cannot see it. As a soiled mirror is incapable of receiving an image, so the impure soul is incapable of receiving the image of God. True, God has created all things for the purpose of making Himself known through His works, just as the invisible soul is discerned by its operations. All life reveals Him ; His breath quickens all ; without it, all would sink into nothing ; but the darkness of the soul itself is the reason why it does not perceive this revelation." [1]

In the fourteenth chapter of the first book, Theophilus relates of himself that it was through meeting with the Jewish Scriptures that he was converted. Tatian bears the same witness in his own case, and that of Justin is substantially similar. Many other Fathers appeal to the Old Testament in such a manner as to suggest that, if it was not actually the instrument of their conversion, it was well fitted to have been so. This striking testimony to the power of Scripture is all the more impressive when we remember— (1) that these men were highly educated thinkers accustomed to the best of literature ; (2) that defect of style was an unpardonable fault according to the judgment of their day ; (3) that, as a rule, the sacred books of another religion, however critically interesting, generally fall flat from lack of common spiritual associations ; [2] and (4) that, to appreciate

---

[1] Quoted by Neander.

[2] However intensely absorbed a comparative student may be in the Rig Veda, the Tripitaka, or the Zend-Avesta, his attitude, even when wholly sympathetic, is yet unconsciously critical. He is not convinced by Brahmanism, or Buddhism, or Parseeism, though he may accept as divinely given their element of truth.

the prophets' message, the whole mental attitude had to be unlearnt and formed anew. Mr. Dale, in one of his admirable books, tells us of a Japanese philosopher, an earnest seeker after truth, who, on reading S. John's Gospel for the first time, suddenly felt the thrill of a new conviction awakening within him, and, bowing to the divine impulse, became conscious of the spiritual birth, and of a mental repose and joy never before experienced. What this man felt Theophilus and Tatian had felt centuries before; and if professing Christian half-believers would only approach their Scriptures in the same frame of mind as they did, we cannot doubt that the same result would follow now. The attitude of pure receptivity of truth, we hope, is not rarer than it was; but it is forestalled and, as it were, discounted by the pressure of external authority; and that readiness to catch the first tones of a heavenly voice, of which then no one was ashamed, seems to have succumbed to the despairing persuasion that such a voice is nowhere to be heard.[1]

In one respect Theophilus contrasts unfavourably with Justin Martyr. His treatment of mythology is harsher and more severe; for, though he admits that it contains testimonies to the truth, he speaks of these as wrung from it unconsciously, almost against its will, much as the evil spirits in the Gospels are spoken of as confessing the Deity of Christ. Justin's attitude is gentler and more appreciative, though he, like all the Fathers, adopts the uncritical theory that Paganism borrowed from revelation, and dressed it up to suit the prejudices of its votaries. In his scriptural interpretation Theophilus inclines to the mystical and allegorising views prevalent in the East generally, but destined to be superseded at Antioch by a truer and more reasonable exegesis. His *History, Catechetical Treatises*, and controversial pamphlets *Against Hermogenes* and *Against Marcion* are unfortunately lost.

---

[1] καλεῖ τε πρὸς ἀκούοντας οὐδὲν
ἐν μέσῳ δυσπαλεῖ τε δίνᾳ.—*Æschylus.*

Lightning Source UK Ltd.
Milton Keynes UK
UKHW021810261118
332986UK00013B/1305/P